Managing Virtual Teams:
Getting the Most From Wikis, Blogs, and Other Collaborative Tools

M. Katherine Brown

Brenda Huettner

Char James-Tanny

Wordware Publishing, Inc.

Library of Congress Cataloging-in-Publication Data

Brown, M. Katherine, 1965-.
    Managing virtual teams : getting the most from wikis, blogs, and other
    collaborative tools / by M. Katherine Brown, Brenda Huettner, and
    Char James-Tanny.
        p. cm.
    Includes bibliographical references and index
    ISBN-10: 1-59822-028-4 (paperback)
    ISBN-13: 978-1-59822-028-5
    1. Virtual work teams--Computer network resources.   2. Teams in the workplace--
    Computer network resources.   3. Business communication--Computer network
    resources.   4. Project management--Computer network resources.
    I. Huettner, Brenda.   II. James-Tanny, Char.   III. Title.

    HD66.2.B76 2006
    658.4'022--dc22   2006037027

© 2007, Wordware Publishing, Inc.

All Rights Reserved

1100 Summit Ave., Suite 102
Plano, Texas 75074

Printed in the United States of America

ISBN-10: 1-59822-028-4
ISBN-13: 978-1-59822-028-5
10 9 8 7 6 5 4 3 2 1
0611

All inquiries for volume purchases of this book should be addressed to Wordware Publishing, Inc., at the above address. Telephone inquiries may be made by calling:

(972) 423-0090

Contents

Acknowledgments

It has been said that books are not written in a vacuum. A book on the subject of virtual teams by three authors who live in different time zones definitely proves that statement.

We would like to thank Mike Markley, Judy Herr, and our editor, Beth Kohler, for their assistance in reviewing the book. Brian Walker shared information on accessibility for different applications. Thanks also to Paula Berger for her support and advice.

We are also grateful to our friends and colleagues in the Society for Technical Communication and IEEE-Professional Communication Society for their years of advice, mentoring, support, and encouragement.

Kit would like to thank her family, particularly her grandmother Virginia Brown, for their support and encouragement, and Merlin the wonder dog for keeping her sane. Keri Webster, Stephanie Bates, Jean Labrenz, Dave Antonie, Sarah and Todd Harris, Elton and Kathy Hall, and Elizabeth Greene have been stalwart friends and advisors. Many thanks to Lisa Claypool-Lund, Dave Hoekstra, and the rest of the Loomis Social Club for the many years of friendship, support, twisted humor, and gaming. Without you, Kit would not be the person she is today.

Brenda would like to thank everyone who has inspired her in so many ways. The desire to learn new things and the urge to share that knowledge comes from her parents, James Phalon and Mary Phalon Ondrick, who though very different from each other, both contributed to her today. The opportunities to fulfill that desire and satisfy that urge come from the constant support of friends, family, and colleagues, new and old.

Char thanks her son, Jesse Freeman, for having so many interests and making life so fascinating (not many authors get to keep baby corn snakes warm while researching the latest application features!), and her husband, Jim Freeman, for making our home into a virtual working environment (because otherwise, there would be no "backyard office"). The group at HOT made sure that I knew what was going on in the world when I did not have time to read the latest news sites, and kept me entertained with links, videos, and games. And I truly appreciate all those on my buddy lists who answered questions, provided late-night conversations, and made me laugh... you know who you are.

Thanks to the following for allowing us to use their works: Laurel Wagers, editor of *MultiLingual* magazine, for granting permission to use significant portions of the following 2006 articles by M. Katherine (Kit) Brown: "Working on multicultural teams," "Integrating localization into change management," "Developing an effective request for proposal," and "Effective in-country reviews: best practices"; Dr. Bernard Bass for his "Key Dimensions of Leadership" table, which appears in Chapter 1; the San Francisco chapter of the Society for Technical Communication for the "Ten Proven Ways to Get Along with People" article in Chapter 6; TECHWR-L for allowing us to use a 2001 article by M. Katherine (Kit) Brown that appeared on TECHWR-L (http://www.techwr-l.com/techwhirl/magazine/writing/effectivetechreviews.html) for significant portions of the technical review section in Chapter 7; and Roland Tanglao for his "How Blogs Work in 7 Easy Pieces" diagram in Chapter 18.

Introduction

There are lots of good books available today about how to use collaborative tools like wikis, blogs, RSS, and messaging systems. They usually cover the conceptual basics needed to implement the specific tool, and then go into detail about how to implement and manage the various tool features. Tools books are often designed for technical people who already have a grounding or experience in what the tool is and why they want to use it.

There are even more good books available about how to manage teams, how to manage projects, and how to manage cross-cultural or international teams. Typically aimed at managers, these books are packed with theory and many good tips on how to get along with various types of people, but are often vague about the specific tools that are available for project management.

We wanted to write a book that brings these two areas together. Managers need to understand what tools and technologies are available in order to make good choices, and they need to be able to use these tools to support good management practices. As businesses grow increasingly global, and companies are outsourcing to vendors across town, across the country, and across the world, we decided to focus specifically on how to choose and use tools to manage virtual teams.

This book does not specifically recommend any one tool over another. We believe strongly that the "best tool" is going to be different for every situation. Rather, this book attempts to explain the types of tools available, to describe what kinds of things you can do with these tools, and to show a sampling of how some of the current tools compare to each other in order to help you make better choices.

Part I, "Building and Managing a Virtual Team," covers the basics of team and project management with particular emphasis on the unique challenges of virtual teams and plenty of cross-references to the tools you need to be successful. Part II, "Evaluating the Tools," describes the different features of each type of tool, and shows some of the differences (and similarities) between the tools available today.

Caution: New virtual and collaborative tools are being released every day. Rather than attempt a comprehensive list of all available tools, we have chosen a variety of tools that are representative of the functionality that is currently available. Read this book to gain a general understanding of what to look for when evaluating tools, then refer to the references listed throughout the book and to the companion wiki at www.wikiwackyworld.com for more complete lists of tools.

Since we three co-authors were collaborating in a virtual environment, we actually used many of the tools discussed while creating this book. Many of the examples we use throughout the book are based on our experiences as co-authors. The primary tool, a wiki we called "Wiki-WackyWorld," became a critical resource not only in our planning and writing efforts, but in our delivery to our reviewers and to our publisher. Now that we have finished writing the book, we are opening the site so that you can see a real-life example of a wiki at work. Appendix A lists many of the features available on WikiWackyWorld and how to use them.

Appendix B is a glossary of many of the terms used throughout the book.

If you have comments or questions about the book, or about the topic of virtual collaborative tools, go to our wiki site at http://www.wikiwackyworld.com to participate in our growing community. You can email us at authors@wikiwackyworld.com.

Kit Brown
Brenda Huettner
Char James-Tanny

Part I

Building and Managing a Virtual Team

A recent study by the American Business Collaborative found that over 80 percent of the workers surveyed are involved in some way with virtual work teams. These teams include those who work from home, those who work at a customer site, and teams who work in offices across town, across the country, or across the world.

In all cases, the primary challenge to the arrangement was found to be cultural. When you are working with someone who is not physically in your office, it is much harder to drop by for a chat, call last-minute meetings, or share hardcopy information. However, you can make adjustments to your processes and work habits to increase teamwork and productivity in a virtual environment. Processes need to be more explicit in the virtual environment precisely because the water cooler and coffee area conversations occur less frequently for virtual teams. Even casual interactions depend on technology, such as instant messaging. Frequently, you will have to make adjustments to the IT (information technology) infrastructure or policies to make effective use of such tools.

The chapters in Part I of the book describe the typical steps for planning, setting up, managing, and evaluating a successful virtual team. While the focus is on the team interactions, we also include recommendations for the tools that work well for each step along the way, and cross-reference, where appropriate, with the tools chapters in Part II.

- Chapter 1 provides an overview of the way teams work and how virtual teams may differ from colocated teams.

- Chapter 2 describes the process of setting up a team and explains the factors that you need to consider when choosing team members.

- Chapter 3 looks at the types of tasks that every team needs to perform, regardless of project or location, and then offers suggestions on tools that might help with those tasks.

- Chapter 4 discusses issues that may occur once your project is underway by focusing on improving communication between your team members, even though they may be in different cities, countries, or time zones.

- Chapter 5 looks at ways you can track your progress and identifies the types of tools available to help you do so.

- Chapter 6 focuses on the interactions between your team members, addresses some of the things that may go wrong, and offers some suggestions for what you can do to minimize conflict.

- Chapter 7 discusses the different types of reviews you will encounter throughout the course of a project and how to conduct reviews in a virtual environment.

- Chapter 8 helps you to prepare for the inevitable changes that occur during the course of any project, whether changes are in your team, the project goals, or the design.
- Chapter 9 discusses ways to measure the success of your team and to prepare for making your next project even more successful.

If you have any questions, comments, or suggestions, please visit our wiki at http://www.wikiwackyworld.com for the latest updates, corrections to the book, and more. And please feel free to modify wiki pages and participate in our wiki community by entering comments, adding pages, or editing content that is already there.

Chapter 1

Understanding Team Dynamics in a Virtual Environment

" *Virtual teams must be especially conscious of their dynamics. Behavioral clues are spread out not only in space but usually over longer timeframes than they are with comparable collocated teams. Virtual teams need to design for this supercharged eventuality.*

— Jessica Lipnack and Jeffrey Stamps,
Virtual Teams: Reaching Across Space, Time and Organizations with Technology

For as long as two beings have worked together toward a common goal, teams have existed. For as long as companies and institutions have had multiple offices, virtual teams have existed. What has changed is the ease with which teams can communicate across space, time, and organizations (Lipnack and Stamps, 2000). And, since

Lipnack and Stamps made that observation in the first edition of their book 10 years ago, technology has continued to advance exponentially to where most companies now take email, high-speed Internet access, and instant messaging for granted, and are beginning to devise ways to integrate wikis, blogs, RSS feeds, VoIP (Voice over Internet Protocol), and other collaboration technologies into their daily work.

Not surprisingly, however, the people side of the equation has evolved much more slowly, as evidenced by the fact that most organizational development consultants still use some variation on Bruce Tuckman's model of team lifecycle, which Tuckman originally developed in 1965. It is important to remember, as we embark on this journey, that technology is at best a tool and a facilitator of efficiency. The best technology in the world cannot fix the oh-so-very human issues that sometimes sabotage even the best teams.

Lifecycle of a Team

Tuckman's model defines several stages: forming, storming, norming, performing, testing (added later by Lipnack and Stamps), and adjourning. This model still characterizes most teambuilding theory and practice, in part because it provides a practical, replicable view of the team lifecycle, and like most natural systems, seems to follow an "S" curve, with easily identifiable periods of stress and conflict (Lipnack and Stamps, 2000). Peter Senge, author of *The Fifth Discipline* and other books about applying systems theory to organizational development, validates the "S" curve idea in his description of the slowing and growing phases of team lifecycles.

As a manager, you can use the team lifecycle to help you determine the most effective course of action in particular situations, so that you can be proactive about managing the natural stress points that occur during the lifecycle.

The stages of the lifecycle are as follows:

- **Forming**: The "trial balloon" phase. Someone has a bright idea and starts building interest, sponsorship, and alliances. During this phase, many discussions occur, serving to build support and consensus about the vision. The leader is selected and begins pulling together a team. Toward the end of this phase, you might get a "honeymoon" period. Everyone is excited about the project, getting to know each other, and busy ensuring that all the infrastructure and executive support is in place so that the project can succeed. Managers can harness this initial burst of energy and productivity by setting appropriate expectations, ensuring a clear path free of bureaucratic obstacles, and directing activities.

- **Storming**: Similar to the first year of marriage, this stage lays bare all the differences and conflicts about vision, expectations, work style, and communication style. During this phase, the guidelines are honed, compromises are made, and often, real bonding takes place. Managers can help shorten this period of conflict by facilitating discussions, documenting decisions and guidelines, modeling expected behaviors, ensuring that everyone is heard, short-circuiting power struggles, and when necessary, redirecting people to the larger purpose.

- **Norming**: Teambuilding begins in earnest as individuals become comfortable with each other and their roles. The team begins identifying "low-hanging fruit," those activities or solutions that are easy to implement and have a positive impact on the direction and pace of the project. Managers can assist the team by providing opportunities for social interaction and encouraging open discussions and creative problem-solving, as well as identifying the "go-to" people for specific activities.

- **Performing**: The "zone." The team is working well together, knows where it is going and how to get there, and works interdependently. Managers can maximize the benefit of this stage by ensuring that roadblocks get removed, verifying that the team has all the tools it needs to accomplish the tasks, ensuring that the criteria are established and known, and working to delegate tasks appropriately.

- **Testing** (added by Lipnack and Stamps): The "verification" phase. As pieces of the project are completed, they are verified against the specifications and other components of the project. Problems are identified and corrected. Managers can facilitate the testing phase by ensuring that the tools and processes are working correctly and that open communication exists between the developers and the testers.

- **Adjourning**: The "wrap-up." The team is finishing its tasks, evaluating how things went, and preparing to move on to other things. Conflict often occurs during this stage because of deadline stress, and because of the uncertainty associated with transition and change. Managers can ease the transition by making sure that team and individual efforts get recognized, providing an opportunity to discuss the project and evaluate lessons learned, and providing clear direction on what team members should focus on next. (See Chapter 7 for information on conducting reviews.)

Characteristics of an Effective Team

Most of the work done by companies today is accomplished by cross-functional teams, many of which are also geographically dispersed and multicultural. But what distinguishes an effective team from one that merely limps along or falls apart? Technology is not enough. Lu Ellen Schafer, in her training program "How to Make Remote Teams Work," describes five essential components:

- Shared team objective
- Knowledge of what to do
- Equipment to do it
- Ability to do it
- Desire to do it

Without all of these components in place, teams will struggle and, ultimately, will fail.

Shared Team Objective

"Only a few things about teams are sure, and one is this: *successful teams have clear goals.*" So begins the chapter on goal setting in Glenn Parker's book, *Cross-Functional Teams.* Without a shared vision and goals to support that vision, teams will fracture along political or functional lines and the project will fail. It is from this shared objective and vision that the project goals arise.

The project sponsor and team leader must set clear expectations and goals from the very beginning, and encourage the team to refine the goals so that the team gains ownership of the project, gains synergy, builds cooperation, and reduces the areas of conflict. Parker recommends the SMART approach to goal-setting:

- **Specific**: Each goal identifies a specific problem that you are trying to solve. The specificity helps establish a direction and focus. For example, "Company A wants to reduce localization costs."

- **Measurable**: You must be able to determine whether or not you have successfully achieved the goal. For example, "Company A wants to reduce localization costs by 20 percent."

- **Attainable**: The team must be able to achieve the goal. You want the goal to be challenging but achievable. You might need to do some research to determine whether the goal is achievable and, if so, in what time frame. For example, reducing localization costs by 20 percent in three weeks is probably not attainable; however, doing it in the next product release cycle might be.

- **Relevant**: The goals of the team must mesh with those of senior management and with the overall corporate strategy. For example, if the company's globalization strategy targets China as the next new market, and the software product is not double-byte enabled and there are no plans for making it so, the team goals are not aligned with the corporate objectives.

- **Time-bound**: Without a deadline, the project will not be given the appropriate priority. However, the deadline needs to be realistic (something that upper management often forgets in the push to compete). As a manager and team leader, part of your job is to "push back" on unrealistic deadlines and other requests. This goal strongly correlates with the goal of being attainable. Many good projects have failed because the team was not given enough time to succeed.

Each goal should be documented and tied to the overall team vision and objective. In addition, the goals should be prioritized, so the team knows which goal is most important in the event that a trade-off needs to be made.

Knowledge

The team must understand what it needs to do and what the parameters are for doing it. Expectations must be clear and explicit (and preferably documented on the project's wiki or intranet so everyone has access to them). The team needs to know what standards it is using, as well as which arm of the resource triangle is most flexible:

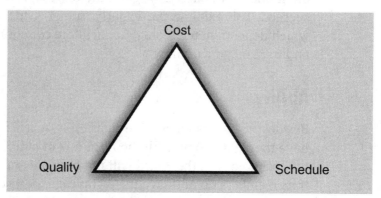

Figure 1-1: The resource triangle

There is an old saying that "you can have it fast and cheap or fast and good, but you cannot have it good, fast, and cheap." Management must communicate to the team which of these components is most flexible. For example, most medical manufacturers will sacrifice the schedule to ensure that quality and safety are high. On the other hand, many software vendors will sacrifice features and quality to get the product out the door on time. Guy Kawasaki is famous for describing this software industry phenomenon of "don't worry, be crappy" and "churn, baby, churn" in his book *Rules for Revolutionaries*.

Teams must also know what types of decisions they can make. If a team is not empowered to make a decision that affects the outcome of the project, its members are less likely to take ownership and to be fully engaged. Responsibilities and lines of authority need to be clearly drawn from the beginning of the project.

Equipment

If teams do not have the right tools for the job in the form of equipment, technology, processes, infrastructure, and so on, it does not matter how good the team is; it will not succeed. This axiom is particularly true of virtual teams, which depend on technology to facilitate communication and to manage workflow.

Ability

Besides a clear vision and the right tools, teams need to have the right people with the right mix of abilities. All the technology in the world will not help a team succeed if its members do not have the technical expertise or the time to complete the project. In many cases, managers can provide the necessary training or build research time into the schedule so that team members can learn as they go.

Desire

As Lou Holtz (a former American college football coach) once said, "Ability is what you're capable of doing. Motivation determines what you do. Attitude determines how well you do it." You can have information, tools, and capability at your disposal, but if you are not *willing* to do it, you will fail. In team situations, one or two cynics can derail the entire team. Managers can monitor and coach but cannot instill desire in someone else. Desire must come from within.

Search and rescue personnel have long puzzled over an interesting phenomenon that occurs when people are lost in the wilderness. Often, the lost person is found dead, propped up against a tree or rock, without a scratch on them, as if they had just given up. Other times, a person will suffer serious injuries, and yet survive for days or weeks until they are found or rescue themselves. No one really knows why some people have the drive and others do not in these situations. The same is true in team situations.

Where strong desire and determination persist, people can overcome all kinds of adversity, including lack of ability, in order to succeed.

Characteristics of an Effective Team Leader

According to Lipnack and Stamps, "Virtual teams can be successful only if people cooperatively manage the coordination involved in membership and leadership," meaning that managers must give up the ideas of power and control, and replace them with service leadership. In the old days, the people who held onto the knowledge, data, and so on held the power in an organization. Today, the people who readily disseminate information, connect people with each other, and facilitate hold the real power in an organization.

The following information originally appeared in *Transformational Leadership* by Dr. Bernard Bass and Dr. Ronald Riggio. It is reprinted here with the publisher's permission. When reading the list and definitions, keep in mind that it was originally created for a North American audience, and that you might need to make some cultural adjustments to relate them to your particular locale.

Table 1-1. Key dimensions of leadership

Leadership Dimension	How Do You Demonstrate This?
Charisma	Make others proud to be associated with you. Instill faith, respect, and trust in you. Make everyone around you enthusiastic about assignments. Have a special gift of seeing what is really important for [the team] to consider. Transmit a sense of mission to [the team].
Individual Consideration	Coach, advise, and teach [team members] who need it. Treat each [person] individually. Express appreciation for a good job. Use delegation to provide learning opportunities. Let each [person] know how he/she is doing. Actively listen and give indications of listening. Give newcomers a lot of help.
Intellectual Stimulation	Get [teammates] to use reasoning and evidence, rather than unsupported opinion. Enable [the team] to think about old problems in new ways. Communicate ideas that force [the team] to rethink some of their own ideas that they never questioned before.
Courage	Be willing to persist and stand up for your ideas even if they are unpopular. Do not give in to group pressures or others' opinions to avoid confrontation. Be willing to give negative feedback to a [teammate] or superior. Have confidence in your own capability and act independently. Do what is right for the company/[team], even if it causes personal hardship/sacrifice.
Dependability	Follow through and keep commitments. Meet deadlines and complete tasks on time. Take responsibility for actions and accept responsibility for mistakes. Work effectively with little contact with the boss [or project manager]. Keep the boss [or project manager] informed on how things are going, take bad news to him/her, and readily admit mistakes to boss [or project manager].

Leadership Dimension	How Do You Demonstrate This?
Flexibility	Maintain effectiveness and provide stability while things are changing. See what is critical and function effectively within changing environments. Remain calm and objective when confronted with many and different situations or responsibilities at the same time. When a lot of issues hit at once, be able to handle more than one problem at a time and still focus on the critical things. Be able to "change course" when the situation dictates or warrants it.
Integrity	Adhere firmly to a code of business ethics and moral values. Do what is morally and ethically right. Behave in a manner consistent with your professional responsibilities. Do not abuse management privileges. Gain and maintain the trust and respect of others. Serve as a consistent role model, demonstrating and supporting corporate policies/procedures, professional ethics, and corporate culture.
Judgment	Reach sound and objective evaluations of alternative courses of action through logical and skillful intellectual discernment and comparison. Put facts together in a rational and realistic manner to arrive at alternative courses of action. Base assumptions on logic, factual information, and consideration of human factors. Know your authority and be careful not to exceed it. Make use of past experience and information to bring perspective to present decisions.
Respect for Others	Honor and do not belittle the opinions or work of other people, regardless of their status or position in the organization. Demonstrate a belief in the value of each individual, regardless of their background, etc.

Note that the original used the term "subordinates," which has been changed to "the team" or "teammates" here.

True leaders empower their teams by their behaviors (for examples of how these characteristics look when a manager is under pressure, watch *Star Trek* — no, really). True leaders perform the following actions:

- Remove roadblocks.
- Act as an advocate for the team with upper management.
- Facilitate open, honest communication.
- Model behaviors that they want from the team.
- Act instead of react.
- Facilitate decision making and discussions with team.
- Recognize the strengths of each team member and focus those strengths to the benefit of the team.
- See the big picture and communicate each member's role in that context.
- Encourage independent thinking and trust their team to make good decisions.
- Gather team members with complementary skill sets and draw from the strengths of each member.
- Share leadership appropriately with other team members.

These characteristics are particularly important on virtual teams. Virtual team members must operate with a certain amount of autonomy because they might be separated by several time zones, resulting in a delay in feedback. It is often easier to "beg forgiveness" than it is to ask permission when the team leader or supervisor is six time zones away. Leaders and managers must trust that their teams are acting in the best interest of the project and the company, and should listen carefully to strenuous objections. For example, one of the reasons cited in the accident report for the *Columbia* space shuttle disaster was that upper management did not take seriously the concerns expressed by several project engineers when the foam hit the shuttle.

As teams work together, often informal roles develop. One person might be really good at planning social functions, while another person might have an aptitude for troubleshooting. Smart team leaders and managers take advantage of these diverse skills by delegating these tasks to the people who enjoy doing them and who are good at them. Doing so enriches everyone's experiences and builds ownership. Lipnack and Stamps described the following virtual team leader roles, originated by Reuben Harris:

- Coordinator
- Designer
- Disseminator
- Tech-net manager
- Socio-net manager
- Executive champion

In a virtual team, each of these roles might be played by a different person, or one person might play several of the roles, depending on the size and complexity of the team.

Challenges and Opportunities with Virtual Teams

All teams experience challenges in culture, logistics, communication, and so on, but with virtual teams, those challenges are exacerbated by not being in the same room or locale. While this chapter touches on many of the issues, the other chapters in Part I provide additional details and recommendations.

Culture

Figure 1-2: Cultural iceberg

As with the icebergs that float on the ocean, it is not the obvious, visible differences that get even experienced people into difficulties when working with other cultures, but the nuances that lurk below the surface of most people's conscious awareness. And cultural differences exist, not only in virtual teams, but also within the same locale, office, or social group (and sometimes even within the same family). The structure of the iceberg is a common and apt analogy for describing culture:

- **Above the waterline**: About 15 percent to 20 percent of culture is readily visible. These characteristics include things like language, ethnicity, dress, laws, art, architecture, and other attributes that are immediately obvious when meeting a person from a particular culture or when you set foot in a particular locale that is representative of a culture.

- **At the waterline**: About 5 percent of culture is on the edge of one's awareness. These are things that might not be obvious until they are pointed out, but most people are conscious that they exist and can generally adapt their behavior appropriately. Examples include table manners, level of formality, personal space, hierarchy, and so on.

- **Under the surface**: About 75 percent to 80 percent of a culture lurks below the surface of most people's awareness. These characteristics are the deeply ingrained attitudes, beliefs, prejudices, expectations, and so on that comprise an individual's world view. In many cases, even people who are self-aware and thoughtful have difficulty articulating and explaining these attributes, precisely because they are so deeply ingrained. These attributes are typically intrinsic to the culture, the things that "everyone knows," such as the level of independence from family that is appropriate, rules for contract negotiation, methods for resolving conflict, and so on. If you have ever had the experience of finding yourself feeling very uncomfortable in a seemingly innocuous situation with someone, chances are that your discomfort resulted from differing cultural expectations or beliefs.

In most situations, you get what you give. If you approach a situation with an open mind, a friendly attitude, and a genuine desire to understand and work with the other person, the other person will respond in kind. When inevitable misunderstandings occur, have a sense of humor about them and patiently work through the misunderstanding. Encourage your team to stretch beyond individual comfort zones and to learn about and accommodate cultural differences, while remembering that, at our core, we are more alike than different — we all want food, shelter, clean water, for our children to be better off than we are, and to leave the world a better place than it was when we arrived.

Logistics

With virtual teams, even casual conversations require orchestration and tools. While instant messaging, WebEx, web cams, and other technologies can facilitate communication with the virtual team (see Part II), it is not quite the same as wandering by someone's office on the way to lunch. When planning a project with a virtual team, you need to be more explicit about everything you do, from communication times and milestones to holiday schedules, rules for out-of-office notifications, format for posting to the wiki, and so on.

As the adage goes, "To err is human; to really mess things up requires a computer." Never underestimate the uncanny ability of technology failures to wreak havoc on your project schedule, communication, and general sanity. For example, two weeks before the deadline for this book, Kit discovered the hard way that one of her computer's RAM chips was bad. Two days before the deadline, her ergonomic keyboard died. Char had a speaking engagement in the United Kingdom shortly before the deadline, and discovered that she could not get access to the

Internet from her hotel because the hotel was being remodeled and the Internet access was down.

Communication

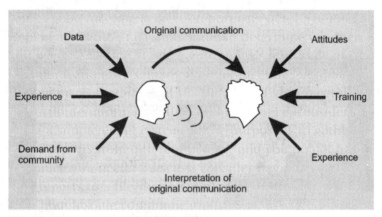

Figure 1-3: Communication feedback loop

When people communicate face-to-face, about 70 percent of the information exchanged is nonverbal. This nonverbal information is lost when the people communicating cannot see or hear each other, but must rely on written exchanges. Add to that the increased noise-to-signal ratio inherent in virtual communication, and it is easy to see how minor misunderstandings can escalate into full-blown wars.

Virtual teams must be vigilant about closing the feedback loop, being proactive about communication, avoiding jumping to conclusions, establishing a clear escalation path, and maintaining a sense of humor.

Chapter 4 goes into more detail about communication, and Chapter 6 provides a list of 10 proven ways of getting along with people.

Project Management

Virtual project managers spend much of their time facilitating communication among team members and ensuring that processes contribute to team efficiency. While typical project estimates usually include an overall project management charge of about 10 percent to 15 percent of the project cost, virtual teams may require a higher percentage at the beginning of the project, especially if many team members have never worked virtually before. However, effective project management is vital to ensuring the success of the team.

The advantage of a virtual team from a project manager's perspective is that, with the appropriate tools, the virtual team can take advantage of time zones and holiday schedules to keep things moving on the project 24/7. For example, if a team member in Europe submits something for review at the end of her day and needs a quick turnaround, the team members in North America, Asia, and Australia/New Zealand can often have a response by the time the European arrives at work the next morning.

Chapter 5 provides tools and best practices for managing virtual projects.

Personnel Management

Supervisors and managers in matrix organizations have an interesting challenge in managing their employees because the employees often spend more time with their respective project teams than they do with the functional group. The supervisor must depend on the project managers and other reports to assess the employee's capabilities, needs, and job performance.

When the employee is virtual, the challenge can be doubly difficult because the supervisor cannot do "management by walking around," at least not easily. Other traditional management strategies also do not work when the employee is working outside the office, and the supervisor must have a high degree of trust in the employee, as well as being comfortable with a certain lack of control, for this situation to work. Like project managers, supervisors with remote employees spend much of their time facilitating communication.

The advantage to the supervisor for having virtual employees is that the employee tends to be highly motivated and self-directed. Several studies have also shown that virtual employees tend to be more productive than people who work in an office, probably because they can focus on the work rather than on the politics and distractions of the office.

Chapter 2 provides information on hiring and Chapter 8 offers ideas on integrating new team members.

Summary

"Communicate, collaborate, coordinate, and communicate some more" is the mantra for successful virtual teams. By understanding the team lifecycle, and the characteristics of effective teams and managers, and by working to build a cohesive team environment, virtual teams can be very successful. The remainder of this book delves into specific best practices and tools that you can use to create and manage your own virtual team.

Related Resources

Bass, Bernard M., and Ronald E. Riggio. *Transformational Leadership*. 2nd ed. Mahwah, NJ.: Lawrence Erlbaum Associates, 2005.

Brown, M. Katherine (Kit). Monthly column in *Multi-Lingual*. 2006.

Buckingham, Marcus, and Donald O. Clifton. *Now, Discover Your Strengths*. New York: Free Press, 2001.

Gibson, Christina B., and Susan G. Cohen, eds. *Virtual Teams That Work: Creating Conditions for Virtual Team Effectiveness*. San Francisco: Jossey-Bass, 2003.

Huettner, Brenda P., and Ken Jackson. "How to Hire Technical Writers: A Manager's Viewpoint." *STC Annual Proceedings*, 1996: 109-112.

Katzenbach, Jon R. *Teams at the Top: Unleashing the Potential of Both Teams and Individual Leaders*. Boston: Harvard Business School Press, 1998.

Kawasaki, Guy, and Michelle Moreno. *Rules for Revolutionaries: The Capitalist Manifesto for Creating and Marketing New Products and Services*. New York: HarperCollins, 2000.

Kayser, Thomas A. *Team Power: How to Unleash the Collaborative Genius of Work Teams*. Burr Ridge, Ill.: Irwin Professional Publishing, 1994.

Lipnack, Jessica, and Jeffrey Stamps. *Virtual Teams: Reaching Across Space, Time and Organizations with Technology*. 2nd ed. New York: Wiley, 2000.

Parker, Glenn M. *Cross-Functional Teams: Working with Allies, Enemies, and Other Strangers*. San Francisco: Jossey-Bass, 2003.

Schafer, Lu Ellen. "How to Make Remote Teams Work." Training materials from a seminar given to Hewlett-Packard in Palo Alto, Calif., 2000.

Senge, Peter M. *The Fifth Discipline: The Art & Practice of the Learning Organization*. 2nd ed. New York: Doubleday/Currency, 2006.

Snyder, Bill. "Teams That Span Time Zones Face New Work Rules." Stanford Graduate School of Business (http://www.gsb.stanford.edu/news/bmag/sbsm0305/feature_virtual_teams.shtml), 2003.

Tate, C. W. "The Art of Managing Difficult People." *Nursing Standard*. 20 (19; January 2006): 72.

Tuckman, Bruce. "Development sequence in small groups." *Psychological Bulletin*. 63 (1965): 384-389.

Setting Up a Virtual Team

> " *A company is only as good as the people it can attract and keep. Everything else flows from that, so create an environment to make those people as successful as they can be.*
>
> — David Ogilvy, advertising company founder

> " *...to know even one life has breathed easier because you have lived; this is to have succeeded.*
>
> — Ralph Waldo Emerson, from his essay on success

Organizations use virtual teams for myriad functions, ranging from cross-functional project teams to task forces and line management. The concepts for setting up each type of team are the same, though the particular roles and responsibilities may vary from team to team.

In an ideal world, managers would be able to select the tools, personnel, and projects that they want to work on, and would have complete control over all aspects of the effort. In reality, managers must usually work within the confines of the existing organization, infrastructure, and available personnel to meet the project deadlines that upper management imposes, and hire only when they need to fill the gaps in their teams.

Hiring

With virtual teams and teleworking opportunities expanding exponentially, managers are increasingly faced with hiring employees, contractors, or consultants who will work and live far from the boss's office. Ideally, managers will bring the top two or three candidates on-site for a final interview and screening. Often, however, managers do not have the opportunity to meet the potential employee or contractor in person, but must rely on prescreening and telephone interviews to determine whether the candidate is a good fit. In such situations, prescreening becomes even more important, and you may want to consider hiring a recruiter or employment agency that is familiar with the locale.

Note: Hiring (and firing) requirements and practices vary from country to country, so if you are not familiar with the local requirements, be sure to work with your human resources department or a reputable employment agency. Not following the regulations could result in huge fines, disciplinary action, or even jail time, depending on the egregiousness of the action and the local law.

Before You Need to Hire

Before you need to hire someone, you can improve your chances of finding a good fit by doing the following:

- **Network with colleagues**: Just as networking is the best way for job seekers to find a job, it is also the best way to find out who is available and who is good at what they do, especially when looking for contractors. Get involved with local professional organizations, chambers of commerce, and so on. Keep a list of the names and specialties of people who are frequently recommended (you can set up a secure manager's area of the project wiki or intranet site to store this information). Find out which employment agencies and recruiters are the best to work with. Act as a mentor for university students majoring in your discipline (even if there is no local university, most mentorships can be carried out via email and the telephone). Agree to requests for informational interviews and keep the person's résumé on file, even if you do not currently have an opening; you never know when that person might be useful to your organization.

- **Track industry trends**: Often when one industry experiences a downturn, others need to hire. Skills are often transferable between industries, and hiring someone from another industry can provide a much-needed injection of new ideas and methodologies into your organization. Business publications, such as *Inc.*, *Fortune*, *Business Week*, and *The Wall Street Journal*, help you identify potential opportunities and threats, as well as provide ideas for strategy and process related to your industry. Such ideas can help you devise interview questions, re-examine the skills you are looking for in a candidate, or give ideas for training and teambuilding.

- **Investigate and establish relationships with recruiters and employment agencies**: Researching employment agencies and recruiters in your area before you need them enables you to be proactive about your search for new team members. If you wait until you are in dire straits, you have less room for negotiation and likely will not get as good of a fit. In addition, by doing your homework up front, you can eliminate unscrupulous agencies from the mix and focus on the ones that provide you with excellent service.

Note: Using recruiters and employment agencies can significantly reduce the time required to bring in a qualified candidate. However, you need to make sure that you have done your prehiring homework (as detailed below) before engaging an agency.

- **Evaluate your needs**: What skills do you need on your team? Are there certain character traits that would fit better with your team than others? When you picture the ideal candidate, how do you see that person interacting with the team, and what do you see him or her contributing? Do you need someone with lots of experience, or would an intern work better? How much supervision do you anticipate providing? What kind of manager are you? Is it important that the candidate have previous experience working on virtual teams? Using a strategic planning tool, such as SWOT analysis (see the following sidebar), can give you a quick way of assessing your current status. When building a team, it is important that the team members have complementary strengths and skills. Homogeneity tends to lead to group-think, and the product will not usually be as good as one produced by a more diverse group. Online surveys work well for gathering information from the team, as do less formal methods, such as instant messaging and teleconferences. And, consider setting up a secure manager's area of the team wiki to collect and manage the information you gather. (See Chapter 3 for more details on needs analysis.)

■ **Develop an organizational chart**: When setting up a team, it helps to create an organizational chart so that you can clearly see functional and reporting relationships. Even if you do not have a specific person in mind yet, you can include a spot for that function. The organizational chart also helps you to visualize what skills or functions you might be missing. (See also the section in this chapter titled "Establishing Team Structure and Roles.")

■ **Develop a written job description**: If the human resources department does not have a written job description, create one yourself. Doing so will help you clarify what capabilities you need and want for a particular function, as well as help you determine the level of seniority needed to adequately perform those functions. Post the job descriptions for each team function on the wiki.

■ **Prioritize hiring checklists**: No candidate will have 100 percent of the experiences and skills that you advertise, so determine which skills are must-haves and which ones are good to have but optional. For example, if you are hiring a senior design engineer, it might be imperative that he or she have a degree in mechanical engineering, but less important whether or not he or she has managed people before.

SWOT Analysis

SWOT analysis stands for Strengths, Weaknesses, Opportunities, and Threats. You can use this tool to fairly quickly identify your team, department, or organizational status. The analysis does not have to take long; simply list each area in a text document or on the wiki and make a bulleted list of all the items that belong in each area. Once the analysis is complete, you can use the results to compare your current status to where you want to be, using the project plan or corporate strategic plan as the basis for comparison.

- **Strengths**: These are things that your team does well. For example, perhaps you have an excellent wiki setup or have great team synergy.

- **Weaknesses**: These are things that your team does not do well, or restrictions on things that you are allowed to do. For example, the version control is problematic, or the project files are not easily accessible to everyone on the team.

- **Opportunities**: These are outside influences that have a beneficial effect on your team. You typically have no control over when or how they happen, but you can possibly use the occurrence to your advantage. For example, your department gets approved for some capital expenditures that were not in your original budget, or you identify an additional market for your products.

- **Threats**: These are outside influences that have a potentially negative effect on your team. Like the opportunities, you have no control over when or how threats happen, but recognizing them (or the possibility of them happening) enables you to mitigate their deleterious effects. For example, hurricanes and tsunamis can wipe out infrastructure, or a competitor might release a product very similar to the one that you are working on, or rumors in the company indicate a layoff is imminent.

Documenting these things enables you to more clearly envision what you need to do to get to where you want to be.

During the Hiring Process

When hiring virtual team members (or rather team members who will work virtually — since they actually exist but just work in a different location), managers must rely more heavily on prescreening, reference checks, and other clues to determine how well a candidate will fit with the rest of the team. Behavioral cues, such as proactiveness, ability to follow directions, and attention to detail, are all readily apparent during the initial screening process. Think about how well the candidate performs in these areas as you perform the following tasks:

■ **Ask for recommended candidates**. Before placing an ad, use your network of colleagues and coworkers to identify candidates who might be a good fit. If they meet the requirements and indicate interest, place them in the "to-be-interviewed" folder (which can be an electronic directory or a physical file folder, depending on your preference). If you receive enough candidates this way, you often can avoid having to place an ad, which can give you more choices than you really have time to deal with.

■ **Be explicit about the résumé/*curriculum vitae* (CV) requirements**. Different locales have different expectations for what should be included on a résumé or CV, as do different disciplines. Being explicit about your expectations helps to ensure that you receive the information you need to make a good decision, as well as ensuring that the information is in the correct format for you to be able to store and read it electronically. For example, you may want to ask how familiar the candidate is with using wikis, blogs, VoIP, web cams, instant messaging, and other technology that you use with the team. Or you might want to request that the candidates fill out an online application.

- **Prescreen**. Once you have obtained an adequate number of résumés or CVs, sort them into Yes, No, and Maybe piles based on their qualifications and what you already know about them from your colleagues. The Yes pile contains the résumés or CVs for the people you definitely want to interview. The No pile contains the résumés or CVs for people who are clearly not qualified for the job (go ahead and send them a rejection letter — you will not hire them for this position regardless of the rest of the pool). The Maybe pile contains résumés or CVs for people about whom you need more information before deciding (for example, maybe they have most of the experience you want, but are slightly off on one of the skills). Look for errors, omissions, and exaggerations (these may not be immediately obvious) in their résumés/CVs and cover letters. Identify which ones have bothered to find out about the company (with the Internet, there is really no excuse for not knowing something about the company and showing it in the cover letter). If one of them calls or emails to follow up, mark that on the résumé.

- **Search for them on the Internet**. Once you have winnowed the stack of résumés to a reasonable number of Yeses and Maybes, you can often narrow the list further by performing an Internet search for the applicants, particularly if you are looking for senior-level team members. On more than one occasion, managers have discovered that an applicant who looked good on paper was posting rude messages or comments that indicated a lack of qualifications on an email list, or was bashing an employer in a blog (things that are good to know before you hire someone). You can use Google, Yahoo!, Ask.com, or myriad other search engines that abound on the Internet. You may even want to use more than one because different engines contain slightly different information. One caveat — be sure that you are actually reading information about that applicant and not a doppelganger. (For fun, search for your own name and see what comes up.)

- **Schedule a telephone interview.** Scheduling even a 30-minute telephone interview can help you see how the candidate will interact with the team, especially if you ask behavioral and scenario-based questions relevant to virtual teams (see the sidebar titled "Things to Look for When Hiring for Virtual Teams" later in this chapter for suggestions). Start with the candidates in the Yes pile. You might be able to narrow the list to your top three candidates without needing to access the Maybe pile. Consider using VoIP for this interview, particularly if the candidate is located internationally. Most VoIP is free if both people are using the same service and within certain restrictions, such as number of people on the call. (See Chapter 4 for more information.)

- **Get work samples, publication lists, or patent lists, or request a sample project.** Depending on the position you are seeking to fill, work samples and lists of previous work can help you figure out what the candidates excel at, as well as where their experiences are focused. In some cases, due to the nature of the samples, candidates may only be able to provide you demonstrations or to bring samples to an in-person interview, but will not be able to send you copies. You can find out a lot about a candidate's value system and ethics by his or her response to the request for work samples. When you receive publication lists or patent lists, verify the contents to the extent that you are able. If candidates have websites or online samples, link them to a secure area of the team wiki so that the other team members who are interviewing candidates can access the information.

- **Schedule an in-person or video conference interview.** Once you have narrowed the list to your top three candidates, it is time to bring them on-site for an interview. (If you cannot bring the person on-site, try to go to him or her, have a local manager conduct the interview for you, have a video conference interview, or use a web cam if you do not have video conferencing facilities. Seventy percent of communication is nonverbal, and you want to know the candidate as well as possible before making an offer.) These interviews are generally more involved than the telephone interview, and often include several key members of the teams on which the candidate will be working. Some companies intentionally stress the candidate to see how well he or she functions under pressure. Others prefer the kinder, gentler approach. There are advantages and disadvantages to both. During this interview, look for body language and verbal cues for how well things are going and how the candidate is getting along with the team. Assess interest level by listening carefully to the kinds of questions the candidate asks and to the casual comments he or she makes. A smart candidate will be assessing you at the same time you are assessing him or her, so be at your most professional. After the interviews, collect impressions from each of the team members who conducted interviews (using an online survey tool might work well for polling the team about candidate preferences). Often, a clear selection stands out from the crowd and your choice is easy. Other times, two or more candidates can be equally qualified and equally well-liked, in which case, the selection becomes more difficult.

- **Check references**. Most people do not ask someone to be their reference unless they are really sure that the reference will be a good one. Sometimes, however, you can be surprised, especially if you present the questions as open-ended rather than yes/no, so it is a good idea to check the references. And, remember that silence and hesitation sometimes speak volumes. In the United States, lawsuits filed by people who received a poor recommendation from their former employers have caused some companies to develop strict policies about references. In some cases, if you call the human resources department, you will only get the dates of employment and the job title. You can get around this difficulty by requesting personal references as well.

- **Review post-interview behavior**. If you have a couple of candidates who seem equally qualified and have equally excellent references, hire the one who sends a thank-you note, follows up with additional thoughtful questions after the interview, and seems the most proactive in his or her communication. Proactive communication is fundamental to a successful virtual team.

- **Make the offer**. Most companies get a verbal indication of acceptance from the candidate and then send out a letter with the specific terms of the offer. Expect to negotiate, particularly if you are dealing with a senior person. Determine what things you are willing to give a little on. For example, you might not be able to do anything about benefits or retirement plans, but you might have flexibility in salary, vacation time, home-office setup costs, or moving expenses (rare on virtual teams, but something to consider). Figure out how badly you want the person and what your bottom line is, and then make your offer somewhere in the middle.

Note: In some countries, negotiation is expected. In others, negotiation is considered unseemly, but giving too low an offer is usually considered insulting. Make sure you know what is appropriate for the locale in which you are hiring. You can find this information in salary surveys done by professional associations, by asking colleagues who work in those areas, or by researching salaries and business etiquette on the Internet.

After you make an offer and the candidate accepts, you need to ensure that the new person gets off to a good start. See the "Changes to Team Structure or Personnel" section in Chapter 8 for ideas on how to integrate the new person into your organization, and for advice on how to bring in new people mid-project.

Things to Look for When Hiring for Virtual Teams

Working virtually requires that team members exhibit certain characteristics, such as curiosity, enthusiasm, proactiveness, responsiveness, self-motivation, flexibility, strong work ethic, and self-management. Whether or not the candidate is familiar with a particular toolset is less important than whether or not the candidate can work effectively with minimal supervision and has a "can-do" attitude. During the interview, you can assess both the personal qualities and the tools experience of a candidate by observing the following:

- **Comfort with technology**. Set up the interview using the technologies that you would use when working with the team, such as VoIP, web cams, email, instant messaging, and so on. It will quickly become apparent how comfortable the candidates are with working with the technology and how they handle it when things go wrong.

- **Response to difficult situations**. Here is where the behavioral and scenario-based questions come into play. These types of questions show you how candidates analyze a situation and what their priorities are. You are looking for responses that indicate the candidates focus on problem-solving, being a team player, and finding the solution that is best for the team. You can sanitize actual occurrences and use them as questions, or make up situations that might happen on your project. Examples include the following:

  ❑ Tell me about a time when communication broke down on a team that you were working on. How did you resolve the situation? What was the outcome?
  ❑ Walk me through a typical workday for you.
  ❑ Tell me about a time when you had to think quickly to get yourself out of a bad situation.
  ❑ How do you organize your workspace? Your workday?
  ❑ What is your routine when you are traveling for work? How do you keep up with the office?

- ❑ How do you manage distractions when working from home? From an office? What types of distractions are the most difficult for you to overcome?
- ❑ When working virtually, how do you establish a rapport with teammates you have never met?
- ❑ Pretend you are working on a project and are 30 percent to 40 percent into the project. You suddenly realize that you have gone off course for whatever reason. How do you get back on track?
- ❑ Tell me about a time when you and a coworker had a serious disagreement.

■ **Probe more deeply**. Once the candidate tells the story you have elicited, ask probing questions that more deeply examine the candidate's motives and behaviors. If the candidate was being untruthful in the storytelling phase, it will become obvious.

■ **Look for a demonstrated ability to work remotely**. Ask what experience the candidate has with working remotely. Ask probing questions to determine whether the experience was positive or negative and why. Look for someone who communicates proactively.

As with any hiring decision, skills alone are not enough to ensure that a candidate will be successful on your team. The candidates must also possess personality and character traits that fit with the other team members. If you have a choice between someone who is knowledgeable but obviously difficult and someone who is less experienced but enthusiastic, consider choosing the less-experienced-but-enthusiastic person. You will likely have far fewer personnel issues, and may get someone who will build team synergy.

Selecting Team Members from within the Organization

Selecting team members from within your organization follows roughly the same process as hiring someone from outside the company, but tends to be much less formal because you already know something about the people being suggested for the team. You might actually have less say in which existing employees are on your team than you would if you hired someone because other factors, such as availability, priorities, relationship with the functional manager, and so on, contribute to the decision.

Establishing Team Structure and Roles

One of the advantages of virtual teams is that team members tend to focus more on getting the job done than on the office politics and gossip that often derails colocated teams. To facilitate this focus, managers and team leaders must be explicit about expectations, structure, and roles.

Expectations

As a team leader or manager, your expectations, assumptions, and responses to questions and situations set the tone for the project. In addition, team members come to the project with expectations, assumptions, and needs of their own. When establishing the team, it is important to identify such expectations and to ensure that, by the end of the initial meeting (see the section in this chapter titled "Initial Meeting"), the team is focused on the same objectives and has the same expectations about the project.

Think about and document the following areas when defining your expectations:

- Communication between team members, with upper management, with functional groups, with customers, and with other employees
- Vision for the project
- Behavioral expectations (e.g., time, how well people play in the sandbox with each other, conflict management, and so on)
- Escalation pathways for conflicts and disagreements that cannot be resolved within the team
- Recognition and reward
- Percentage of available work time that each person will devote to the project
- Relationship of project to other priorities
- Hierarchy
- Percentage of time for billable work and for administrative work (it is unrealistic to expect much more than 80 percent billable hours, particularly if the job requires intense concentration or creativity)
- Methodology for measuring success (see Chapter 9)

Some expectations may require negotiation with the team, so be prepared to discuss areas of disagreement or misunderstanding during the initial meeting. Be conscious of conflicts that arise as the project progresses due to unspoken or unconscious expectations. As they arise, document team decisions, and ensure that the entire team is aware of the expectation. (See also Chapter 4 for information on communication and Chapter 6 for information on troubleshooting.)

Structure, Roles, and Responsibilities

The structure of the team and its relationship to the corporate hierarchy forms the framework upon which the roles and responsibilities hang. The structure of the team defines how each functional area will work together, as well as who shows up for reviews, who manages changes, who works with whom, and how often meetings are held. (See Chapter 7 for more about the review process.)

Each member of the team should have a clearly defined and documented role and set of responsibilities for the project. These responsibilities might have significant overlap with the person's overall job description. Then again, they might be highly specific to the particular project. For example, one medical company had a major product recall due to a malfunction that was causing serious injury and death. The company pulled its top performers onto the recall team to address the problem. Team members found themselves performing duties that, while outside their typical responsibilities, were necessary to save lives and to find out how to fix the problem.

Be careful of the "other duties as assigned" statements; such phrases tend to be a catch-all and, if you are not careful, can often distract the team from its primary task due to conflicting priorities from project management and line management.

For areas of overlap, be sure to define decision trees to help determine who deals with the issue. (See Figure 2-1.)

The more clear you can be, the fewer conflicts you will have within the team and the more easily team members can direct someone to the appropriate person.

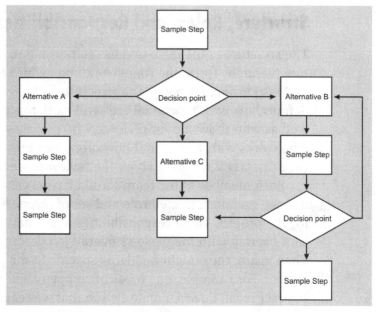

Figure 2-1: Sample decision tree

Leadership

On virtual teams, leadership is shared. While one person might be assigned as the project manager, responsible for the budget and schedule, everyone on the team provides leadership in some area. For example, team members who are experienced with working virtually typically take extra time at the beginning of the project to find ways of establishing rapport with their distant colleagues, and are very proactive about their communication. Other team members are good at planning teambuilding activities, and connecting people comes naturally to them. Still others are highly competent technically and become the "go-to" person on some aspect of the project.

A good team leader actively encourages these unofficial roles because the team becomes more invested in the project if each member feels that his or her contribution matters. As mentioned in Chapter 1, the leader's attitude, particularly at the beginning of a project, sets the tone for the entire team. It is important, therefore, that the leader resolve any conflict or doubt about the goals of the project before setting up the team.

Core Team

The core team on a project typically includes the functional leads from each discipline required to complete the project. These team members get involved at the very beginning of the project and stay involved throughout the process. These core team members typically include the following roles and areas of expertise:

- Project manager
- Requirements analyst
- Design engineer/developer
- Documentation
- Localization manager
- Marketing
- Regulatory affairs (medical or other regulated products)
- Testing/quality assurance
- Manufacturing/packaging

Depending on the complexity of the project, these core members might have additional people working for or with them on the project. However, the team leads are the ones who provide the continuity, attend most of the project-related meetings, and review or collate their functional group's comments before presenting them to the project team.

Associated Subject Matter Experts

In addition to the core team members who stay with the project for its duration, subject matter experts (SMEs) might be brought in to assist with specific aspects of the project. These SMEs typically have specialized skills or knowledge that the project team needs to access for a short period of time. Examples include reviewing the final engineering diagrams for electrical issues, providing assistance with troubleshooting a particularly complex testing issue, evaluating the ethical issues that arise during a clinical trial, and so on. These experts typically work with the core team members on a specific task and then move on to other work. The core team members are responsible for ensuring that the SMEs have the information that they need to accomplish the tasks assigned to them.

Localization and Other Vendors

Companies often hire contractors or consultants to assist with aspects of a project that are outside the company's primary focus. Localization is a primary example. Bringing localization into the project early can reduce costs and problems later on. Particularly for large projects that involve many languages, it is a good idea to include the localization vendor in the initial project meeting and to keep the vendor apprised of project status throughout the project. Many companies assign a localization manager to act as a liaison between the localization vendor and the project team. This localization manager identifies issues that may affect the schedule or localizability of the product. Some companies also have a vendor manager who works with subcontractors on a project to ensure that they have everything they need. This arrangement is particularly helpful if the vendor in question is developing a component that must later be integrated into the product as a whole. (See Chapter 6 for more information on working with vendors.)

Setting the Ground Rules

Once you have established the team structure and have identified the core team, it is time to get the project started. The tone and organization of the start phase has lasting implications on how well the entire project goes, so it is imperative that you carefully plan the initial meeting, teambuilding activities, and guidelines for team interaction. In addition, if you have members of your team who are not experienced in working virtually or in multicultural environments, consider assigning them a mentor who can work with them and guide them as they learn their role. (For information on how to communicate, work with the team, and resolve conflicts during the project, see Chapters 4 and 6.)

Initial Meeting

The initial meeting sets the tone for the project, so during this meeting it is vital to accurately set expectations and ensure that everyone understands the goals, deliverables, and schedule for the project. Perhaps even more important, however, is the rapport building and teambuilding that occurs.

It is best if this meeting can take place in person. The cost of getting everyone together for a few days at the beginning of a big project will be saved many times over with fewer conflicts and better communication. Shared experiences and goals are the fastest ways to build rapport within a team.

If you absolutely cannot hold the initial meeting in person, try to hold a video conference. From a psychological and sociological standpoint, it is important for people to be able to visualize their teammates so that they can "hear" and "see" the human being on the other side of the email, instant message (IM), or telephone. There is a tendency for people to be more blunt, to say things in email that they would never say to someone's face, and for issues to escalate more quickly when most of the interaction is via email or IM if the people involved have never met in person or via telephone. Nothing derails a project faster than flame wars or, conversely, team members feeling that their ideas and information are going into a "black hole," where the recipient never responds to anything he or she receives.

Even if you cannot afford to meet in person, allow time during the initial meeting for everyone to introduce themselves and talk about their role on the project. Be creative about teambuilding activities that can be done virtually. (See the "Virtually" section later in this chapter.)

Note: These meetings require preparation if they are to be successful. Be sure to plan enough time in the project schedule to prepare for the initial meeting.

The following agenda describes what is involved in the initial meeting:

Agenda for initial meeting (also known as the project kick-off)

- **Day 1**: The first day should focus on introducing all the players, providing context to how the team and the project fit into the larger organization, and providing an overview of the project itself. Many companies invest in a teambuilding activity, such as a ropes course, rafting, or other shared experience that requires team members to work together in an adrenaline-producing activity. If your company cannot spend the money to do such activities, you can set up a few team sports activities or board games to engage the team. *Quick Teambuilding Activities for Busy Managers* by Brian Cole Miller has some inexpensive activities that require little preparation time. For each activity, Miller identifies the purpose and the desired outcome, as well as what materials you need, and provides instructions on how to conduct the activity. (Note: Choose your activities carefully and be sure to explain the purpose of the activity; if team members think it is silly, they will not participate wholeheartedly, thus defeating the purpose of the activity.)

- **Day 2**: Now that the team members are comfortable with each other and have a sense of how their counterparts will respond in a stressful situation, it is time to get down to business. Day 2 should be spent establishing the charter, identifying major tasks and milestones, scoping, identifying risks, and generally ensuring that everyone understands the scope, purpose, and roles/responsibilities for the project. If this is the first time that the team has used collaboration technologies, you may also need to spend some time training the team on the technology.

- **Day 3**: Once the project has been outlined and understood, and everyone has an assigned role/responsibility, you can begin assigning specific action items and due dates, identifying dependencies, and helping the team establish both formal and informal lines of communication. If there are IT security requirements for accessing the project web portal, it is a good idea to make sure everyone's laptop computer is set up correctly and that everyone can access the portal. Before adjourning the meeting, set expectations about the next meeting, identify days and times for project status meetings, and establish a tentative date for the next milestone meeting.

Teambuilding Activities

A certain amount of teambuilding occurs naturally as people work together on the project. Over time, team members naturally form alliances and make friends. However, even the most extroverted people experience some anxiety early in the team forming process, wondering how the team will work together, whether or not they will be liked, whether they will like the people they are working with, and so on. You can use teambuilding activities to help alleviate this initial reticence and discomfort by consciously providing shared experiences and goals.

When you are building a team, it is important to ensure that everyone on the team feels included and welcome. Otherwise, your efforts will backfire, and the team will fall apart. Teambuilding activities, when not managed effectively, can trigger core issues for people around rejection, isolation, cliques, and social hierarchy. To avoid these issues, take the following steps, regardless of whether the activity is virtual or in person:

- **Provide a personal welcome to everyone on the team**. Make sure that you greet each person as he or she joins the team. For in-person meetings, introduce yourself and facilitate introductions of the rest of the team. Identify at least one characteristic or ability that you admire about each individual, and make a point of telling him or her.

- **Get the team involved in planning some of the activities**. Ask team members what activities they think would help build team synergy. Then implement them.

- **Pick the sides at random for activities**. Have people count off or just assign people to teams. Doing so avoids the nightmare of someone always getting picked last, and keeps people who are already friendly from always being on the same side in an activity, which can cause clique formation. Mixing up the sides for different activities helps to prevent cliquish behavior.

- **Watch for signs of social isolation**. Many people are uncomfortable in group activities, especially if they do not know anyone. Others may lack social graces. Encourage participation from everyone, and if you see one of your team members standing alone during icebreaker sessions, breaks, or social interactions, make a point of talking to that person for a few minutes. If the opportunity arises, introduce the person to another team member who has similar interests. In the case of virtual teams, if one team member seems exceptionally quiet, you might want to contact him or her individually and find out what is happening. The rest of the team tends to emulate the actions of the team leader, so it is important to ensure that you are being inclusive and welcoming, without being patronizing.

Chapter 2

- **Ensure that everyone has the opportunity to participate equally.** Set up the teambuilding activities so that each member of the team has to contribute something to the effort. For example, in a trivia game, you can make the rule that each person has to speak for his or her side at least once during the game.

- **Vary the type and duration of the activities.** Some people love trivia, some love drawing, some love athletics. Not everyone is good at everything. Choose a mixture of activities that enables everyone to excel at least part of the time. For example, one consulting company had several writers and only one graphic designer. The graphic designer often felt left out of the word play and trivia games that the writers loved, so the manager devised a modified Pictionary game using Play-Doh. The team loved it, and started playing regularly, and the graphic designer felt more included.

- **Provide time to socialize casually after the activity.** Casual social time enables the team to relive and replay the activity through discussion, stories, teasing, and laughter. Often, this social time provides more bonding than the activity itself.

- **Maintain a sense of humor.** Someone once said that "laughter shortens the distance between two people." Shared fun and laughter can provide strong bonds that enable teams to withstand difficult times later on. It is especially important to see the humor in the situation if the activity does not turn out exactly the way you planned, or in other situations where something goes awry. Often, what happens is not as important as your response to what happens.

Teambuilding activities can occur both virtually and in person. Some activities may be incorporated in accomplishing tasks related to the project; others require special planning. In *Quick Teambuilding Activities for Busy Managers*, Miller includes several activities that work both in person and virtually.

In Person

In-person teambuilding activities range from a simple introduction game to a ropes course or other adrenaline-producing activity aimed at building trust among team members. Which one you choose depends on your schedule, budget, and specific goals. Some of the most common activities include the following:

- **Ropes course**: Builds trust and teamwork in physical (and adrenaline-producing) environment.

- **Board games**: Help people see how others react under stress and to competition, and how well team members can play together. Games that require teamwork, such as Pictionary, Cranium, or Trivial Pursuit, are great.

- **Sports**: Foster teamwork and camaraderie. Physical activities help get oxygen to the brain and fuel creativity.

- **Scavenger hunts**: Foster teamwork, problem-solving, and creativity.

There are myriad other activities that you can use as teambuilding activities — the possibilities are limited only by your imagination (and budget).

Virtually

Virtual teambuilding activities are more challenging but typically less expensive than in-person ones. Such activities can be synchronous or asynchronous, depending on what you want to accomplish.

- **Have each team member build a personal page on the wiki or team site**: Helps team members get to know each other and provides training on the tools that the team will be using for the project.

- **Share information and ideas on an ideas page**: Idea sharing fosters creative problem-solving and encourages team members to actively seek information and ideas. You could even set this up as a virtual scavenger hunt. *Fast Company, Worthwhile, Inc.,* and other business magazines provide short articles intended to trigger ideas and "aha!" moments. *Science News Weekly, Popular Mechanics, The Smithsonian, National Geographic,* and other magazines provide information and ideas about things that might only be tangentially related to your business, but which could have a profound impact. For example, when working for a cardiac pacemaker company, Kit found an article about a new advancement in battery design. She cut it out and gave it to the design engineer, who happened to be struggling with a battery problem in the new pacemaker the company was working on. By being constantly on the lookout for new ideas, you open yourself to opportunities and to information you never knew you needed. For the broadest dispersal, set up an ideas page on the team wiki where everyone can contribute links, thoughts, and files. Blogs are also good for this type of idea generation because people can comment on the ideas.

- **Virtual game show**: Using a webinar and instant messaging, you can do a virtual game show for teaching company facts, history, terminology, and so on.

- **2 Truths and a Lie**: This game is harder to play online than in person because it is harder to determine whether someone is lying when you cannot see them. However, this can be a fun "get to know you" game, where participants tell two truths and a lie about themselves and the other participants have to guess which are true and which is a lie.

- **Trivia challenge**: Great for familiarizing people with the company culture, history, and so on, as well as for training on specific tools.

- **Who Am I?**: Each team member is given a list of characteristics or hobbies and has to match the descriptions to the correct team member. Good for getting to know your teammates better.

- **One Positive Thing**: Everyone is given a list of the team members, and has to name one thing that they like about each person. The facilitator collects them and reads them aloud. At the end of the meeting, the facilitator collates the responses and then gives each team member the positive statements about them.

Building a Team Culture

The challenge for managers of multicultural teams is to build an atmosphere of camaraderie, mutual respect, effective communication, and productivity despite differing worldviews and physical environments. In essence, as a manager or team leader, you must take a disparate group of people and cultures, and develop a team culture that is an amalgamation of the best of each culture and strength that the individual team members bring with them.

Managers can facilitate building a team culture by doing the following:

- **Budget for periodic in-person meetings**. If the project is going to last for more than a year or is highly complex, budget for periodic in-person meetings for at least the functional leads. In addition, the project manager should plan to visit each of the other locations at least once during the project. (These visits should be part of the project plan and not scheduled only to discuss problems. If the only time the team meets in person is when there is a problem, it has a significant dampening effect on the entire team, and the project manager will not be very popular.)

- **Facilitate an open discussion about team expectations**. During the initial meeting, after some teambuilding time, ask team members what kind of team they want to be and what they want the work environment to be like. This helps identify what the team members expect from themselves, each other, and you. Encourage members to speak freely by using active listening and by incorporating suggestions into the team guidelines.

- **Be explicit with rules and expectations**. One challenge to working with other cultures is that the rules are generally implicit; that is, "everyone knows to do X, not Y." However, in multicultural teams, behavior X might not be the same in situation Y for everyone. For example, the importance of being on time varies from culture to culture, as do many other aspects of doing business. Making these expectations explicit in the beginning helps to alleviate potential conflicts.

- **Encourage social interaction**. People tend to be more productive when they feel a connection to their teammates. Fun, social interaction builds that connection and encourages proactive communication with the other team members. Such interactions can range · from checking in at the beginning of a meeting to an off-site teambuilding event. Be creative. One team we know always collected souvenirs (the sillier, the better) when traveling and sent them to team members.

- **Be proactive**. The biggest complaint in post-project evaluations is communication. It is impossible to over-communicate. Follow conversations with an email summarizing agreements and action items, and ask the recipient to confirm his or her understanding. Identify potential challenges and opportunities, and plan as a team for the possibilities. Check in regularly with team members; doing so helps maintain the team connection and keeps remote team members from feeling isolated. Perform random kindnesses for members of the team. At one company, the birthday list was published on the intranet, and one manager took it upon herself to send a brief, personal "happy birthday" email each day to every person in the company whose birthday it was. On several occasions, people came up to her teary-eyed, saying that she was the only person who remembered their special day. Never underestimate the power of kindness.

- **Recognize both team and individual efforts**. Recognizing a job well done is an important aspect of team leadership. It is important to provide recognition thoughtfully and carefully. The adage to "praise in public, chastise in private" becomes more important on virtual, multicultural teams. Actively seek ways of building "face" for your team. (See "The Importance of Saving Face" sidebar.) Be sure, when you recognize team efforts, that you include everyone who participated in the activity for which the reward is being given. Leaving someone out, even inadvertently, will cause more problems than not giving recognition at all. Be careful how you recognize individual team members. You do not want to set up a competition between members. Whatever you do, do *not* cause one of your team members to lose face, especially in a public situation. If you have an issue with someone, discuss it privately.

- **Provide a centralized repository for project information**. If you have team members in Asia, Europe, the South Pacific, and North America, you have maybe an hour or two of overlap each day. Place project-related information on an intranet site (also called a "team room") where everyone can access it 24/7. Incorporate other collaboration technologies, such as instant messaging, wikis, and blogs.

- **Facilitate rapport-building**. Hold a Culture Day (this can be virtually or in person), where everyone can bring food, music, history, and other information about their native culture. Build a "face book," where everyone sends a picture and writes a short description of their job and some of their hobbies. Celebrate birthdays and other personal milestones. If possible, plan an exchange, where some team members travel to work in another team member's office for a couple of weeks. (You might have to think of an alternative if some team members work from home.)

- **Be considerate**. Incorporate national and religious holidays, as well as vacations, in your project planning. When scheduling conference calls, rotate the time so that no one always has to get up early or stay up late to participate. Promise only what you can comfortably provide, but always suggest alternatives if you are unable to meet a request. If you make a mistake, apologize immediately and make amends.

The Importance of Saving Face

The concept of "face" is difficult to explain because it is one of those things that is so deeply ingrained in our psyches that we "know it when we see it." Wikipedia (2006) describes it as "someone's public self image. It is the presentation of the self which they would like to project for others." However, this definition does not really fully express the emotional and cultural importance of this concept. In addition, some cultures place greater value on face than others, to the point where wars have been fought over a perceived loss of face. What might be a momentary or temporary embarrassment in one culture can have lifelong or even generational repercussions in another.

Collectivistic cultures, which place a high value on relationships, obligation to the group, and group harmony, tend to place more emphasis on face. On the other hand, individualistic cultures, which place a high value on problem-solving, personal responsibility, and the contractual obligation, tend to place less emphasis on face. However, context is key, and even in an individualistic culture, you can cause problems if an individual feels threatened or is not treated with respect.

The best way for managers to deal with this delicate issue is to actively seek ways to build face for the team and to encourage team members to actively seek the "win-win" situation. Sarah Rosenberg (2004) recommends three things in negotiations:

■ Ensure that both parties feel validated and respected, and that the other person is making positive overtures to resolve the situation.

■ Ensure that both parties feel that the concessions they are asked to make are fair and equitable.

■ Ensure that neither party feels exploited.

Patricia Digh (2006) explains, "Helping someone save face involves giving them a way to exit the situation with their dignity intact. It involves creativity, patience, and sometimes looking the other way. And it puts the impulse on giving, where it should be."

Summary

Being proactive and conscious about how you set up the virtual team sets the tone for the project and helps to ensure its success. By acknowledging and accepting cultural differences, facilitating communication, and generally treating people as you would be treated, you set the tone for the rest of the team. The rest of the chapters in this part provide best practices for managing the teams during the project.

Related Resources

Bass, Bernard M., and Ronald E. Riggio. *Transformational Leadership*. 2nd ed. Mahwah, NJ.: Lawrence Erlbaum Associates, 2006.

Brown, M. Katherine (Kit). Monthly column in *Multi-Lingual*, 2006.

Digh, Patricia. "The delicate, and important, art of saving face." *The Christian Science Monitor* (www.csmonitor.com), August 7, 2006.

Gibson, Christina B., and Susan G. Cohen, eds. *Virtual Teams That Work: Creating Conditions for Virtual Team Effectiveness*. San Francisco: Jossey-Bass, 2003.

Kayser, Thomas A. *Team Power: How to Unleash the Collaborative Genius of Work Teams*. Burr Ridge, Ill.: Irwin Professional Publishing, 1994.

Lipnack, Jessica, and Jeffrey Stamps. *Virtual Teams: Reaching Across Space, Time and Organizations with Technology*. 2nd ed. New York: Wiley, 2000.

Miller, Brian Cole. *Quick Teambuilding Activities for Busy Managers: 50 Exercises that Get Results in Just 15 Minutes*. New York: American Management Association, 2003.

Parker, Glenn M. *Cross-Functional Teams: Working with Allies, Enemies, and Other Strangers*. San Francisco: Jossey-Bass, 2003.

Rosenberg, Sarah. "Face." *Beyond Intractability*. http://www.beyondintractability.org/essay/face/, February 2004.

Schafer, Lu Ellen. "How to Make Remote Teams Work." Training materials from a seminar given to Hewlett-Packard in Palo Alto, Calif., 2000.

Sellin, Robert G., and Elaine Winters. *Cultural Issues in Business Communication*. 2nd ed. Charleston, S.C.: BookSurge Publishing, 2005.

Wilson, Shauna. *InterneTeaming.com: Tools to Create High Performance Remote Teams*. Portland, Ore.: Inkwater Press, 2005.

Chapter 2

Chapter 3

Evaluating Your Needs

> *To do his work well a workman must first sharpen his tools.*
>
> — Chinese proverb

Before you can get the most out of tools like wikis and blogs, you need to understand what you are going to use them for. Just as it is a waste of money and time to purchase and train your team members on a complex system that they do not really need, it is also a waste to have your team working harder than necessary for the lack of the right tool. Once you have established your team (covered in Chapter 2), you can begin to choose the types of collaborative tools you need to accomplish your goals. This chapter steps through some of the questions you need to answer in order to choose the most appropriate tools for your project. These questions include the following:

- What are you trying to accomplish?
- What are your current capabilities?

- Who is on your team?
- Which tool is appropriate for each task?

What Are You Trying to Accomplish?

Before you can choose a tool, you need to define the types of tasks you want to accomplish. Just as you would not use a hammer to cut a board in half, you should not use a wiki to communicate one-to-one, because wiki pages are generally viewable by multiple team members. Do not use a message board for urgent or time-sensitive information, because team members may not read the message boards regularly. Most projects require a variety of tools for different purposes.

One way to begin is to determine the types of output you need to create, the team members who need input into each, and the team members who need to receive each output. Though the specifics will vary according to the needs of your project, a sample list of output types and the needs for each might look like the following table.

Table 3-1: Determining the tools to use for specific tasks

Output	Who receives it?	Who contributes?	Consider this tool:
Team discussion	All team members	All team members	Email list Message board Intranet Chat room Conference call Web-based meeting tool Survey tools

Output	Who receives it?	Who contributes?	Consider this tool:
One-to-one discussion	One team member	One team member	Phone call VoIP Email Instant messages Chat rooms
Status reports	All team members	One team member or a small subset of team	Announcement list Message board Blogs Intranet
Documents, specifications, software code, prototypes	Team members, management, customers	Many team members	Wiki Message board Email list

What Are Your Current Capabilities?

In the ancient world, leaders employed messengers to take information long distances across treacherous terrain, often through hostile territory. Messages (and messengers) were lost frequently along the way, and it often took months to receive a reply, if one arrived at all. Today, communication to opposite sides of the globe is virtually instantaneous, and we begin to fret if someone does not respond to our email fairly quickly. We also tend to take this level of access for granted, forgetting that all parts of the globe do not have equal access to technology. When setting up a virtual team, it is important to recognize and accommodate the conditions under which all team members function in their jobs.

For example, a few years ago, a software company in the midwestern United States purchased a testing and quality assurance company that had an office in Manila, Philippines. While the Manila office had T1 lines within the building and high-speed access within Manila, the lines going out of the country could only support 28K to 56K modem speed. The U.S. office needed to regularly transfer large files to the Manila office for testing. Needless to say, file transfers were painful at best, with many project teams resorting to sending CDs via courier or overnight mail.

Before you can choose a collaboration tool or set of tools, take an inventory of the hardware and software your team is using. You might already have some of the infrastructure in place to allow for collaborative technologies. With just a basic Internet connection, you can access tools like Skype (VoIP) and most of the instant messaging packages (like Yahoo! or AIM). If you already have intranet pages, you can easily add wiki or blog technologies.

Use the following checklists to identify potential issues so you can involve the appropriate executives in getting the issues resolved. It helps if you can identify costs of *not* resolving such issues.

Hardware/Software Issues

- **Bandwidth**: Does everyone on the team have access to high-speed connections to the Internet? Are there time restrictions on access? If the office has high-speed access, does the country's infrastructure support that level of access? Are alternatives, such as a secure wireless network, available? If most people on a team have high-speed access, and one or two remote team members have dial-up access, communication and resource sharing can quickly break down. The team members with slower connections might not be able to handle large files in a timely manner, and might not be able to keep up with or participate in synchronous conversations if everyone else on the call or in a chat room can "speak" faster than they can.

- **Disk space**: As we are all starting to see, more of our information is being transmitted and stored digitally, and our electronic storage needs are increasing. Particularly if you plan to record/store conferences, training sessions, or any type of video, you need to consider the amount of hard drive storage available to each of your team members.

- **Equipment**: Does everyone have the equipment and software they need to do their jobs effectively? How old is each person's equipment? Are there export restrictions for getting someone updated equipment? What operating systems are team members using? Does each team member have his or her own equipment, or do people have to share? Do team members who travel frequently have laptop computers and cell phones, PDAs, or whatever tools are appropriate? Some tools, like web conferencing, assume all participants have a certain level of hardware already in place. Will you need to buy additional cameras? Do you need to upgrade sound or video cards?

- **Software**: What versions of the applications are team members using? While each team member has different needs depending on his or her function, the equipment and software needs to be compatible so everyone can work together more effectively, share files as needed, and so on.

- **Version control system**: If you need many people to share the same files, you might be able to use an existing version control system such as CVS, Documentum, or SharePoint, tools specifically designed to allow and control file sharing. Check around your company to see which tools other groups might be using. By using the same system other departments are using, you might be able to reduce training costs as well as increase the portability of your outputs.

- **Storage devices**: Most computers now come equipped with multiple USB ports, enabling team members to quickly network or to share files via portable USB drives. However, before purchasing a bunch of USB drives for your team, make sure the drives actually fit in the ports provided. While the connector is standard, some computers have ports placed in awkward locations that do not accommodate certain shapes of drives. Some drives and peripherals are shaped so that when installed in one USB port, they can block access to other nearby ports. Also, the size and speed of the newer drives might not be compatible with older equipment and operating systems.

- **Security protocols**: What security protocols exist for each site? How do security protocols affect your team's ability to communicate, share resources, and so on? Differing security protocols between offices can make it difficult to, for example, share files or access project team information. The first time you set up a virtual team, you might need to work with the IT managers in each office to devise a security policy specifically for remote workers.

Communication Issues

- **Internet/intranet access**: Does everyone on the team have consistent, reliable access to the Internet/intranet? What browser and version are they using? Can traveling team members access the Internet using dial-up access if necessary? (Remember that high-speed access is still not readily available in many parts of the world.) What security requirements do you have for accessing a corporate intranet remotely? When you have remote teams scattered across the globe, the easiest way to share files is through an intranet site, wiki, or FTP site, so ensuring adequate access and bandwidth is key to the team's success.

■ **Virtual Private Network (VPN) access**: Can remote or traveling team members access the file server and network using VPN or other technology? What are the security protocols for approving such access for team members? If you are storing project files and other information on a secure server behind the corporate firewall, remote team members might not be able to access the secure information unless they have VPN access.

■ **Conference calling plan**: Does your conference calling plan offer international toll-free numbers? Does the email include the meeting time for all time zones represented in the call? Toll-free international numbers make it easier for remote team members to call in from home when you have early or late calls. Including the time zones in the call announcement helps to prevent misunderstandings and shows you are considering the needs of all your team members.

■ **Wireless access**: What is your company's policy about wireless access? Is a secure wireless network available? Are the laptop computers used by your team wireless-enabled? Wireless access enables your team members to more easily connect when they are traveling. Many coffee shops, Internet cafés, hotels, airports, and conference centers now provide wireless access, though it can often be very expensive. In addition, some companies now sell a portable wireless network that enables travelers to log in for free wherever the company has a presence.

■ **Company privacy**: Even if you do not think you need to worry about security, you still need to determine how private or public your team communications can be. Some of the tools discussed in this book can be had for free if you use the vendor's server (and view the associated advertising). Others are open source, and allow free use without advertising. And of course, some are commercial products available for purchase. Depending on your company's needs, the free tools might be sufficient. Or you might decide to host your tools on your own servers if you want to reduce the amount of data transmitted to public servers, your information has high security needs, or you prefer to maintain your own servers.

Who Is on Your Team?

Before you decide which tools to use, take an honest inventory of the background, experience, capabilities, and unique needs of your team members. Much of this information you will remember from when you first built your team (see Chapter 2). Once you know your team's current knowledge, you can determine how much training your team needs.

When building your team, you probably chose people specifically because they have a certain type of experience or knowledge. If you can build a team that already knows how to use a variety of tools effectively, you might not have to worry too much about additional tool training. On the other hand, your team members might be familiar with your product and your industry, but if they cannot use the tools, they will not be able to accomplish much.

In addition to the time and cost considerations of training programs, you need to build some extra time into your schedule to get everyone up to speed on the tools you select. For example, the first time you hold a conference call, some of your team members might be unable to dial in to the standard phone line, and need to get an alternative access number. If you are using instant messaging software, you have to take the time to ensure that everyone on your team recognizes each other's login names.

Though the virtual tools allow you to communicate with anyone pretty much anywhere in the world, you still need to keep track of where everyone is while working on your project. For example, a virtual meeting scheduled for 3 p.m. in Boston might not be too much trouble for someone in London (where it would be 8 p.m. that evening) but would be quite an effort for someone in Hong Kong (where it would be 3 a.m. the next morning). A handy tool for keeping track of times around the world can be found online at http://www.timeanddate.com/worldclock/meeting.html. Simply enter the cities where your team members live, and the site displays a color-coded table that shows when most people are sleeping in each time zone.

Which Tool Is Appropriate for Each Task?

After you have a solid picture of the tasks you want to accomplish, your current capabilities, and the specific needs of your team members, you can begin to choose the specific collaborative tools you want to use. The ultimate choice depends on many factors, but the rest of this chapter gives you an idea of some of the possible approaches you might want to use for a variety of output types.

For documents such as a **specification**, **outline**, or **project deliverable**, you are likely to have multiple

Chapter 3

people contributing as authors, editors, or approvers, and the output is likely to go to many recipients. The following tools can be used for a variety of deliverables.

- **A wiki page** that everyone on your team can edit. You will probably want to enable change tracking to identify who does what. Note that a wiki can also be used to upload files in whatever format you need (such as Word or FrameMaker), but team members would have to download the files to view or edit them. If you use a wiki page to upload and download documents, establish your own change tracking system to prevent team members from writing over each other's work. (See Chapter 15, "Information Sharing Tools.")

- **A message board or forum system** where team members can post comments or questions. This type of tool allows you to store and easily refer back to previous comments, and automatically tracks which comments come from each team member. Forum and message boards make it easier to categorize discussions, since you can have one board for each area, and you can view responses to each comment in a topically sequential or "threaded" view. However, team members generally need to check the boards periodically to view new topics and recent responses. Many message board systems also include RSS feed functionality that can be set up to send information about the new messages or responses to team members with RSS reading capability. (See Chapter 18 for information on RSS feeds.)

- **An email list** that sends the same document to everyone on the list. Email lists generate multiple copies of the document (one on each team member's system), so you need to have a change tracking system in place.

Project status reports are typically created by one team member and distributed to many readers. This includes any mechanism where the team members learn about what the other team members are doing. Generally, status reports are stored by date, and each subsequent report is stored as an additional file. This lets you maintain a record of the things that work and do not work throughout your project. There are lots of options here!

- **Intranet pages**. If your team maintains intranet sites anyway, the team members probably already know how to post status reports to their pages. If you already have a technology that works, there might not be a need to add new collaborative technology.

- **Blogs**. When using a blog for status reports, consider whether or not you want team members to be able to post comments. This feature can usually be turned off if not needed. If you want to keep the ongoing status of your team within your team, you can easily set up a group of blog users so that only team members can view and post comments.

- **Wiki pages**. One of the strengths of wikis is that many people can edit the content, which might not be appropriate for status reports. However, like blogs, wikis can easily be set up so that only team members can view or post comments to pages. Or you can set it up so that some pages, like status reports, are displayed as static pages that cannot be edited by anyone other than the poster.

- Many teams use a **verbal format** for status, often in a team status meeting. Some collaborative tools like VoIP or web conferencing include the ability to record your discussions, while others might include a text chat component that can be used to store and track your meeting content on the fly. The entire meeting can be done as a webinar, created once and then

Chapter 3

stored for later viewing. This is particularly useful for projects that cross multiple time zones or where the team members work during different hours each day.

One-to-one discussions can include administrative duties, such as employee reviews, or project-related topics, such as determining an approach before bringing in the rest of the team or simply setting up more involved meetings.

- **Phone calls**. The proliferation of new tools does not mean that we need to abandon the old ones. For many purposes, a phone call or even an in-person conversation might still be the best approach. A phone call has the benefit of immediacy (assuming that both people are available at the same time) and, depending on the parties' locations, can be very inexpensive or even free.

- **VoIP**. VoIP offers no record tracking, but it is instant and often easier than IM for people with poor typing skills.

- **Video conferencing**. While this includes most of the benefits of in-person meetings, it requires fast connections, can be difficult to schedule, and may be more expensive than other options.

- **Instant messaging and chat rooms**. Like phone calls, instant messages and chat rooms have the benefit of immediacy, plus they can be logged or recorded. This is useful for tracking exactly what you decided and when, as well as allowing other people to read the conversation later if necessary. Some instant messaging packages, like Skype and AIM, also have voice capabilities.

Note: For potentially difficult or contentious conversations, always use in-person, video conferencing, or the telephone rather than text-based approaches. Nonverbal cues communicate up to 70 percent of any message, and can easily get lost in text-only tools.

In many-to-one situations, you might be trying to brainstorm at the beginning of a project, troubleshoot in the middle, or possibly conduct some sort of post-project review. Or you might just be trying to agree on a deadline or set up the next virtual team meeting. **Gathering team input** requires team members to be able to provide feedback.

- **Chat room or meeting space**. Bring everyone together in a virtual space for discussion or decisions. The benefit here is that everyone can see what everyone else is saying (or typing) and you can turn tracking or logging on to maintain a record of the decisions made.

- **Email list**. Email recipients can respond either to the person gathering the input or "to all" so that everyone sees their answers. The first option sometimes causes people to miss parts of an email conversation, while the second may result in receiving more of the discussion emails than wanted. Email is asynchronous, so everyone can participate even if they are not actively online at exactly the same time. This is also a drawback, as you cannot be sure when each person will actually read his or her email, and thus cannot be sure that all feedback comes within a specific time frame.

- **Dedicated survey tool**. Survey tools, like Zoomerang or Survey Monkey, can keep responses anonymous, which might provide you with more honest feedback than other methods, and can also allow you to limit the possible answers. Survey tools are

Chapter 3

usually quite simple to set up and can be free or low cost. However, they do require the team members to go to an external site, which can raise security issues. This is typically a one-way response; that is, the participants send in an answer to the survey question, and whoever gathers the information must distribute the results if they want the participants to see them.

- **Survey on a wiki or blog**. Some wiki and blog packages include survey functionality or make it very easy to add surveys to the site. Others require some programming knowledge but can be customized to your needs. This type of survey would be just as secure as your site and administrator set it up to be, and you can also set it up so that respondents can see each other's answers.

Once you know which type of tool you need to use, you can choose from many software packages. For more details on types of tools and the functionality of each, see the chapters in Part II.

Summary

Before you decide which tool you want to use, spend some time evaluating what you really need to accomplish, what your current capabilities are in terms of hardware, software, and communications, and the experience and needs of the people on your team. Only then can you choose the right tool for each task.

Related Resources

Duarte, Deborah L., and Nancy Tennant Snyder. *Mastering Virtual Teams: Strategies, Tools, and Techniques That Succeed*. 2nd ed. San Francisco: Jossey-Bass, 2001.

Lipnack, Jessica, and Jeffrey Stamps. *Virtual Teams: Reaching Across Space, Time and Organizations with Technology*. 2nd ed. New York: Wiley, 2000.

Chapter 3

Chapter 4

Communicating with the Team

> " *To effectively communicate, we must realize that we are all different in the way we perceive the world and use this understanding as a guide to our communication with others.*
>
> — Anthony Robbins, author, speaker, business strategist

All the tools in the world are not going to be useful if your team does not understand how to use them to communicate effectively. Before beginning any project, it is critical to establish a set of guidelines for team communications including what information to share, which method of communication to use for each, and specifically how you expect to communicate and how often. Then you can determine which tools are appropriate for the various types of interaction your team is likely to use.

Early in the process, establish and distribute guidelines for interteam communications. Enforcing clear, consistent guidelines can help prevent misunderstandings and improve the way information gets shared.

Synchronous vs. Asynchronous Interaction

The primary consideration when choosing a method for communicating between team members is the urgency of the message. If something is extremely urgent (think "fire alarm"), then you need to use a "synchronous" mechanism to ensure that the team members get exactly the same information at exactly the same time. Synchronous tools include conference calls, meeting software, chat rooms, VoIP, and instant messaging software.

Messages with less urgency can be sent with an "asynchronous" tool that team members can access at their convenience. Asynchronous tools let your team members access the content of messages repeatedly, and are good for reference information such as project plans, schedules, or to-do lists. Asynchronous tools include email, message boards, wikis, intranets, and blogs.

One-to-One Conversations

The bulk of your daily interteam communication is likely to be one-to-one. When all team members are colocated, a lot of communication occurs as casual conversations or one-to-one in-person meetings. In a virtual team, however, the one-to-one communication requires a bit more planning.

If all of your team members are online most of the time, instant messaging software (like AIM, Yahoo! Messenger, or Lotus SameTime) can be a quick and easy way for team members to communicate with each other. Messaging tools generally allow team members to set up the software to display whether or not other team members are online and available, and can be set to store a log of each conversation (though many people do not use the logging feature).

VoIP and chat rooms can also be used for one-to-one meetings, depending on the relative cost and ease of access to the team members, though VoIP technologies might be more complex to set up and possibly more costly than is efficient for brief discussions.

One-to-Many Email

Most of us are fairly comfortable with email communication. It is easy to fire off a short message, and the message can be sent to numerous recipients at the same time. However, sometimes the ease of sending quick notes to many people can be one of the drawbacks of email. If you are not careful, responses intended for a specific person may get sent to the wrong recipients. Many senders have regretted messages sent in anger or been embarrassed by writing a private message (usually something critical or uncomplimentary) and then sending it "to all." As with any written communication, the sender can sometimes "hear" one message while typing, but the person on the other end gets an entirely different message. Humor does not often come across very well, and the nuances of language, like sarcasm, metaphors, or informal expressions, can be easily taken the wrong way. Misunderstandings can easily occur, particularly if your team members come from different cultural backgrounds, whether or not they are using the same language.

Chapter 4

Many of the drawbacks of email can be avoided or minimized by establishing and distributing a set of guidelines for email communication within your team. The guidelines are likely to vary by team and project. For example, if some team members use email software that cannot handle large attachments, you might want to specify alternative methods for file transfers (such as posting to a wiki or using an intranet). If some people have limited or shared storage capacity, consider establishing guidelines for how long (or where) messages are stored.

Establish a subject heading convention that works for your team. For example, you might want to preface each subject line with [project name] for easier sorting, or use more specific tags like [budget], [schedule], or [status] when sending budget, schedule, or status types of email. Or you might decide on a code for very short messages that fit in the subject line so recipients do not need to open the email message at all. For example, [EOM] at the end of the subject line indicates that the entire message is contained in the subject line — there is no content in the body of the email itself.

If email is a primary communication mechanism, establish a policy for how often team members will read their email — once a day, twice a day, once an hour, etc. Similarly, you might want to provide a recommended turnaround time. For example, depending on the specific needs of your group, you might suggest that emails be answered within one working day.

Note: Use caution when setting short time frames, particularly for international teams. An email sent at 9 a.m. on a Friday from Bangalore, India, arrives in Boise, Idaho, at 9:30 p.m. on Thursday evening. It is highly unlikely the recipients will respond before the end of the Bangalore workday unless they begin their workday in Boise before dawn.

Some sample guidelines for using email are listed in the following section.

Sample Email Guidelines

- Email is quick and can be casual, but proper grammar and full sentences are still important. Many email misunderstandings stem from people assuming that the recipients understand their shorthand.

- Proofread your email before you send it. Sometimes leaving out just one word by accident can change the entire message!

- Do not assume the recipients read your email as soon as they receive it. Use other communication mechanisms for urgent information or requests.

- Email is not a secure medium. Do not write anything in email you would not want posted on a public bulletin board.

- Do not overwhelm the team with too much unnecessary email. For example, do not use the "reply to all" feature unless necessary, and never, ever "reply to all" if you are just saying "me too" or "I agree."

- Use prudence when including parts of an original message to which you are replying. While you want to include enough previous conversation so that the recipient understands what you are talking about, there is usually no need to include the full text of every message exchanged.

- Ensure that the subject line matches the topic of your email. Important information can get lost if you are replying to a message on one topic, but discussing a different topic in the body of the email.

One-to-Many Documents

While you could email project documents (such as standards, schedules, or style guides) to the team members, email can cause some problems. When you email a document, you are actually creating a copy of the document for each recipient. Once people receive the document, you cannot be sure how they will store it or whether or not they keep it updated. You might also have trouble finding where the original is stored if you do not have a central file storage mechanism.

Virtual collaboration tools offer several options for one owner to create and distribute documents to many other team members.

Note: If you have a central file system that allows people to download copies, place a note or disclaimer within each document specifying the location of the original document and a reminder that copies (or printed versions) might not be the most recent version.

Most wikis and blogs (see Chapters 14 and 17) have a file repository, archive, or gallery system of some kind. Team members can list the files and download copies as needed, but the original remains available to all on the wiki. You can also duplicate file repository functionality on an intranet page.

Many-to-Many Team Meetings

Running a virtual team meeting requires many of the same preparations and skills as running a meeting in person. A good meeting achieves a purpose. Before you begin to plan a meeting, take some time to determine whether you need a meeting at all — with today's multitude of communication tools, many types of meetings become redundant. For example, if the purpose of your meeting is to distribute information to everyone at once, consider using a simple email instead. If the purpose is to gather status reports from different people, and you do not have too much you need to discuss, consider having everyone post reports to a file sharing application rather than meet.

Though some communications can be covered by other processes, there will be times when you still need to have a variety of meetings. Meetings are appropriate when you need to have a lot of back-and-forth discussion, as when coming to a team decision, or when you are trying to resolve specific conflicts (see "Managing Conflict within Your Team" in Chapter 6). Another common type of meeting is the review meeting, described in more detail in Chapter 7. Meetings can also be very useful at the beginning of a project when team members are just starting to get to know each other. The key is to understand the purpose or goal of your meeting, and ensure that everyone in the meeting works toward that goal.

Chapter 4

Before the Meeting Begins

Whether your meeting is virtual or in person, start by defining the goals for the meeting. Goals should be discrete, and reasonable for the time frame allotted. Do not try to resolve all project issues in a one-hour meeting, but do not tie up everyone for a whole day if you just need to discuss a single, simple issue.

When scheduling a meeting, keep in mind the time zones of your attendees. If you are all in the same city or same part of the country, different time zones might not be too much of an issue. However, if you have to schedule regular meetings across multiple time zones, try to share the inconvenience across your team rather than always have the same person meeting before breakfast or late in the evening.

The other consideration about time zones is to remember that some places recognize daylight saving time — that is, they move the local time forward by one hour during the summer months, then back to standard time in the winter. A three-hour time difference between two locations during "standard time" might switch to only two hours during daylight saving time. For a good reference about time zones around the world, see http://www.timeanddate.com/worldclock.

Invite only people who need to attend the meeting, but make sure you have everyone in the meeting who needs to be there. After all, if a critical decision maker or technical expert is not at the meeting, it often ends up as a waste of everyone else's time.

Ensure that every team member understands the goals of the meeting and has sufficient time in order to prepare for it. The lead time required for virtual meetings might be longer than for in-person meetings, since in addition to the meeting "room" (or virtual space), you need to ensure that all participants have the necessary hardware, connections, and login or password information. If you are going to be sharing files, allow time for files to be uploaded to a central site or for participants to review the files in advance of the meeting.

The standard way to prepare attendees for a meeting is to distribute an agenda either on paper, through calendar software, or by email, or by posting to an intranet, message board, or collaboration suite. An agenda should specify the following information:

- Name and contact information of the person calling the meeting
- Meeting purpose
- Start time and expected duration
- Names of invited attendees
- Meeting location including connection information, phone numbers, URLs, connection passwords or login IDs, or any other information attendees need in order to participate
- List of the topics to be discussed and time limits for each topic

Below is a sample meeting agenda:

Sample Meeting Agenda

Meeting Lead: Brenda Huettner

Attendees: Kit Brown, Char James-Tanny

Location: Skype (voice) and Wiki (file sharing)

Date & Time: August 1, 2006, 1 p.m. Eastern, 2 p.m. Central, 4 p.m. Pacific

Estimated Duration: 1 hour

Prep: Upload current revisions of overall TOC, chapter outlines

Agenda:
- Check-in/greetings
- Review of current chapters
- Assignment of authors to chapters

Action Item: Establish tentative schedule

Allow extra time at the beginning of your first virtual meeting, or the first time you use a new technology or tool, to work out glitches that often occur with new technology. Once your team members are familiar with login or startup procedures, you can reduce the amount of time you spend on connection issues.

Note: If you have a new member join your team, arrange a trial "meeting" to check connections and ensure that the new member is up to speed before a larger group meeting.

During the Meeting

Remember that virtual meetings generally cost more than time — there is often a connection fee, sometimes for each participant. If you have given everyone enough time to prepare, you should be able to stick to your agenda and ensure an efficient and effective meeting.

As you begin, make sure you assign someone to be responsible for taking the meeting notes or minutes. You might want to split the note-taking chore; for example, have one person document decisions and another keep track of action items. If you are going to use any of the automatic recording functions available through many tools, make sure you let all your participants know in advance that you plan to record the meeting and store their input.

Caution: If you are taking notes electronically by typing directly onto a wiki page or even using a word processor on a laptop, make sure you save frequently rather than wait until the end of the meeting. While writing this book, we learned this lesson the hard way when our note-taker was logged out of the wiki page because the system did not recognize typing as activity, and timed out (thus losing all the notes). In this case, the wiki was watching for information being transferred between the user and the server, so frequent saves would not only have prevented the data loss but would have prevented the time-out as well.

Chapter 4

Special Notes for Voice-Only Meetings

If you are holding your meeting as a telephone conference or using VoIP (without associated video or text), review the following guidelines with the team at the beginning of each meeting.

■ Preface all comments with your name — it is not always obvious who is speaking.

■ Never speak when others are speaking; neither one of you will be heard clearly or understood completely.

■ Use the mute feature when not talking (to prevent background noise from interrupting the meeting). Distracting noises can include ringing phones, typing at the keyboard, or drinking or chewing while on the phone. If a team member is calling in from a home office, noises like pets, doorbells, or small children can also disrupt a conference call. Just remember to un-mute when you want to say something!

■ Remember that others cannot see you. Do not rely on physical motions to convey information, such as nodding to show agreement, or shaking your head, or moving your hands around. Facial expressions are lost, too, such as smiles to indicate a joke or quizzical looks to indicate a lack of understanding. In voice-only meetings, it is important to verbalize your whole message.

■ Let the rest of the team know if you have to leave the meeting for some reason so that the meeting will not come to a screeching halt if your response is needed while you are away.

- If you have people participating in a meeting that is held in other than their native language, speak slowly and clearly, and avoid idioms. Someone who is participating in a meeting that is not in their primary language could get lost or confused if people speak too fast or the connection is poor.

Special Notes for Text-Only Meetings

The following guidelines apply to meetings in a virtual meeting space or chat room where team members type their conversation on the screen.

- Ensure that all team members have equally fast connections. Text chat can move very quickly, particularly if there are a lot of participants, and it is easy for someone with a slower connection to get left behind.

- Keep in mind that different people have different levels of skills. A person who uses the "hunt-and-peck" method of typing might not be able to fully participate in a chat room-style meeting, and will likely get frustrated attempting to do so. When working with someone who is participating in a different language, type one thought at a time and wait for a response rather than firing too many text strings at once.

- Because online meeting spaces identify participants by their login name, make sure that participants with non-standard IDs identify themselves at the beginning of the meeting. For example, if you are using the free service from AOL or Yahoo!, a team member using the ID "DoggieDoctor1999" might not be instantly identifiable to all attendees. Identifying attendees can also be a concern in corporate systems that assign temporary or functional IDs (like "tempwriter9" or "group4user3").

- Avoid slang or abbreviations unless you are sure that everyone reading the conversation knows what you mean. Terms that are common in social or casual Internet conversations (AFAIK instead of "as far as I know" or TTYL for "talk to you later") can slow down meetings if people are always stopping to ask what a particular abbreviation means. Worse, abbreviations can cause misunderstandings or hurt feelings. For example, a team member who does not recognize "J/K" as "just kidding" could take away a very different message than the writer who used it intended. On the other hand, abbreviations can be very useful as long as everyone in the meeting agrees to their meanings. Some popular abbreviations are on Wikipedia, the Internet's largest collaborative encyclopedia, at http://en.wikipedia.org/wiki/Internet_slang.

When the Meeting Is Over

Make sure you finish on time. If your meeting runs late, you run the risk of participants leaving early, or they might mentally "check out" and start thinking about where they are supposed to be and what they are supposed to be doing rather than focusing on the content of your meeting. If you cannot accomplish what you need to do in the allotted time, use the last few minutes of the meeting to set up another meeting rather than let the current one run longer than scheduled.

At the very end of the meeting, review the action items participants agreed to. A review helps to summarize the accomplishments of the meeting and makes sure everyone knows what they are supposed to do. Hearing the list of action items all at once, rather than spread out over the course of the meeting, often helps participants to identify missing, duplicated, or completed action items. Each action item should be assigned a single "owner" who will be responsible for seeing that the item is accomplished and a deadline (or at least a time frame) by which to accomplish that item.

In the list of action items, include "produce and distribute meeting minutes." Even if you are recording the entire meeting as a log or an audio file, or capturing presentation slides, it is useful to create a summary document that describes the important decisions and outcomes of the meeting. If you do not have information worth summarizing by the end of the meeting, you probably should not have bothered holding the meeting at all. Ideally, set up an archive on a wiki or intranet site where the minutes can be stored, along with whatever other log or audio files you create. Action item deadlines can be entered into a team calendar or scheduling tool so they can be tracked along with other project tasks.

Meeting minutes are *not* the same as a transcript, because they capture only the key outcomes of the meeting. You might also notice a similarity between the sample agenda (on page 88) and the following sample minutes. It can sometimes save time to start with the agenda document and make appropriate changes based on what occurs during the meeting.

Chapter 4

Sample Meeting Minutes

Meeting Lead: Brenda Huettner

Attendees: Kit Brown, Char James-Tanny

Location: Skype (voice) and Wiki (file sharing)

Date & Time: August 1, 2006, 1 p.m. Eastern, 2 p.m. Central, 4 p.m. Pacific

- All required forms completed and submitted to the publisher
- Wiki set up; all co-authors have login IDs and have been able to edit pages
- Files uploaded: NBI, style guide, co-author schedules
- Assignment of authors to chapters posted to wiki TOC page
- Tentative schedule established and posted to wiki home page

Action Items:

- Each author to write draft of assigned chapters by August 30
- Char will update schedule page by end of business today

Summary

In order for a team to work well together, team members need to communicate well with each other. Particularly in a virtual environment, you must establish the ground rules for good communication. These rules vary by the type of communication (such as one-to-one or one-to-many) as well as by the specific communication mechanism you choose (such as email, conversations, or meetings).

Related Resources

Maxwell, John C. *The 17 Indisputable Laws of Teamwork: Embrace Them and Empower Your Team*. Nashville: T. Nelson, 2001.

Wilson, Shauna. *InterneTeaming.com: Tools to Create High Performance Remote Teams*. Portland, Ore.: Inkwater Press, 2005.

Chapter 4

Project Planning and Tracking

" Even if you're on the right track, you'll get run over if you just sit there.

— Will Rogers, humorist

Whenever two or more people share a task, the total amount of time required to complete that task goes up just a bit because the people involved need to spend additional time coordinating their efforts. Without coordination, they run the risk of duplicating effort or leaving portions of the task undone (or both!). As your team grows, the amount of time needed for this type of coordination effort (or project management) grows right along with it. Virtual teams must not only have a good plan, but also must have a mechanism for tracking the progress against that plan. There are many software packages created just for project planning, and many of the other tools discussed in this book can also serve as project tracking mechanisms.

Planning

Start every project with a plan. If one person has to accomplish a task that will take one hour, you may not need to write a formal plan document, but you still probably have a plan in mind before you begin work. As the project grows larger, extends for a longer period, and involves more people, it becomes more important that the plan be comprehensive and well-documented.

Lots of reference books and courses are available that teach the basics of project planning and cover a wide variety of specific methodologies. There are also many organizations of professional project managers such as the Project Management Institute (http://www.pmi.org), the International Project Management Association (http://www.impa.ch), and the American Management Association (http://www.amanet.org). Whichever methodology or tools you use, a good project plan must incorporate the following elements:

- Scope of the project
- Assumptions on which the rest of the plan is based
- Requirements for project success
- Tasks included in the plan
- Schedule for completion of each task
- Cost estimate

Scope of the Project

This first section is the foundation on which the rest of the plan is based. The scope lays out the high-level vision for the project and provides some of the justification for the effort. The description of the project scope must include the following elements:

- **Purpose**. Why are you doing this project? What will be different when you finish the project successfully? Without a clear purpose, you will not be able to tell if the project is successful or not. For example, a project purpose might be "to shorten the customer's learning curve."

- **Goal**. What are you going to do in order to accomplish the purpose? A project with the purpose of shortening the customer learning curve might have a goal of "simplify the user interface" or "improve available training materials." Note that purpose and goals are *not* the same!

- **Major milestones**. How are you going to accomplish the goals, and by when? You do not need to duplicate the task or schedule sections (those come later in the plan); just summarize them at this point. Sticking with our hard-to-learn software example, the milestones might involve conducting a usability study, revising interface programming, and issuing a new release of the software within six months.

Assumptions

If you are planning a picnic, you make an assumption that the weather will be nice on the scheduled picnic day. If the weather turns stormy, the picnic can be cancelled without anyone blaming the quality or preparation of the food. When planning a project, you make a series of assumptions like "we will have the same personnel for the duration of the project" and "software will be available for testing x days before product release." Documenting these assumptions in the plan accomplishes three things: You get buy-in from management that your assumptions are correct, you increase the likelihood that the assumptions will be borne out as true, and if something does change, you have justification for changing the other elements of your plan (like schedule and budget) accordingly.

Requirements

While the assumptions are somewhat general ("equipment will be available for testing"), the requirements section gets more specific. This section includes the details of the things needed to accomplish the stated goals.

- **People**. Work does not happen by itself; you need people to make your project a success. Include a description of your team in the project plan (see Chapter 2, "Setting Up a Virtual Team"). When describing the people who will work on your project, include the critical non-team members as well. Will you need someone from QA to test your product? Does your company require approval from a legal department before release? Will you be using copy center personnel?

- **Tools**. Imagine an empty room. What does your team need in that room in order to complete the project? Though some things may seem obvious to you (such as a computer and a license for each of the software tools for each of the team members), document them here anyway. Do you need to upgrade software versions to ensure compatibility across team members? Do you need to provide office supplies (ink, paper, etc.) for remote team members? Do you need to buy special hardware or supplies for testing purposes? For example, if the project is building a multipurpose printer, you probably need a variety of types and sizes of paper stock on which to test. Include reference materials that you want team members to use (books, CDs, online libraries such as LexisNexis, or specific server access), and permissions, logins, and IDs needed to access your servers or to get behind fire-walls. Finally, document any special training that team members may need. The cost of a training program is often more than offset by the savings in a team member's time and effort.

As an example, the following table shows some of the tools requirements we had for each writer and for this book project.

Table 5-1: Example tools requirements

	Writers	Project
Hardware	Laptop or desktop computer Microphone and speakers for VoIP Printer	Server to host wiki
Software	Microsoft Word 2002 Skype 2.0 or higher AOL version 9 or AIM Email access	Wiki software Demo versions of other software discussed in book
Other	High-speed Internet access Permission to access wiki Style guide from publisher Standard office supplies (paper, ink, etc.)	

Once you have listed everything you need, you can check to see which of these things you already have. In the above example, some of these things we owned already — each of us owns a laptop, so though computers are required for the project, they would not have to go into the budget. Some we had to purchase, like an external PC microphone.

Chapter 5

Tasks

Describe each of the tasks that need to be performed, including who will perform them. This can easily become the longest part of your plan, depending on how detailed you get. For example, a project plan for a documentation project within a well-established publications department might be fairly brief because the intended audience (the pubs manager and the writers on the team) are likely to understand the tasks already.

Sample Simple Task List

1.0	Research
2.0	Outline
3.0	Write draft 1
4.0	Technical review of draft 1
5.0	Revise draft 1 to create draft 2
6.0	Technical review of draft 2
7.0	Editing review of draft 2 (can be concurrent with 6.0)
8.0	Revise draft 2 to create final draft
9.0	Production
10.0	Post-project analysis

However, if the same project were sponsored by a development department that had not used professional technical documentation services before, the task list would need to be much more detailed.

Also, if the type of project is new to your company or to the decision makers, create a detailed task list to ensure that you are being realistic about what is required.

Sample Detailed Task List

1.0 Research
    1.1 Audience analysis
    1.2 Product training
    1.3 Needs analysis
2.0 Create information plan
    2.1 Information design
    2.2 Document design
    2.3 Style guide, glossary
    2.4 Cover design
        2.4.1 Design artwork
        2.4.2 Review artwork
        2.4.3 Revise artwork
        2.4.4 Specify stock, colors
        2.4.5 Print
3.0 Write content specification
    3.1 User guide contents
    3.2 Reference manual contents
    3.3 Quick-reference card contents
    3.4 Help system contents
    3.5 Review content specification
    3.6 Revise content specification
    3.7 Obtain sign-off
4.0 Write user guide
    4.1 Write first draft
        4.1.1 Chapter 1
        4.1.2 Chapter 2
        4.1.3 Chapter 3
        4.1.4 Chapter 4
        4.1.5 Chapter 5
        4.1.6 Introduction
    4.2 Review first draft
        4.2.1 Technical review
        4.2.2 Editorial review
    4.3 Revise and write second draft
    4.4 Review second draft
        4.4.1 Technical review
        4.4.2 Editorial review
    4.5 Create index
5.0 Write reference manual
    5.1 Write first draft
        5.1.1 A-E

5.1.2 F-J
5.1.3 K-O
5.1.4 P-T
5.1.5 U-Z
5.1.6 Introduction
5.2 Review first draft
    5.2.1 Technical review
    5.2.2 Editorial review
5.3 Revise and write second draft
5.4 Review second draft
    5.4.1 Technical review
    5.4.2 Editorial review
    5.4.3 Create index
6.0 Create quick-reference card
    6.1 Design layout
    6.2 Add text and graphics
    6.3 Review card
    6.4 Revise card
    6.5 Prepare for printer (specify stock, color
        separations, etc.)
7.0 Help system
    7.1 Main topics
        7.1.1 Write topic text
        7.1.2 Review topic text
        7.1.3 Revise topic text
        7.1.4 Check links
    7.2 What's this topics
        7.2.1 Write topic text
        7.2.2 Review topic text
        7.2.3 Revise topic text
        7.2.4 Check links
    7.3 Production
        7.3.1 Developer effort
        7.3.2 Encode topics
        7.3.3 Check links
8.0 Post-project tasks
    8.1 Archive completed documents
    8.2 Establish maintenance procedures
    8.3 Evaluate successes/failures
    8.4 Recommend process improvements

Chapter 5

It is often difficult to determine just how detailed a task list needs to be. Certainly, you do not want to spend more time creating the list than it will take to accomplish the tasks! The sample list above goes to three levels (7.3.2). For any project, the lowest level should be small enough for one person to accomplish but big enough to measure in hours.

This might seem like a lot of effort up front, but it will serve you well over the course of the project. In addition to helping you create a more accurate schedule, a detailed task list helps to better track the progress of the project (see "Tracking Your Progress" later in this chapter). A task list is the input to the "Work Breakdown Structure," or WBS, which is the foundation of many project management software packages. If you take the time now to create a detailed task list, it can also become a template for later, similar projects.

Schedule

Once you have a task list in place, simply assign a time frame to each task to determine your project schedule. Sounds easy, right? The difficult part is knowing how long each task will take. If you are working with or for an organization that has done many similar projects in the past, you may have access to the statistics or metrics about those prior projects. Metrics can give you a good starting place and help to improve your estimation accuracy over time.

But most of the time, you just have to make an educated guess. There are two ways to approach scheduling. If you get to pick your deadline, assign each task a start date and a duration (how long it takes to accomplish that task). The start date for each will usually follow from the end date of the task before it. If you are using project management software, these are called dependencies, or indications of tasks that must be complete before the current task can begin. For example, you cannot begin a review task until the development task is complete. When you enter all this information into project management software, the system calculates the end dates and total time spent for you.

In real life, however, you will often be given a deadline by upper management, or have a deadline based on some external event like a major trade show. If you have an external, unmovable deadline, use a percentage method to determine approximate start and end dates. A project that has a research phase, a development phase, a testing phase, and a production phase may break down to 15 percent research, 60 percent development, 15 percent testing, and 10 percent production. If your deadline is 12 weeks away, you know that the research must be complete and the development must start after 1.8 weeks. Remember that virtual teams may require some extra time for communication issues. Go through your task list and determine how long each task should take, and then compare your task durations to the schedule time frames based on percentage. If you have a conflict, such as a task that takes four weeks to accomplish but is due in just one week, you then have two choices: You can either reduce the scope of the project to decrease the number of tasks you take on or you can add more people to your team.

Note: Be cautious when adding people to alleviate a tight schedule. Some tasks cannot be speeded up by assigning more workers. *"Crash programs fail because they are based on the theory that, with nine women pregnant, you can get a baby a month."* — Wernher von Braun, rocket scientist

Chapter 5

Project management software does a pretty good job of assigning work only to workdays (that is, skipping weekends), and most packages include a function that lets you specify major holidays. If you have an international team, make sure you are taking into account the holidays for each country. For example, many people in the United States do not work on Independence Day on July 4, but people in England do not celebrate that holiday. Labor Day is a holiday on May 1 in Hong Kong, Peru, and Finland; on November 23 in Japan; and on the first Monday in September in the United States. For a quick reference of international holidays, see http://www.earthcalendar.net. You can view the lists of holidays by date, by country, or by religion.

In addition to allowing for holidays, try to take into account any other times that people may be unavailable for work. For example, if your project is scheduled to last a year, do not schedule 52 weeks of effort for a person who gets four weeks of vacation per year. There may also be delays if your industry has a large annual conference that most of your team will attend (this can cost you a week or more) or if you have team members in an area with high potential for severe weather. For example, the northeast part of the United States often gets severe snowstorms that can knock out power (and communications) for days in January and February.

No schedule can be 100 percent accurate, but the more you can allow for various delays, the more accurate your schedule will be.

Though project management software does an excellent job of calculating schedules and lets you easily track progress throughout a project, you do not have to use dedicated software. For very small projects with a small team and short time frame, you may be able to use tools like Microsoft Word and Excel to create and distribute your schedule. Whichever method you use, ensure that all team members have the software required to read your output.

Cost Estimate

At this point, you know how long your project will take, how many people will work on it, and which tools you will need to purchase. You just need a few more items to create the cost estimate for the project.

Time is money, and for most projects, the cost of your team's time will be the largest percentage of your expenses. When calculating the cost of a person's time, salary is just the starting point. You will need to add in other costs associated with that person (called overhead or "burden"). Expressed as a percentage, it includes all the other expenses that are associated with each person, such as benefits, insurance, taxes, office space, etc. Some companies use a single percentage for all employees, while others distinguish between types of workers to determine more accurate numbers. For example, an engineer who makes $60 per hour in salary might need a 25 percent burden, resulting in a $75 per hour cost to the project. Your company's financial department will be able to tell you what percentages to use.

If your project will be using sources outside of your company, include the estimates from those sources in your costs.

Chapter 5

Tracking Your Progress

All team members need to know where their efforts fit into the larger project, how they are doing compared to the other team members, and how the team is faring compared to initial project estimates. Ensure that you have processes in place to allow team members to perform the following basic tasks:

- Update progress on individual tasks. This category may also include bug tracking or similar types of error management software.

- View overall project status.

- Adjust the plan as needed.

- Maintain an archive for documenting actions and decisions.

- Calculate and store metrics that may help improve accuracy of estimates for future projects.

All of these can be accomplished by a combination of individual applications like word processing software, calendar software, spreadsheets, and file sharing systems, or can be quickly and easily processed by dedicated project management tools. There are many different packages available, with a wide variety of capabilities and a wide range of prices.

Before choosing a package, determine which features you need, some of which are described below:

- **Output types**. Most packages let you enter tasks and milestones, and then generate a variety of charts and reports. Two common charts are Gantt charts and PERT charts, which are graphical representations of tasks and schedules. Higher-end project management systems increase the options for output and may include capabilities for custom reports and graphics.

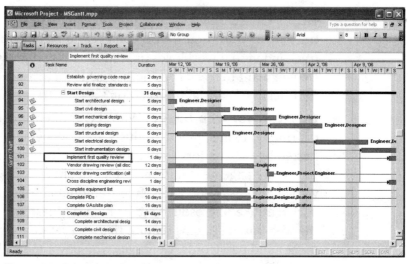

Figure 5-1: Gantt chart for an engineering design project

- **Compatibility**. Consider the existing software within your team, and also the project management needs of other teams with which you might need to share information. Look at the compatibility of output files with other software packages. Can a person without the project management software view the output? Can the output be easily pulled into other applications, like word processing or spreadsheets? If you are already using a database product like QuickBase, you may want to stick with that tool for the project management tasks rather than invest in purchasing and learning new software.

- **Security**. Some project management packages now have file management functions like the ability to check files in and out, which can be useful when many people are accessing the same task and scheduling files. Particularly with the newer web-based project management systems, consider the level of security, passwords, and IDs.

- **Other tasks**. How detailed do you want to get in the tracking of your project? Do you need to be able to track individual workloads as well as team progress? Do you want to track specific issues? Is there a need for tracking financial information?

- **Desktop vs. web-based**. With the proliferation of distributed teams, many products are now being hosted by the vendors so that users can access their project management information from any web-enabled system. Unlike the traditional desktop packages like Microsoft Word or Kidasa Milestones, the web-based systems require that you set up user names and passwords. Generally, you pay a monthly service fee rather than purchase the software outright. Web-based systems make virtual collaboration a bit easier than desktop systems do, but they might not have all the security functionality that some companies require.

Table 5-2: Examples of project tracking software

Tracking Software	Description
@Task (http://www.attask.com)	Web-based; files can be checked in and out
eProject (http://www.eproject.com/ products/index.htm)	Web-based; files can be checked in and out, has forum/message board capability
Kidasa Milestones (http://www.kidasa.com)	Desktop; limited document and resource management functionality
Microsoft Project (http://www.microsoft.com/)	Desktop; many outputs, customizable and compatible with most other tools, does not have check-in/check-out capability

Incorporating Progress into Your Plan

The plan you create does not go away just because it has been approved. Once you begin implementation, you will need to measure your progress against your initial estimates. No plan is ever 100 percent accurate, but by measuring your estimates against the actual results of your project, you can create a more accurate plan the next time around.

When you begin tracking a project, ensure that you are keeping track of the information that will be most useful to you later. Much of this may be determined by your upper management — are they more concerned with hours spent or dollars spent? Do they want to track individual productivity, or are they more concerned with process improvement? Are they more interested in evaluating the process with a view to improving future projects, or are they focused on measuring the specific output values (quality, cost, on-time) of the current project?

For most projects, the raw data can be divided into three categories:

- **Input**. The cost of the project and the amount of effort expended, usually tracked as number of hours devoted to each task or expenses accrued, such as software purchases, outsourced services, or travel.

- **Process**. A measurement of things that happen during the course of the project — the number of review cycles, for example, or the number of mistakes made or bugs fixed. These measures can include variance measurements — that is, how far over or under budget you are, or how far ahead or behind the estimated schedule.

■ **Output**. A measurement of the finished project — the number of widgets produced, the number of lines written, the pages of text printed.

If you are using a standard project management package, many of these numbers will be automatically stored for you as long as you input the raw data. Otherwise, you will need to track them manually, as did the users of the first Gantt charts back in 1910 (see Figure 5-2).

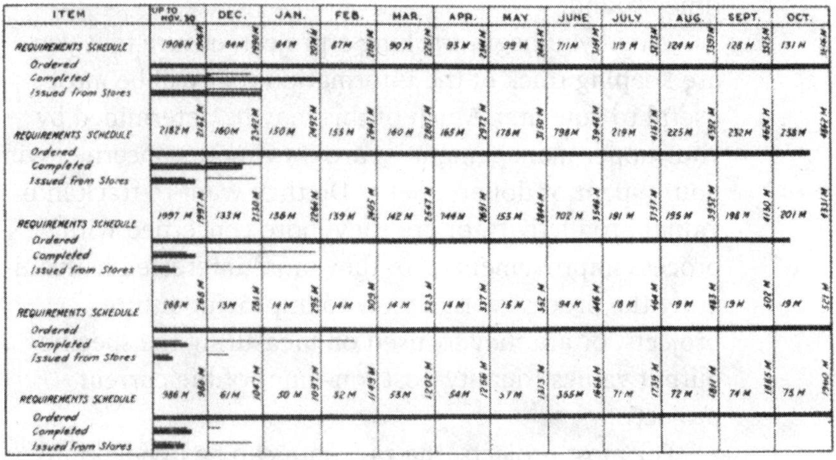

ITEM	UP TO NOV. 30	DEC.	JAN.	FEB.	MAR.	APR.	MAY	JUNE	JULY	AUG.	SEPT.	OCT.
REQUIREMENTS SCHEDULE / Ordered / Completed / Issued from Stores	1906M	84M	84M	87M	90M	93M	99M	711M	113M	124M	128M	131M
REQUIREMENTS SCHEDULE / Ordered / Completed / Issued from Stores	2182M	160M	150M	155M	160M	165M	178M	798M	219M	225M	232M	238M
REQUIREMENTS SCHEDULE / Ordered / Completed / Issued from Stores	1997M	133M	138M	139M	142M	144M	153M	702M	191M	195M	198M	201M
REQUIREMENTS SCHEDULE / Ordered / Completed / Issued from Stores	208M	13M	14M	14M	14M	14M	15M	94M	18M	19M	19M	19M
REQUIREMENTS SCHEDULE / Ordered / Completed / Issued from Stores	986M	61M	50M	52M	53M	54M	57M	355M	71M	72M	74M	75M

Figure 5-2: Gantt chart from *Industrial Management* magazine, 1918

The key here is to be diligent in keeping up to date with the status of your plan. Record the actual hours expended, the actual number of lines written, or whatever measure is appropriate for your project.

In the example of this book project, we began by counting chapters, and then moved on to counting pages. Though we did not measure the number of hours expended, we did have a scheduled due date.

For most projects, particularly ones of longer duration, update your actual numbers fairly frequently but at least once a week. Note that at this point you are simply storing information, not yet analyzing it in any way. When you begin the analysis of the numbers, by looking at percentages or by comparing values in different categories, you are actually creating the metrics by which you can evaluate the success of your project (see Chapter 9, "Evaluating Project Success").

Summary

Every project needs a project plan. Ideally, project plans need to include the scope, assumptions, requirements, tasks, schedule, and costs for the project. The more detailed your plan, the better you will be able to track your progress as time goes by.

Related Resources

Garton, Colleen, and Erika McCulloch. *Fundamentals of Technology Project Management*. MC Press Online, 2004.

Project Management Institute. *A Guide to the Project Management Body of Knowledge*, (PMBOK Guide). 3rd ed. PMI Publications, 2004.

Chapter 5

Chapter 6

Collaborating and Troubleshooting

“ *Difficulties increase the nearer we get to the goal.*

— Johann Wolfgang von Goethe

“ *In the middle of every difficulty lies opportunity.*

— Albert Einstein

At this point in the project, needs have been evaluated, the team selected, communication guidelines established, and project tracking mechanisms put into place. Now, the team must begin producing. Frequently, several team members are assigned different components of the same deliverable and must work collaboratively to produce the design documents, specifications, product documentation, and so on for the project. Often, the team realizes that it is lacking in a particular area of expertise and must hire contractors to assist. In addition, as the team settles down to the real work of the project, differences in work style, communication style, and culture become apparent and challenges arise.

Working Collaboratively

Working collaboratively means different things to different teams. It can range from everyone being assigned a separate component to work on, with integration occurring at specified stages in the cycle, to everyone working on the same component until it is done, and then moving to the next component. Most teams use a combination of the two, depending on the complexity of the component. When teams are colocated, it is relatively easy to have them camp out in a conference room to work collaboratively on a problem or design. With virtual teams, however, this method is impractical, if not impossible. Teams must be creative about how they collaborate.

Wikis can be a very powerful tool in assisting virtual teams in collaborating on a component. For example, if several team members are working on the same component, they can all contribute content and commentary simultaneously in a wiki. On the other hand, sending a document by email allows for simultaneous review but sequential incorporation of comments, and it typically takes more time to accomplish the review.

Agile Environments and Virtual Teams

"Agile" teams (usually found in a software environment) are set up with short cycles and rapid response to customer requests. When originally envisioned, it was expected that teams would be colocated and would work face to face as they produced each component. Virtual teams, of course, require modification of this idea.

Instant messaging windows can act as a virtual office, showing who is in and who is unavailable, and providing for that "water cooler" discussion that is so vital in an agile environment. Wikis can shorten the review cycle and help teams track project-related information. Web-based project tracking and bug-tracking applications help the team maintain visibility on what needs to be done and allow each member to track his or her own progress toward the tasks assigned.

Working with Vendors

Unless your team is really large, you probably need to use the services of people outside the team for some of the tasks required to complete your project. For example, if you are writing a book, you need a printer. If you are writing a software program, you need CDs and packaging. And if you are designing a piece of hardware, you need materials, subassemblies, and production services. In some cases, you may need to hire a vendor or contractor to participate on your team from the beginning, while in other cases, the vendor is needed only for a specific set of tasks on the project.

Regardless of the type of vendor, you need to perform the following tasks before hiring one:

1. **Define the task** or tasks you are assigning to the vendor. For some vendors, such as those who copy CDs, the task may seem obvious. But even for simple tasks, make sure you specify everything that you want the vendor to do. For example, will the CD vendor be responsible for a quality check? For attaching a label? For printing the label? For providing sleeves

Chapter 6

or boxes for the CDs? For shipping costs? Define each task, deliverable, and outcome, including any deadline requirements you have.

2. Using your task definition from step 1, **get quotes** from at least two (preferably three) vendors. Be prepared for the vendors to ask for clarifications or request changes to whatever specifications you listed. This process alone can be a terrific learning experience!

3. **Ask for and check references**. You want to verify that the vendor has a record of satisfied customers. For most vendors, you can also request a sample of their work to check the quality for yourself. This does not mean that they do your work for free; you should be able to determine quality based on work they have done for others.

4. **Choose your vendor**. When comparing vendors, consider how the vendors differ in their approach and process. For example, say you are using a vendor to print a document. The cost for spiral binding is more than the cost for stapling the pages together, but the spiral binding looks more polished. If you are printing copies for use within your team, you may prefer the cost savings. If the document is getting wider distribution, you probably want the more expensive binding. You also want to consider the capacity of the vendor compared to your needs. A one-person shop can probably turn things around very quickly and is likely to give you extremely personalized service, but might not be able to handle a large volume or might not have the specific expertise you need.

5. **Write your agreement as a contract**. Be sure to include invoicing requirements, payment schedule, any major milestones that must be met, and specific

deliverables. Specify what you give to the vendor (and when) and what you expect from the vendor in return (and when).

If you go through these steps and find a vendor that works well with your team, you can bring the vendor back for future projects. Reusing the vendor reduces the learning curve (and your cost) on subsequent projects.

Though the steps for each type of vendor are similar, there are a few specific things to consider depending on the type of vendor. The following sections describe some of the types of vendors and questions you may want to ask for each.

Localization/Translation

(Adapted from "Developing an effective request for proposal" by M. Katherine (Kit) Brown in the March 2006 issue of *Multi-Lingual*. Reprinted with permission.)

Effective localization depends on building and maintaining a good relationship with your localization vendor. When hiring a localization vendor, it is important that the initial request for proposal (RFP) be as complete as possible. RFPs provide the localization vendor with critical information about the project and about the company requesting the proposal. However, many RFPs lack the information necessary for the vendor to develop an adequate proposal or quotation.

An effective RFP enables you to more effectively evaluate and manage the localization project. Benefits include the following:

- Provides a consistent description of the project, including potential issues
- Ensures that you are comparing like to like when evaluating multiple vendors

Chapter 6

- Requires you to clearly define the scope and schedule for the project
- Enables you to clearly define expectations at the beginning of the project

Components of an RFP

RFPs do not have to be long documents; generally two to five pages (plus source files) provide enough information for the vendor to develop a proposal. The following outline describes the components that should appear in every RFP that goes out for competitive bid:

- **Introduction**: Provide a paragraph or two summarizing your business and the project. Describe your expectations (what is most important — quality, cost, or schedule?). Identify the key players, including contact information and roles.

- **Development process graphic**: This graphic should provide an overview of your company's development cycle and how localization fits into the cycle. Are you expecting to provide content for localization throughout the project or at the end? Where does localization fit into the release schedule? Are you expecting simultaneous release in all languages, or will the product releases be staggered? Do you even have a product release schedule, or is everything done using a streaming release model?

- **Scope**: Identify how big and how complex the project is. Which languages do you need? What formats do the deliverables need to be in? How many words, graphics, documents are being translated? Will the localized versions be fed into a content management system or publishing system, or do they need to be formatted? Does the localization include software strings? Firmware? Testing for user interface issues in the localized versions? Does a translation memory exist for this content, or is it the first time the content has been translated?

- **Schedule**: Provide an overview of the project schedule, with the localization areas highlighted. When do you anticipate getting the first round of content to localization? When do you want to see in-country reviews? When is the source content final? When do you expect the product release? Are you doing simultaneous release in all languages?

- **Tools required**: Identify what tools are being used to create the content. This information will help the localization vendor more accurately estimate the effort this job will require. For example, some languages are not supported by some applications and require a workaround. Some applications are less localization-friendly than others. The high-end features available in some applications do not work well in all languages. A competent localization vendor will be able to identify these issues for you in the proposal and will recommend workarounds.

- **Sample files**: Provide a list of the source files that you are including with the RFP, and identify the tool used to create them. For graphics, provide the original file (such as CorelDraw, Adobe Illustrator, or Adobe Photoshop format). For software products, consider providing a working copy of the software, as well as the RSC, XML, or string files, so that the vendor can quickly identify interface issues. If you provide a PDF of the content, also provide the original source file (such as Adobe FrameMaker, Adobe InDesign, Quark, Microsoft Word, and so on) so that the localization vendor can identify any problems related to formatting. If you have screen shots of a software product,

Chapter 6

include the specifications used to develop the screen shots.

- **Templates, style guides, glossary**: Provide the localization vendor with the templates, style guides, list of text strings in the user interface, and glossary. This information enables the vendor to ensure consistency in developing the localized versions. Has the glossary been translated previously? If so, provide the translated versions. Are you using a terminology management system? If so, which one?

- **Preferred format and due date for proposal**: Tell the vendor how you want the proposal structured and when it is due. By requiring a particular order of information, you can more easily compare proposals from multiple vendors. Identify the level of detail you want on the cost breakdown. Identify how you want to receive the proposal (email, regular mail, in person, presentation). Tell the vendor when the proposal is due, and provide at least a week so that the vendor has time to contact you with questions. For complex projects, you may want to arrange a meeting with each vendor to ensure understanding of the project.

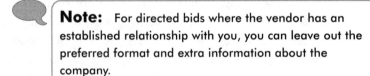

Note: For directed bids where the vendor has an established relationship with you, you can leave out the preferred format and extra information about the company.

Evaluation Checklist

Once the vendor has provided you with a proposal, you can use the following checklist to evaluate how well it meets your needs:

- Did the vendor follow the directions?
- Is the proposal complete and comprehensive?
- Does the proposed solution meet your needs? Does it fit your budget?
- Does the proposal consider any special issues that you listed in the RFP?
- Does the proposal clearly identify how the vendor's process meshes with yours?
- Are the cost estimates in line with the other vendors? If not, is there a special service that the vendor recommends, which may account for the difference?
- How does the vendor handle translation memory? Content management? QA? Changes?
- Is the vendor responsive to providing additional information or clarification?
- Does the vendor include a list of assumptions and risk assessment for the project?
- Does the vendor provide innovative solutions to issues with your files or processes?

Creating an effective RFP can save you time and money on your localization projects by ensuring that you receive an accurate quote and an effective solution to your localization needs. By clearly identifying expectations, scope, and schedule, you can help ensure that the relationship with the localization vendor gets off to a good start.

Chapter 6

Production or Hardware

When the vendor is making something physical for you, such as books, CDs, or hardware, you need to focus on consistency of quality from one unit to the next and the ability of the vendor to deliver in the time frame you need. Ask the following questions:

- Does the vendor have the type of certifications your company needs (such as ISO 9000 or 9001)?

- Is the vendor's shop capable of producing the volume of product you need in the specified time frame?

- Is the vendor's system compatible with yours, or is a conversion step required? This is likely to impact both time frame and cost.

- What is the vendor's quality control process (and is it sufficient for your needs)?

Documentation

If your team needs to hire a documentation vendor, it is critical that the vendor be brought in as early in the project as possible. Do not wait for the product to be complete and then expect a manual in just a few days! Documentation drafts can help point out inconsistencies or missing components, identify areas that need improvement, and serve as a basis for usability testing and quality assurance testing. When hiring a documentation vendor, use the following questions as a starting point for discussion:

- Can the vendor coordinate well with your existing project plans?

- What is the vendor's process for delivering drafts, requesting reviews, and finalizing documents?

- How much time will the vendor require from the subject matter experts? A good vendor will probably need more time than you expect for information gathering and review cycles.

- Who is responsible for creating graphics? Will that cost extra?

- Who will hold the copyright? Who will obtain permission to use copyrighted materials if necessary?

- What will the final deliverable be? A PDF file? Source files (in Word or FrameMaker or a similar format)? Printed documentation?

- Is the work billed on time and materials or flat fee?

- What components and information does the documentation vendor require?

- Will the vendor work remotely or on-site?

- What supporting information, access, and so on does the vendor need?

Contractors/Consultants

If you need to use a vendor to round out your team, you actually are doing two things at once. You are evaluating the vendor and you are "hiring" an employee (see Chapter 2). In this case, add the following questions to your interview list:

- How does the invoicing/payment schedule work?

- Who will pay the expenses of the team member? For example, is the vendor responsible for providing the team member with hardware and software, or will they ask you to pay for the expense of upgrades as needed? If travel is involved, will the vendor pay for it or charge your company for it?

Chapter 6

- Is a process in place to replace a team member if needed? This situation might occur because the team member is not capable of doing the work or because of conditions beyond anyone's control, such as family issues or health crises.

Caution: In the United States, there are tax implications based on whether a team member is an employee (W-2) or a contractor (1099). If the U.S. Internal Revenue Service determines that your project held too much control over the work of contractors, it might categorize those people as employees and demand that your company pay appropriate taxes (and sometimes fees). An outline of these rules is at http://www.irs.gov/businesses/small/article/0,,id=99921,00.html. Consult your HR department, tax advisor, or legal counsel when in doubt!

Challenges for Virtual Teams

Just as a little rain must fall in every ecosystem, so challenges arise in every project. Awareness of the common challenges that virtual teams face can help you mitigate those challenges when they arise.

Do Not Leave Anyone Behind!

When you work surrounded by the latest technology every day, it is easy to forget that most of the world does not have as easy access to technology as you do. Infrastructure is still catching up in many parts of the world, and high-speed access may not be readily available (though this is changing rapidly with the improvement of wi-fi availability and the commoditization of computer technology). Some challenges you might be able to alleviate by updating equipment; for others, you must be creative in finding ways to work around the problem. The following issues might arise when working with virtual teams whose members are located in less developed parts of the world:

- **Import/export restrictions dictate the level of technology available**: Many governments strictly regulate the type and level of technology available for import into certain countries. These restrictions mean that team members located in certain countries might have a difficult time getting updated versions of software or in obtaining the most recent versions of hardware. Check with the Customs department in your home country before shipping equipment to team members in other countries.

- **High-speed access to the Internet is limited or unavailable**: In areas where the infrastructure is antiquated, team members might have high-speed access within the walls of the office, or possibly even in the city where they are located, but the lines going out of the region might not be able to handle the load. For example, as recently as 2000, Manila, Philippines, had high-speed access available within the city, but the lines leaving the country could only support 28 Kbps. Many parts of Africa, Asia, and the Middle East are completely lacking in infrastructure for Internet access of any kind. While satellite and wi-fi access is increasingly available, coverage is often spotty at best. In addition, such access can be prohibitively expensive.

- **Telephone service is spotty**: Land lines in many parts of the world are antiquated or nonexistent. In other areas, one is charged by the minute for even local calls, making dial-up Internet unrealistic where high-speed access is not available. Interestingly, there is a trend in many areas to skip directly to cellular or satellite telephone service because the infrastructure is less expensive to deploy.

Chapter 6

- **Rolling blackouts dictate work schedules**: In some areas, electricity is available only for a few hours per day. Team members in these areas must rely on generators or alternative energy to do their work.

- **Government regulations restrict access to certain websites**: Not all countries believe that citizens should have access to information that the government does not agree with. Not all countries believe that citizens should have freedom of speech. Many countries monitor communications and transactions.

- **Currency exchange and banking laws can create difficulties**: Some countries regulate what currency their citizens can receive payment in, and transaction fees can be exorbitant, particularly when using paper checks. In addition, credit cards can be difficult to obtain in some countries. Many people use electronic fund transfers instead of credit cards for online transactions. This can cause issues if your corporate expensing processes do not accommodate this difference.

- **Safety and security are a concern**: In addition to robberies, which are common worldwide, remote team members might face daily life-threatening situations ranging from terrorist attacks and kidnappings to shootings and bombings from warring factions. Survival is a daily challenge in these war-torn areas, and team members in these areas might be understandably distracted at times.

Before you say, "Why would I consider hiring someone who lives in such a 'primitive' environment," consider for a moment that many of these issues can occur anywhere at any moment under the right circumstances, such as a natural disaster or a coup. By being aware of their possibility, you can mitigate the effects and develop workarounds.

Dimensions of Culture

As mentioned in Chapter 1, much of culture is implicit and unconscious; this is true of beliefs ranging from worldview to what is considered effective leadership. Geert Hofstede devised a system of cultural dimensions based on research conducted at IBM with employees in offices worldwide. Hofstede's system attempts to categorize cultures based on these dimensions, and while some might argue that IBM is a limited and skewed sample pool to draw from, these dimensions are widely accepted and recognized by cultural experts. For each dimension, Hofstede attempts to be culturally neutral and nonjudgmental:

- **Power distance** (relationship to authority): Cultures with high power distance tend to be more hierarchical and authoritarian, while cultures with a lower power distance tend to be egalitarian.

- **Individualism vs. collectivism**: Individualistic cultures often take the good of the one over the good of the many, and value personal achievement, initiative, and recognition. Collectivistic cultures believe in the good of the many over the good of the one, and value group stability, cooperation, and harmony.

- **Masculinity vs. feminity**: Masculine cultures tend to value power, achievement, and wealth. Conflicts often get resolved by aggression. Feminine cultures tend to value relationships, environmental protection, and quality of life. Conflicts are resolved by negotiation.

- **Uncertainty avoidance**: Cultures with high uncertainty avoidance value data gathering and full (often lengthy) discussions of all the ramifications of a potential course of action. Such cultures like to know all the rules of the game, carefully study their opponents (or business partners), and only make a move when they are sure of the decision. Cultures with low uncertainty avoidance value risk-taking and tend to leap first and figure out the details later.

- **Long-term vs. short-term orientation**: Long-term orientation means examining decisions for how they will affect the seventh generation from now. In other words, these cultures try to understand the consequences of their decisions on future generations. They tend to view themselves as stewards of the resources. Cultures with a short-term orientation tend to look only at the immediate gain and do not worry about the consequences in the future. They tend to consider themselves resource owners.

As you might imagine, such cultural differences can also give rise to differing expectations and assumptions about what makes a good leader. Cornelius Grove and colleagues conducted a massive, global, 11-year study on what makes an effective leader. The following table lists some of the more interesting traits that the GLOBE team found:

Table 6-1: Examples of global leadership traits

Universal Positives	Universal Negatives	Culturally Dependent
Charismatic/inspirational	Irritable	Cunning
Team-oriented	Dictatorial	Sensitive
Participative	Malevolent	Evasive
Humane-oriented	Self-protective	Class conscious
Trustworthy	Autonomous	Ruler
Motivating		Provocateur
Communicative		Risk-taker
Informed		
Coordinator		
Just		

The GLOBE researchers themselves caution, "Keep in mind that a critical question remains unanswered. How does a leader in this or that society actually demonstrate...[these qualities]?" And "therein lies the rub." While certain concepts might be agreed upon as universally positive, the way they are demonstrated in a particular culture might be very different.

It is easy to see where conflicts can arise when two cultures with such different worldviews come to the bargaining table. Knowing that these different perspectives exist help you to modify your own behavior when working with someone whose worldview differs from your own.

Managing Conflict within Your Team

When two or more people in the same office have a disagreement, they can sometimes just sit down in a room somewhere to talk things out. Or the manager can call the people involved into a meeting and hear both sides of the story at once, allowing the team members to hear each other's arguments. In a virtual team, however, these in-person meetings are often difficult or impossible to set up. But if conflicts are left unaddressed too long, they can adversely affect the relationships between team members and the ultimate success or failure of the entire project. In addition, conflict tends to escalate more quickly on a virtual team than it does for colocated teams because team members have little visibility into the challenges that their teammates are facing in their daily lives.

In any team, conflict can result from differing work styles or expectations, from team members having different goals or methodologies, or even, sometimes, from hidden agendas. When you add the challenges of a virtual team, you are also adding the problems that come with more complex communications and the possibility of team members making assumptions about each other that may not be accurate. Finally, when you have a multicultural virtual team, you add in potential conflict based on cultural differences.

So what can you do besides issuing an order to "play nice"?

First, recognize that your goal is to manage the conflict, not necessarily resolve it. Conflict is a normal part of everyday life and can even be productive when it points out problems or helps you identify new ways of doing things.

Second, some types of conflict, like sexual harassment and discrimination, require very specific actions on the part of the employees, managers, and company. Get help from your human resources department or legal department! It is important to also keep in mind that what one culture considers rude or offensive might be perfectly acceptable in another culture or context. For example, Americans have large personal space requirements compared to other cultures, and touching in a business setting is typically limited to handshakes, unless the colleagues know each other very well. In France, on the other hand, a kiss on each cheek is the typical greeting between male and female colleagues.

For the most part, however, conflict will be minor clashes of work styles, personality differences, or cultural misunderstandings. Some of this may be covered by the team communication guidelines you set up at the beginning of the project (see Chapters 2 and 4), and the team members involved may be able to achieve agreement or compromise on their own or with just a bit of coaching. In other cases, however, the project manager may have to step in to prevent conflict from escalating. If you have to do this, keep a couple of key points in mind:

- **Get the facts**. Remember that there are (at least!) two sides to every story, so make sure you understand the situation from both sides of the conflict. Often, conflict arises over one issue (such as a team member who is consistently late to meetings), but turns out to be caused by some entirely different issue (such as scheduling the meetings too early in that team member's time zone).

- **Stick to the issues at hand**, and try not to let anyone get too personal. That same person who is consistently late may be perceived as careless, lazy, or inconsiderate of the team's time, but these issues, assuming they exist, should be handled outside of your project team. Within the project, focus on the issue that impacts the project (in this case, chronic lateness to meetings). If the conversation degenerates into personal attacks, it gets very difficult to recapture a genial team atmosphere.

■ **Get together with everyone involved**. If at all possible, conflict resolution is best handled face-to-face. If that is not possible, try to use video conferencing or, at the very least, VoIP. Remember, a lot of information is communicated by facial expressions and tone of voice, things that do not come through well in text-based tools like email. It can be helpful for everyone to see each other, particularly when dealing with team members who are emotionally committed to their side of the conflict, or when one or more of the people involved are operating in a second language. More than 70 percent of communication is nonverbal, particularly in an emotional exchange. Whatever you do, do *not* try to resolve a touchy issue by email or written communication alone. Such efforts quickly degenerate into flame wars.

■ **Acknowledge cooperation, even if it is small**. Start with something that works well or something that everyone agrees upon. This is similar to the salesman's strategy of getting you to say "yes" at the beginning of a conversation with questions like "Isn't it a nice day?" or "Did you have a nice weekend?" This gets you in a positive mood, and theoretically sets the tone for his sales pitch, making it more likely for you to continue to say "yes" to whatever he is offering. In conflict management sessions, you may have to look hard to find something positive, such as "Thank you all for being here" or "We all agree that we need to address this situation." Practice nonviolent communication by being respectful and remaining calm, regardless of the provocation.

- **Ask leading questions**, and give everyone a chance to contribute to the solutions. Let each "side" describe their view of the problem, then ask them what the next appropriate action might be. Remind them, if necessary, to remain calm, to avoid personal attacks, and to focus on the issue at hand. Use active listening and reflect back what you hear to show that you are paying attention and working toward understanding. Stay neutral and nonjudgmental.

- **If necessary, take a time out**. If people get too emotional, they cannot hear what the other side is saying. Sometimes, it is helpful to allow for a "cooling-off" period, so that people can take a deep breath and recover their composure. Some people also need time to consider what has been said or recommended before making a decision or changing their behavior. *Never* cause a team member to lose face. (See "The Importance of Saving Face" in Chapter 2.)

The following list first appeared in the October 1991 issue of *Active Voice*, the newsletter of the San Francisco chapter of the Society for Technical Communication (STC). It behooves all of us to remember these guidelines when we are working with other people, particularly when that person is located on the other side of the world.

Ten Proven Ways to Get Along with People

(Reprinted with permission from *Active Voice*, the newsletter of the San Francisco chapter of the Society for Technical Communication, October 1991.)

1. Refuse to talk negatively about others; do not gossip and do not listen to gossip.

2. Have a forgiving view of people. Believe that most people are doing the very best they can.

3. If someone criticizes you, see if there is any truth to what s/he is saying; if so, make changes. If there is no truth to the criticism, ignore it and live so that no one will believe the negative remark.

4. Before you say anything to anyone, ask yourself three things: Is it true? Is it kind? Is it necessary?

5. Make promises sparingly and keep them faithfully.

6. Never miss the opportunity to compliment or to say something encouraging to someone.

7. Forget about counting to ten. Count to one thousand before doing or saying anything that could make matters worse.

8. Let your virtues speak for themselves.

9. Keep an open mind; discuss, but do not argue. (It is possible to disagree without being disagreeable.)

10. Cultivate your sense of humor; laughter is the shortest distance between two people.

Chapter 6

Summary

Every project runs into difficulties, and every team will face conflict of one kind or another at some point. Remember that your vendors are part of your team and critical to your project's success. With proper planning you can avoid some problems, and if all team members focus on the good of the project, you can work through those problems that you cannot avoid.

Related Resources

Brinkman, Rick, and Rick Kirschner. *Dealing with People You Can't Stand: How to Bring Out the Best in People at Their Worst*. 2nd ed. New York: McGraw-Hill, 2002.

Brown, M. Katherine (Kit). "Developing an effective request for proposal." *MultiLingual*. (March 2006): 26-27.

The Dalai Lama, and Howard C. Cutler. *The Art of Happiness at Work*. New York: Penguin Press, 2003.

Ferraro, Gary P. *Global Brains: Knowledge and Competencies for the 21st Century*. Charlotte, N.C.: Intercultural Associates, Inc., 2002.

Frakes, Cindy. "Creating Documentation in an Agile Programming Environment." Presentation given at LavaCon, October 2006.

Grove, Cornelius. *Leadership Style Variations Across Cultures: Overview of GLOBE Research Findings*. Grovewell, LLC (http://www.grovewell.com/pub-GLOBE-leadership.html), 2005.

Hofstede, Geert. *Culture's Consequences: International Differences in Work-Related Values*. Vol. 5, *Cross-Cultural Research and Methodology*. Abridged ed. Beverly Hills, Calif.: Sage Publications, 1984.

House, Robert J. et al. *Culture, Leadership, and Organizations: The GLOBE Study of 62 Societies*. Thousand Oaks, Calif.: Sage Publications, 2004.

Rosenberg, Marshall B. *Nonviolent Communication: A Language of Compassion*. Del Mar, Calif.: PuddleDancer Press, 2003.

Sanders, Tim. *Love Is the Killer App: How to Win Business and Influence Friends*. New York: Three Rivers Press, 2003.

Chapter 6

Chapter 7

Conducting Reviews

> " *Evaluating is itself the most valuable treasure of all that we value. It is only through evaluation that value exists: and without evaluation the nut of existence would be hollow. Hear it, you creators!*
>
> — Friedrich Nietzsche, in *Thus Spoke Zarathustra*

> " *I have but one lamp by which my feet are guided; and that is the lamp of experience. I know of no way of judging the future but by the past.*
>
> — Patrick Henry, speech to the Virginia Convention, Richmond, Virginia, March 23, 1775

Mention reviews to a project team and chances are good that you will hear a collective groan or team members will vie to tell you the best review horror story. Adding the complexity of the virtual team environment to the mix can completely derail the process if you have not planned and set expectations appropriately.

However, reviews are a vital and inevitable, though sometimes onerous, part of team projects. Effective reviews help us produce higher quality products, documentation, and services; help us perform our jobs more effectively; and identify lessons learned so that we can continuously improve our collective performance on subsequent projects. Hopefully, by the time the project team needs to hold a review, the team has already established a rapport and is working together effectively. (See also the other chapters in Part I.)

In this chapter, we will discuss best practices for the following types of reviews:

- Content reviews
- Performance appraisals
- Project reviews

Content Reviews

(Adapted from "Conducting Effective Technical Reviews" by M. Katherine (Kit) Brown that appeared on TECHWR-L [http://www.techwr-l.com/techwhirl/magazine/writing/ effectivetechreviews.html] in 2001. Reprinted with permission.)

We have important reasons for conducting content reviews:

- Content reviews can provide a system of checks and balances from a variety of subject matter experts (SMEs) on the team, which helps bring technical accuracy and completeness to the documents and products that we produce.

- Content reviews can help improve the product's design and catch problems or bugs, which can enhance both the product and the accompanying documents.

- Content reviews can help reduce product development costs, minimize problems for product users, and reduce technical support calls or needs.

Most people on the project team would agree with these reasons, but despite these common goals, technical reviews still go awry for a number of reasons:

- Poor communication
- Lack of preparation
- Lack of management support
- Unclear expectations and objectives for the review
- Insufficient time planned for the review
- Lack of follow-up
- Wrong people involved, or right people involved at the wrong time

As project leaders, we can — and should — take steps to facilitate communication throughout the review process, which is the core of a successful review. Conducting an effective review requires commitment from the project team, from management, and from yourself, as well as proactive communication, consistency, and organization throughout the process.

Content reviews fall into three main categories:

- **Technical reviews**: Gathering formal input from subject matter experts (SMEs) on the product, documentation, or service being developed. This type of review includes editorial reviews by the documentation team.

- **In-country reviews**: Reviewing the localized product and associated documentation to ensure technical accuracy and appropriateness for the local market.

- **Sign-off (approval) reviews**: Circulating final versions of the design or documentation for approval before the product is shipped or distributed.

Regardless of the type of content review you are doing, the following best practices apply, though the specifics of how they are implemented may vary depending on the type of review:

1. Get involved early in the project.
2. Identify and involve the correct individuals for the review team.
3. Develop a project plan and schedule, and assign responsibilities.
4. Provide clear instructions for each review.
5. Clearly identify the purpose, audience, and scope of any documents or products that you are sending out for review.
6. Provide sufficient time for the review.
7. Follow up after the review with the resolution of action items and comments.

The following sections explain each type of review and how these best practices apply.

Technical Reviews

Formal technical reviews are typically scheduled at various milestones in the project schedule, though individual team members may be collaborating informally throughout the project. Typically, these milestones occur during requirements development, alpha product testing, beta product testing, and pre-market release. These formal reviews enable the project team to evaluate how well each part of the project is fitting together, and to obtain the input of subject matter experts (SMEs) who may not be official members of the team.

The best technical reviews involve team members from all the major functional groups on the team (for example, quality assurance, marketing, product development, documentation, regulatory affairs, research, training, technical support, and localization), as well as any specialists who can provide input into specific aspects of the item under review. Each of these team members brings a unique perspective to the item under review, and because of this unique perspective, might see issues or opportunities that other team members miss.

While this collaborative process takes time and commitment, it results in significantly higher quality, improves the long-term success of the product and company, and reduces the risk of embarrassment or liability once the product is released.

Get the Right People Involved Early

The key functional groups should be represented on the project from its inception. Other team members may be brought in later as the need arises, but the core team should be involved from the requirements development stage on. This involvement can prevent significant design issues from arising by accessing the varied talents of the team.

In addition, project and line management must support and enforce the technical review process so that teams do not start taking shortcuts. Get to know the team members who are responsible for deliverables, and establish a rapport with them. Educate them about your needs, work with them to establish goals and roles, and work with them to establish consequences for team members who are unprepared or do not participate as expected. With multicultural, multisite teams, negotiating these expectations and then documenting the agreement are particularly important for ensuring team buy-in and for accommodating cultural differences in attitudes toward leadership and teamwork. (See also Chapter 2.)

By this point in the project, you should have a rapport established with the rest of the project team as well. Reviews, particularly early ones, can be contentious, so it is critical to have a solid team structure and relationship in place beforehand. Particularly with virtual teams, the importance of this early relationship-building cannot be stressed enough. In most cases, you will not be able to meet in person for every review, though you can simulate an in-person meeting by using video conferencing and other meeting technologies. (See Chapters 4 and 13.)

Identify the Review Team

Work with the line managers to recruit a cross-functional review team with members who offer expertise from all areas of product, document, and business development.

- **Know the key players**. Typically, you want to include the functional leads at the review meeting. These leads are responsible for collecting comments from the other members of their functional group.

- **Identify the secondary reviewers**. Know which team members are the experts in which topics. These reviewers can also help evaluate aspects of the design or documentation to help ensure accuracy before the official review process.

- **Plan, as much as is possible, to have a consistent primary review team**. Bringing new people into the review cycle in the middle of a project causes the review process to grind to a halt because the new person inevitably wants to rehash decisions made by the project team. If you must add a new reviewer during the project, take the time to provide him or her with the list of issues, constraints, and solutions that have already been identified and responded to. This will help bring the new person up to speed and will reduce the need to rehash issues.

Plan and Prepare

Have each functional lead develop a project plan and list of deliverables for his or her portion of the project. Have the team members review the plans so that they know how their work meshes with the rest of the project schedule. Work with the functional leads to incorporate the deliverable schedule with the rest of the project schedule.

Encourage team members to use all of the resources available. For example, the technical writers who are creating the product documents should use the design specifications, functional specifications, meeting notes, or other project documents as a starting point for answering their own questions. Ensure that the team members have access to prototypes as soon as they are available, and use them throughout the product development cycle. Work with the functional leads to ensure that subject matter experts are available for questions during product and documentation development.

Each functional lead should preview work on his or her group's deliverables before sending them to the rest of the project team. By doing so, you can often eliminate more obvious problems or ones that would detract from technical review goals. Then, incorporate needed changes and resolve any issues before sending your work to the project team.

Provide Clear Objectives and Instructions for Each Review

Educate the project team on what to review — and what not to review. Different stages of a project require a different focus, and team members should be informed of the goals and needs throughout each review pass. Use a memo like that in Figure 7-1 to track this information.

Sample Review Cover Memo

To: Wiki project reviewers

From: Kit Brown

Date: August 1, 2006

Date Due: August 15, 2006

Subject: Requirements specs for the Wiki A project

Purpose/Scope: Review for completeness and technical accuracy, as well as integration with the existing portal.

Checklist:
1. Do the requirements make sense?
2. Do they match the business rules and fit with the customer requests for features?
3. Have we forgotten any features that will make it easier for the user?
4. Do the specifications flow logically and are they consistent with the existing portal?
5. Are there any places where we can improve usability? If so, where?
6. Do the requirements include requested changes from the bug database?
7. Is the purpose of the proposed feature clear?

Other Comments:

_____
_____
_____
_____

Thanks for your assistance!

Figure 7-1: Example review memo

Clearly Identify the Purpose, Audience, and Scope

Identify specific issues that need to be addressed in each review. For example, if the lead engineer needs to provide you with information on a particular aspect of your deliverable, indicate that you want her to pay particular attention to that aspect and specify what issues to look for.

Establish sign-off protocols. Before the project begins, establish procedures for the required sign-off, and

Chapter 7

establish criteria that the deliverables must meet at each review phase.

Provide Sufficient Time for the Review

Plan review time into the project schedule. If it is not in the project team's schedule, it likely will not happen.

Work with reviewers (individually and collectively) to find out what review schedule(s) would best meet their needs. Using a wiki or other collaborative tool can significantly reduce the turnaround time on comments by enabling the reviewer to directly alter the information, regardless of physical location.

If practical, schedule a review meeting. Be specific about the time (be sure to identify which time zone you are using), place, and agenda, and provide a copy of the deliverables and any review instructions. As you work with the team, you may find that some team members work better if they know they will have to discuss their comments at a specific time.

Establish realistic deadlines for returning comments. Do not expect a thorough review if you give the team a 30-page document at 3 p.m. on Friday and schedule the review for 9 a.m. on Monday.

Give reviewers at least 48 to 72 hours to review even a short document or small component, and a week for anything over 20 pages or for complex components. Even though the deliverable is your primary responsibility, it is likely a secondary responsibility for other team members. In addition to planning the reviews into the project schedule, warn the team ahead of time that they will be receiving something to review on x date. Reminders help them remember to plan time into their schedules.

Break large projects into manageable chunks. Unless it is the final check on a specification or document, provide reviewers with only a few chapters or sections at a time. Or in the case of online help, provide them with a set of related topics.

Manage the Meeting

If you hold a meeting, establish and announce a finite time for the meeting. Typically, people's attention tends to wander after about two hours. Even if you are not finished with the review, end the meeting on time and schedule a new time to finish the review. If you are almost done and time is up, you can take a vote to see who wants to continue. If the review is likely to be contentious or difficult, you may want to bribe the team with treats. Sharing food or other treats helps to break the tension and contributes to a convivial atmosphere. (For people who will participate via conference call, consider sending them a treat specific to your locale.)

When scheduling a meeting with people scattered in different time zones, be sure to "share the pain" by alternating the times so that everyone periodically has a time that is best for them. Also, be sure to include Greenwich Mean Time (GMT) in your meeting time (for example, London is GMT 0, while France, most of Germany, the Netherlands, and so on are GMT+1, the east coast of North America is GMT–5, and Tokyo is GMT+9). For team members outside North America, the Pacific, Mountain, Central, Eastern, and Atlantic time zones mean absolutely nothing. See Figure 7-2.

Assign someone else to be the review leader. This person should be someone who understands the purpose and goals of the review, who can push people along through the review, and who can guide people back on topic when they stray; in other words, someone who is an effective facilitator. This facilitator should also take a minute at the beginning of each meeting to remind the team of review etiquette. This is particularly important with video and teleconference meetings, as it is more difficult to pick up on nonverbal cues during such meetings, and it is important to solicit input from all members of the team.

The World Clock Meeting Planner - Results

The table below shows actual time in the cities chosen, as well as the corresponding UTC-time.

Change cities
Change date: Month: September ▾ Day: 26 ▾ Year: 2006 ▾ [Show]
Change interval: Every hour ▾ [Show]

UTC-time	Bangalore	Boise	Boston
Monday, September 25, 2006 at 19:00:00	Tue 12:30 AM	Mon 1:00 PM *	Mon 3:00 PM *
Monday, September 25, 2006 at 20:00:00	Tue 1:30 AM	Mon 2:00 PM *	Mon 4:00 PM *
Monday, September 25, 2006 at 21:00:00	Tue 2:30 AM	Mon 3:00 PM *	Mon 5:00 PM *
Monday, September 25, 2006 at 22:00:00	Tue 3:30 AM	Mon 4:00 PM *	Mon 6:00 PM *
Monday, September 25, 2006 at 23:00:00	Tue 4:30 AM	Mon 5:00 PM *	Mon 7:00 PM *
Tuesday, September 26, 2006 at 00:00:00	Tue 5:30 AM	Mon 6:00 PM *	Mon 8:00 PM *
Tuesday, September 26, 2006 at 01:00:00	Tue 6:30 AM	Mon 7:00 PM *	Mon 9:00 PM *
Tuesday, September 26, 2006 at 02:00:00	Tue 7:30 AM	Mon 8:00 PM *	Mon 10:00 PM *
Tuesday, September 26, 2006 at 03:00:00	Tue 8:30 AM	Mon 9:00 PM *	Mon 11:00 PM *
Tuesday, September 26, 2006 at 04:00:00	Tue 9:30 AM	Mon 10:00 PM *	Midnight Mon-Tue *
Tuesday, September 26, 2006 at 05:00:00	Tue 10:30 AM	Mon 11:00 PM *	Tue 1:00 AM *
Tuesday, September 26, 2006 at 06:00:00	Tue 11:30 AM	Midnight Mon-Tue *	Tue 2:00 AM *
Tuesday, September 26, 2006 at 07:00:00	Tue 12:30 PM	Tue 1:00 AM *	Tue 3:00 AM *
Tuesday, September 26, 2006 at 08:00:00	Tue 1:30 PM	Tue 2:00 AM *	Tue 4:00 AM *
Tuesday, September 26, 2006 at 09:00:00	Tue 2:30 PM	Tue 3:00 AM *	Tue 5:00 AM *
Tuesday, September 26, 2006 at 10:00:00	Tue 3:30 PM	Tue 4:00 AM *	Tue 6:00 AM *
Tuesday, September 26, 2006 at 11:00:00	Tue 4:30 PM	Tue 5:00 AM *	Tue 7:00 AM *

Figure 7-2: World clock meeting planner
(http://www.timeanddate.com/worldclock/)

The facilitator should ensure the following to orient the team on the progress of the review and to keep things on track:

■ **Go through the details of each component to be reviewed**. Pause for 15 seconds or so as each item is announced. If no one has a comment, move on.

■ **Keep discussions focused**. Sometimes tangential issues arise during the discussion. In this case, acknowledge the issue, assign an action item and due date, and arrange for the item to be resolved — either with an individual or at another meeting. During the review meeting though, stay focused on the topic at hand.

- **Keep comments constructive**. The comments should be about the deliverable and what will improve it, not about someone's personality flaws or competence. The facilitator needs to challenge unconstructive comments and ask the commentator to turn the comment into something constructive.

The recorder for the review session should be the person whose deliverable is being reviewed. Because this person is responsible for incorporating changes, he or she cares more than anyone else on the team about how clear the comments and solutions are. By being the meeting recorder, this person can focus on listening rather than talking, and can ensure the notes about changes needed are clear for his or her needs:

- **Use a review form** or set up an area of the wiki to capture the issues and information. The form should contain space for the name of the document, the date, team signatures, and the issues list, as shown in Figure 7-3. (Refer to the companion wiki at

Technical Review
Direct Issues Form

Use this form to document issues related to the item or product under review. Direct issues are those that affect the actual wording, organization, or content of the product.

Name of Document:			
Date of Review:		Review Number:*	
Review Leader:			
Recorded By:			
Reviewers:			
Approval Status (circle one):	Approve as Is	Approve with Changes	Requires Another Review

*Review Number = where is this item in the development cycle? 1st review = substantive, technical accuracy, completeness; 2nd review = technical accuracy and completeness; 3rd review = final approval

Issue #	Description	Location
1	Example: graphic needs to say FY 2009, not FY2004	Pgs 21-22 of UC43

Figure 7-3: Example review form

http://www.wikiwackyworld.com/wiki/tiki-index.php for other examples.)

- **Track both direct and indirect issues**. Attach the form to the document and use the form to record indirect issues. Mark up the document itself with direct issues.

- **Assign action items to appropriate people**. If an issue requires further action, assign someone to take care of it and provide a deadline. Then, follow up with a reminder after the meeting. For some meetings, it might make sense to divide the action items and follow-up responsibilities among several team members. (See Chapter 4 for more information on conducting meetings.)

- **Resolve direct issues in the meeting, if possible**. If the project team disagrees about how to present a piece of information, for example, discuss it and come to agreement about wording or presentation during the meeting. Remember, if the team gets stuck on a particular sentence or specification, it means that the idea will not be clear to the final audience either and needs to be reworked. Do not take it personally.

- **Determine whether or not another review is required**. If there are minimal changes, suggest that the leader check the changes and sign off, rather than convening another meeting. Doing this requires a high degree of trust among the team members. Be sure to send the team the final copies (or send out the location on the network or intranet).

- **Ensure that the appropriate people sign the review form after the meeting**. The signatures give you a paper trail in case of problems. For remote team members, allow an electronic signature via email or other mechanism.

- **Save the forms, and make a backup in case problems arise after the project is completed**. It is also a good idea to save the marked-up copies at least until the end of the project. Sometimes, people forget what they said and want to make changes at the sign-off stage that contradict their original comments. Having the marked-up copies can help alleviate this problem.

- **Make second reviews "changes only," unless the deliverable changed significantly as a result of the first meeting**. This will keep the review process moving and prevent revisiting every issue every time. Providing a list of decisions that arose from the previous review along with the updated copy can also prevent the spin cycle that sometimes occurs.

Follow-up

The facilitator or recorder should follow up on action items and issues:

- Send reminders about action items.

- Resolve issues promptly.

- Go over complex comments with the reviewer who made them, if necessary, as quickly as possible after the meeting.

- If you do not incorporate a particular comment, document the reason.

- Follow your document control procedures.

- Thank your reviewers for their time. This small courtesy will go a long way toward ensuring help on future projects. In addition, if someone was particularly helpful, you may want to further acknowledge her contributions with a special public thanks or a message to her boss.

While some of these suggestions may seem to add to your workload, doing them consistently builds trust, helps keep the team in synchrony, and often prevents much larger issues later on. With proactive communication, consistency, and organization, a technical review can indeed be effective. In short, communicate, be prepared, be clear, and follow through. As a result, you can improve the accuracy and completeness of the deliverables you produce, improve the product itself, maximize users' experience in using the product and documents, and reduce product development costs.

In-country Reviews

(Adapted from "Effective in-country reviews: best practices" by M. Katherine (Kit) Brown in the April/May 2006 issue of *MultiLingual*. Reprinted with permission.)

Remember all those home electronics manuals that you cannot make sense of? In most cases, the confusion arises from a combination of a bad translation and a lack of in-country review. While having your VCR/DVD recorder flashing 12:00 is not the end of the world, not correctly understanding a machine's operation could be the end of someone's world. That is why in-country reviews are critical to the quality assurance process during localization.

In-country reviews can be difficult because they are often poorly managed and become a bottleneck to the process. Back in the day when the localized versions of a product were released months after the original version, and before the EU instituted stringent requirements about local language versions of safety, mechanical, and medical information, localization vendors and clients could work around the problem. Today, however, simultaneous language releases are *de rigueur*, and local language versions are expected by customers even for products where translation is not required.

Problems that Can Arise

Problems resulting from a poor in-country review range from the mildly annoying, such as the blinking clock mentioned above, to the potentially fatal, such as an operator losing an arm in a piece of machinery because she did not understand the safety instructions, or a patient overdosing on a drug because his physician misread the dosage requirements.

While most countries are not as litigious as the U.S., poor or nonexistent translations can result in huge liability for international companies, not to mention the fines, bad publicity, and ethical black eye. Aside from the fact that it is rather bad form to maim or kill one's customers, most customers, if given the choice, will always choose a product that is provided in their native language, even if it costs a bit more than the competitors' products.

Companies that fail to realize this bit of human nature lose market share, dilute their brand, blemish their customer service record, and open themselves to lawsuits. Any one of these issues is much more expensive than the localization would have been.

Why In-Country Reviews Go Wrong

The number one reason that in-country reviews go wrong is upper management does not understand the importance of the review, and therefore does not put the appropriate infrastructure in place to facilitate its success. Frequently, the international offices are primarily sales and distribution offices, rather than development offices. Since most salespeople work on commission, they are not getting paid when they review the translations. As you can imagine, volunteer work tends to fall rapidly down the priority list.

The second reason that in-country reviews fail is that the people selected to do the in-country reviews lack either the language skills or the technical skills to conduct an adequate review. In addition, they may not have a good understanding of what such a review entails or how much time it requires in order to do a good job.

The third reason that in-country reviews fail is that the reviewers lack the time to perform the review because the reviewers' time was not planned into the original product development schedule. The in-country reviewers typically work for the client company, not the localization vendor, so the localization vendor has little control over what the reviewer does.

Reviewer Skills Needed

The ideal in-country reviewer has the following skills:

- Native speaker of the target language
- Fluent in English
- Training in linguistics
- Deep technical knowledge of the product
- Deep understanding of the target customer's technical skills, preferences, and so on
- Good project management skills
- Flexibility
- Ability to work well with others (they must be willing and able to work with both the documentation team and the localization vendor and to provide feedback constructively and on time)

Best Practices

Because the in-country reviewers usually work for the client, it is the client's responsibility to develop an effective process for managing these reviews. While most localization vendors can provide recommendations, ultimately the directives must come from senior management at the client company:

- **Engage upper management**. Many times, the international offices are semiautonomous business units over whom you have little influence or control. By getting upper management to understand the business case for in-country reviews, you can improve the likelihood of success.

- **Define the in-country review as part of the person's job**. In defining the task as part of the position, be sure to include the skills required to do the job effectively. If it is not part of the job description, it will always get a lower priority. At one company, the French reviewer was also the medical director for the office who was responsible for all the French clinical trials and regulatory compliance. You can imagine how difficult it was to get the reviews back in a timely fashion.

- **Consider hiring a localization manager for each international office**. If you have a significant volume of documentation or software products, this person can facilitate the reviews and ensure that they happen in a timely and effective manner. The advantage of this approach is that you will have a professional who specializes in linguistics, understands project management, and knows the product well. This person can also act as a verification step that the documentation meets local regulations and can funnel any issues back to the documentation team. In addition, the localization manager can act as a resource for the global marketing and regulatory teams.

- **Provide a written checklist of expectations**. While the in-country reviewer should certainly mark egregious language errors, the primary focus is on the technical accuracy of the translation, whether it meets local regulatory requirements, and whether it meets the needs of the local customer base.

- **Plan for the in-country review in the project plan for product development**. Ideally, the in-country reviewers should be consulted on their availability during this key phase of the project and should be kept apprised of schedule changes and product changes that will affect the review cycle. For example, planning an in-country review for August may make your European reviewers very unhappy, as most Europeans take the month of August for vacation. Respecting and planning for international holidays and vacation schedules help to make the review go more smoothly.

- **Provide a liaison from the documentation team to the in-country reviewers and to the localization vendor**. This liaison can establish a rapport with the in-country reviewers, as well as with the localization vendor, and can provide assistance when there are questions about the product or the content. This liaison should be a senior member of the project team who understands the product, the documentation process, and the localization issues.

- **Ensure that the in-country reviewers have access to the same translation memory tools as the localization vendor**. This greatly facilitates the process, as well as improving terminology management.

- **Ensure that both the localization vendor and the in-country reviewers have the appropriate contact information**. On more than one occasion, the review process has stalled or has gotten delayed because contact information was outdated or unavailable. Verify the contact information with every project, and identify a secondary person in case the primary one is unavailable.

- **Define success**. Work with the in-country reviewers to define success for both the review and for the quality of the localization. Ensure that reviewers provide feedback on any localization issues in the English content as well. Such feedback helps you to continuously improve the quality of all language products.

- **Be appreciative**. Ensure that the in-country reviewer knows that you appreciate his or her efforts. Such appreciation builds rapport.

In-country reviews do not have to be onerous if you clearly define the process and the reviewer's responsibilities, and if upper management recognizes the importance of the reviews and provides the infrastructure to support them.

Sign-off (Approval) Reviews

By the time the deliverable is ready for official approval, it has been through several technical reviews. The approval review should largely be a formality, and used as a final verification that the deliverable incorporates the appropriate specifications, change orders, and review comments. For regulated products, such as medical devices, engineering designs, legal documents, etc., you may have to obtain the signature of the official responsible party, such as the project manager or professional engineer (PE). This person may need to see the relevant specifications, change orders, and the last set of review comments, so ensure that all of these things are available either on the project intranet portal or wiki, or in printed form (make copies of any handwritten comments that you give to the signatory(ies) and keep the original in your files).

Performance Appraisals

Despite the fact that most management books emphasize the importance of regular, formal performance appraisals, many companies do them badly or not at all. There is even a website called www.worstreview.com (http://blogs.successfactors.com/worst-review-contest/the_worst_reviews_ever/), which holds an annual contest for the worst reviews. In *Now, Discover Your Strengths,* Marcus Buckingham and Donald Clifton estimate that less than 40 percent of the employed population is in a job that draws primarily on their strengths. Considering that most people spend two-thirds of their waking hours at work, such a statistic is particularly depressing. The performance appraisal, in its current incarnation, perpetuates this situation by focusing on areas for improvement rather than areas of strength. The good news is that we, as managers and team leaders, can use this information to ensure that our teams use the strengths of individual members to do high-quality work.

While most project managers lead teams of people who do not report directly to them, project managers are often asked to participate in performance appraisals for people on their teams. If you are reading this book, you already care about the success of your team and of the project. This caring attitude carries through to your daily interaction with the team, as well as to your approach to performance appraisals. Incorporating some best practices can ensure that your team functions effectively and that individuals feel challenged and empowered in their jobs.

Best Practices

As operant conditioning (the use of consequences to change voluntary behavior) studies repeatedly show, people respond more effectively and consistently to regular, positive reinforcement than they do to punishment. This is particularly true of virtual teams, which by their nature require members to be self-directed and engaged in order to be successful. In a virtual team, the manager or team leader's primary responsibilities are to remove roadblocks and to facilitate the team's ability to get the work done. Collaboration and negotiation are the primary tools required to accomplish this, particularly if the virtual team is also multicultural. An effective performance appraisal begins with establishing regular contact with each team member and documenting expectations so that nothing in the formal, year-end review comes as a surprise.

During the project, you can do the following:

- **Document expectations, goals, position descriptions, and so on**. Define what you mean by leadership, teamwork, and other concepts that might mean different things in different cultures. Negotiating a team culture is important for ensuring mutual respect and understanding among the team members.

- **Hold regular team meetings**, and allow time to check in with each member at the beginning of the meeting. This helps build trust and a convivial, collegial atmosphere. Personal relationships are particularly important to people from high-context cultures, in which most information and expectations are implicit and understood by the members of the culture. Community is more important than the individual, and tradition and ritual are integral parts of the society. Examples include most Asian, Latin American, Native American, and Middle Eastern cultures.

Providing time to connect will help people from this type of culture feel comfortable on the team.

- **Establish regular one-on-one discussions** with each team member. This time allows you to get to know your team and to provide feedback in a private, informal way. Remember, these sessions should not always focus on problems or issues. They can also be a time for sharing ideas. Also, many people feel uncomfortable with publicly providing the team leader with constructive feedback or bringing up issues. A one-on-one meeting gives those team members a forum for expressing issues and providing feedback. As a leader, you need to be sure that you are responding to things that come up in the meetings and listening without being defensive, or you will shut down the process.

- **Provide feedback in real time**. Telling a team member that he should have contacted Joe Schmoe in shipping about the packaging design six months after the fact helps no one. Waiting until the performance appraisal to congratulate a team member on her major industry award is likewise demoralizing. Instead, tell the person immediately that he or she did a great job or needs to consider doing something differently. Remember also to praise in public and to reprimand in private. Nothing is more demoralizing than losing face in front of one's colleagues.

- **Look for opportunities to build face** for your team. Actively look for things that they are doing well, practice service leadership, and focus on strengths. Creating opportunities for your team to look good also makes you look good. (See the sidebar in Chapter 2 titled "The Importance of Saving Face.")

- **Request monthly reports** of accomplishments and issues from each team member. This will help you remember what each person has contributed when it comes time for the formal appraisal.

- **Maintain a positive, constructive attitude** even when things go wrong. While it is important to be honest with your team, it is also important to put setbacks and challenges into the most positive light. Your team will reflect your attitude and response to the situation. It is often not what you say, but the way you say it that matters. For example, if you find a major problem with the product that requires the team to work over a holiday weekend, you can either get mad and yell about it, be upset about it, or be calm and say something like, "I know that this is a huge setback and that you guys were wanting to enjoy your weekend. However, it's better that we found it now than after the widget went to market. I appreciate your sacrifices this weekend, and will bring in some treats to help us through. Let's work together to figure out the best way to handle the situation. Ideas?" Acknowledging the issue, showing appreciation, and involving the team in the solution helps to alleviate the anger and frustration that the team might be feeling. Focusing on problem-solving helps the team invest in the process.

- **Do not play favorites**. Treat everyone on the team equally and with respect. While it is human nature to connect better with some people than others, displaying that preference can kill the team synergy and can cause competition rather than cooperation.

Chapter 7

During the annual formal appraisal, you can do the following:

- **Provide two weeks' notice** that you are scheduling the review and ask the team member to provide a self-appraisal. Send him or her the previous review and goals so that there is a reference point. Remind him or her to also look at the monthly reports.

- If possible, **conduct the appraisals in person** (video conferencing is a poor second, but better than nothing). About 70 percent of communication is non-verbal, and in-person discussions help facilitate understanding, particularly when either person is using a non-native language.

- **Give the team member a copy of your review** before the meeting. This enables the team member to digest the review and to identify questions or concerns before the meeting.

- During the meeting, **discuss any discrepancies and disagreements** between the self-appraisal and your appraisal. Everyone who observes a situation will have a different idea about what happened; the reality is usually somewhere in the middle. (This is one reason why eyewitness accounts are frequently discredited in legal proceedings.)

- **Negotiate the goals together** during the appraisal. Make sure that both of you understand them and agree to them. Where possible, give the team member choices. People who feel that they have some control over their job and their life are much more likely to work to their highest ability.

- **Focus on strengths**. Buckingham and Clifton provide some excellent suggestions for how to identify and work with a person's strengths. Reward what people do well, and look for ways to capitalize on those strengths. If necessary, consider shifting people's duties around to better access their strengths. You will get a more productive team and happier team members because people generally like doing the things that they are good at.

■ If necessary, **help the team member transition to another job**. Sometimes people are placed in positions that do not interest them or in which they have little expertise, and they fail despite their best efforts and yours. If you are focusing on strengths, you can mentor this team member into a better fit for his or her skills. Bending over backward to help someone succeed in a position that does not suit his or her skills or temperament does not do anyone any favors, and only prolongs the suffering on all sides. It is much kinder in the long term to help him or her find another position or focus. It is important to do this with integrity and caring, and by preserving the other person's dignity to the extent possible. You never know when the situation might be reversed, so it is best to avoid destroying professional relationships if possible.

Ultimately, following the Golden Rule by treating others with the respect and care with which you want to be treated will help ensure that each member of the team functions at his or her highest level.

Project Reviews

Project reviews analyze the project status and success from a project management perspective. Conducting periodic reviews to assess the state of the project enables you to capture and implement lessons learned, identify potential risks early, and provide for continuous improvement on future projects.

There are two types of project reviews:

- Milestone reviews
- Post-project evaluations

Milestone Reviews

Milestones are points in the project schedule when major portions of the project are due. Conducting a milestone review at each of these points helps to ensure that the project stays on schedule and on target. Such reviews also help to identify risks and complications early so that they can be resolved before they get out of hand. It is important for everyone on the project team to be honest about status and complications, and if there are problems, it is imperative that the project manager keep the team focused on problem-solving instead of finger pointing and blaming.

Who Should Attend

Milestone reviews should include all the functional leads for the project. The functional leads should poll their teams before the meeting to identify any issues or items for the agenda. Many managers use a standard survey form to collect the feedback in an organized way. These surveys should be short and should allow for some open-ended responses and ideas for resolving issues. (See the companion wiki for an example.)

If the project management and team leads have been holding regular status meetings, none of the information provided should be a big surprise. The purpose of the milestone meeting is to determine whether or not a course correction is needed and to resolve any issues that are interfering with functional groups working together.

Setup

Ideally, these meetings should occur in person. However, if that is not possible, use video conferencing so that nonverbal cues can be more easily interpreted. People are often uncomfortable sharing negative news in such groups, so, if possible, use a roundtable format so that everyone can see everyone else, and spend a few minutes at the beginning of the meeting doing some teambuilding or reconnecting. This activity is particularly important if team members have not seen each other in a while, or if they have not worked together for long. If several people are coming from out of town for the meeting, consider doing some off-site activities in the evenings, such as sightseeing, dinner, or sports or cultural activities, and encourage local team members to participate. These outside activities help create shared experiences, and a lot of decisions get made less contentiously when people are having fun together.

Consider rotating the location of the meetings so that each team lead has an opportunity to host a meeting. Seeing the physical environment where someone else works can help everyone be more understanding and tolerant of teammates. For example, team members at corporate headquarters typically have more luxurious surroundings because of the office's visibility to upper management, but they might also have a vice president micromanaging them and causing conflicting priorities.

Chapter 7

On the other hand, someone in a satellite office might have a small, noisy cubicle with little privacy, but has easy access to the development team and can bring the dog to work.

Reporting

Ask the functional leads to write a progress report before the review. In the report, the leads should include the following information:

- Current status and percentage complete
- Accomplishments since last report
- Challenges
- Estimated hours remaining for each task
- Identification of any dependencies that might be causing schedule or cost issues

The reports should be short (one or two pages), and the functional leads should arrive at the milestone meeting ready to discuss their reports.

Agenda

Several team books, such as *Virtual Teams* and *Team Power*, recommend that these meetings last three days to allow adequate time for teambuilding, particularly early in the project. (See Chapter 2 for an explanation of the initial meeting.) While spending three days at the beginning of the project to get it started is important, you may not need that much time for milestone reviews if everything is going fairly well. On the other hand, if the project is at a crucial stage where the team needs to discuss and decide many potentially contentious issues, you may want to schedule a whole week for the meeting.

Projects typically set milestones for requirements development, alpha review, beta testing, pre-release, and product launch. Depending on the project, you might have more or fewer reviews. Each milestone is an opportunity for holding a milestone review to ensure that the project is going the way it is supposed to and that any risks are identified early so that they can be mitigated. Not holding these reviews usually results in some major component not fitting in with the rest of the project or, in some cases, a disaster. Examples include the *Columbia* space shuttle disaster, the Boston "Big Dig" transportation tunnel system, the lack of warning about the Indian Ocean tsunamis, and the aftermath of hurricanes Mitch and Katrina, to name but a few.

A few days before the meeting, the attendees should receive copies of the agenda and of everyone's reports, so that they know what they need to prepare. If the meeting is likely to be contentious, you may want to bring in an outside facilitator to help you keep the meeting on track.

The agenda should include the following elements:

- Introductions and teambuilding
- Overview of project purpose, scope, and description of milestone (as a reminder of the meeting topic; this should take less than 15 minutes)
- Expectations for the meeting
  - ❑ What do you expect to accomplish?
  - ❑ What are you going to do during the meeting?
  - ❑ How will you handle disagreements, discussions, etc.?
  - ❑ Who is responsible for taking meeting minutes?
  - ❑ What are the meeting logistics? (location of toilets, times for breaks, meals, and so on)
- Status from each functional lead
  - ❑ Reports should include both positives and challenges
  - ❑ Summary of survey results of functional group

- ❏ If the functional group is dependent on someone else for something, that should be identified
- Team assessment of project thus far (discussion based on status reports and other information)
- Lessons learned
- Risk assessment
- Process changes required
- Analysis of next steps
- Issue resolution
- Assignment of action items

Each milestone review should follow a similar format so that the team becomes familiar with the process and can be more efficient at conducting the review.

Post-Project Evaluations

As the name implies, this review occurs at the end of the project, usually after the product has shipped. This review should involve all the primary players and as many of the supporting players as are available. Ideally, it occurs immediately following the conclusion of the project while both the successes and failures are still fresh in everyone's mind. The purpose is to gather lessons learned and best practices so that your team can do even better the next time. No matter how well a project went, there is always room for improvement, and a well-done project provides an excellent opportunity to codify best practices.

Unfortunately, even when the project is successful, such evaluations often degenerate into finger pointing, blaming, whining, and so on. It is absolutely critical that you have a strong facilitator, preferably from outside the team, to lead the meeting and to keep the meeting from degenerating.

Preparation

At least three weeks before the evaluation, send out a survey asking the project participants how they think it went and ideas they have for future projects. The survey should contain both multiple-choice and open-ended questions. Allowing people to remain anonymous often provides you with more honest and complete responses than you would get otherwise. Survey Monkey (www.surveymonkey.com) is a good tool for this task. (See Chapter 9 for more information on metrics.)

Setup

For a small team, you might be able to use a roundtable setup. For a large team, you may have to set up the meeting auditorium style. Because the purpose of this meeting is to collect lessons learned and best practices, consider using a focus group format. If the meeting will last more than two hours, provide snacks and breaks so that everyone stays physically comfortable.

Agenda

Depending on the complexity of the project, the meeting could be as short as a couple of hours or as long as a day. The agenda should include the following topics:

- Introductions
- Overview of project, highlights, and challenges
- Summary of survey findings
- Focus group discussion
    - Lessons learned
    - Best practices discovered
- Categorization and prioritization of focus group results
- Action items
- Wrap-up (always end on an up note)

In addition to a strong facilitator, be sure to assign someone (again, preferably from outside the project team) to take copious notes so that the knowledge does not get lost after the meeting.

Follow-up

It is critical that the project manager follow up on each action item after the post-project evaluation. While it is true that sometimes it takes time to see results from codifying a best practice or from changes made due to lessons learned, the evaluation loses its power if the team never hears what changes were actually implemented and how. In addition, upper management loses credibility if it pays to have all the team members in a room to discuss the good, the bad, and the ugly, only to ignore the advice of the people who took the time to engage.

Following up can be as simple as sending an email to let the team know the status of the action items. If something requires significant expenditure, people understand if it takes a while to implement. What they do not understand and do not like is feeling like their ideas went into a black hole. Close the feedback loop, even if you have to say that upper management declined to make the change requested or that the solution is still in progress. Keeping the team informed short-circuits the rumor mill.

Summary

As we have seen, there are many types of reviews, and many points along the project path where reviews can be not only useful but critical to the success of your project. The team will work together more efficiently if all the team members know where they stand in relation to each other and to the goals of the project.

Related Resources

Brown, M. Katherine (Kit). "Effective in-country reviews: best practices." *MultiLingual* (April/May 2006).

Brown, M. Katherine (Kit). "Conducting Effective Technical Reviews." TECHWR-L (http://www.techwr-l.com/techwhirl/magazine/writing/effectivetechreviews.html), 2001.

Buckingham, Marcus, and Donald O. Clifton. *Now, Discover Your Strengths*. New York: Free Press, 2001.

Kayser, Thomas A. *Team Power: How to Unleash the Collaborative Genius of Work Teams*. Burr Ridge, Ill.: Irwin Professional Publishing, 1994.

Lipnack, Jessica, and Jeffrey Stamps. *Virtual Teams: Reaching Across Space, Time and Organizations with Technology*. 2nd ed. New York: Wiley, 2000.

Parker, Glenn M. *Cross-Functional Teams: Working with Allies, Enemies, and Other Strangers*. San Francisco: Jossey-Bass, 2003.

Schafer, Lu Ellen. "How to Make Remote Teams Work." Training materials from a seminar given to Hewlett-Packard in Palo Alto, Calif., 2000.

Chapter 8

Managing Risk and Change

" *It takes a lot of courage to release the familiar and seemingly secure, to embrace the new. But there is no real security in what is no longer meaningful. There is more security in the adventurous and exciting, for in movement there is life, and in change there is power.*

— Alan Cohen, inspirational author

" *Technological change is like an axe in the hands of a pathological criminal.*

— Albert Einstein

" *The important thing is this: To be able at any moment to sacrifice what we are for what we could become.*

— Charles DuBois

At the risk of stating the obvious, change is inevitable. So why do so many companies and organizations do such a poor job of planning for and managing change?

In this chapter, we will discuss best practices for managing change in the following situations:

- Changes to team structure or personnel
- Product design or documentation changes

(Although organizational change can also affect virtual teams, it is not the focus of this book. Several resources on organizational change are included in the list of related resources at the end of this chapter.)

Changes to Team Structure or Personnel

It is midway through the project, the team is functioning well together, and the project is on schedule. One of your key team members comes to you and says that she is moving to another company. How you handle this situation can determine the ultimate success of your project.

While managers hope that the project team stays stable throughout the project, smart managers plan for the possibility that key team members might leave, or worse, have an illness or accident that precludes them from finishing the project. While no one likes to think about the worst-case scenario, doing so enables the team to recover from all but the most serious catastrophe. (See also Chapter 2, "Setting Up a Virtual Team.")

Planning for Personnel Changes

At the beginning of the project, analyze the team structure and project milestones. For critical areas, consider doing the following:

- **Perform a risk analysis**. Identify potential events, such as a key team member leaving, determine the likelihood of the event, and detail its impact to the project if it occurs. Then, identify at least three things you can do to mitigate that risk. For example, if the software architect leaves during the requirements phase, it could seriously delay the project. However, if he or she leaves three weeks before product release, it may not cause as big a problem. Knowing the risks to your project can help you prevent problems later on.

- **Assign backups or "understudies" to key personnel**. The success of a project should not depend on one or two key people. Assigning backups to mission-critical functions can mitigate the problems that arise from losing key personnel in the middle of a project, and have the added advantage of providing cross-training and experience to team members.

- **Identify team members' key motivators** and use them as an incentive for staying with the project. Some people will work for food or beer. Some people only care about monetary incentives. For others, it is the satisfaction of a job well-done or the challenge of solving a difficult problem. For still others, it is the camaraderie of working with interesting and intelligent people. As a manager, it is important to understand each team member's key motivators so that you can keep them engaged even when things get tough. It is equally important to understand each team member's stress triggers so that you can minimize them as much as possible (at least in the context of the project). Some people want detailed instructions to ensure that they are working to the project requirements; others think that too much detail is burdensome, or perhaps even insulting. You need to evaluate the triggers for each team member and remove any roadblocks so that your team can perform to its highest potential.

- **Create an atmosphere of trust and camaraderie**. A recent newspaper article identified "relationships with coworkers" as a primary reason for staying or leaving. Just because it is work does not mean that the team cannot have some fun (within appropriate boundaries, of course). In fact, shared experiences and a sense of humor go a long way to create this atmosphere. And if people are happy and having fun, they are less likely to leave.

- **Assume that everyone is doing his or her best**. Most people, even when they appear to be failing at something, are not actively malicious. It is better to assume the best, and to ensure that you have all the facts before passing judgment. Make sure that the team member has all the skills, equipment, and understanding required for the job. Practice service leadership by checking in with each team member and working together to find out what each person needs in order to improve. Particularly if you have team members operating in a second or third language, make sure that they fully comprehend the tasks and requirements. You have to balance the needs of the individual with the needs of the team, however. If you are unfortunate enough to have someone on your team who is malicious or generally behaving badly, you may need to work with an organizational psychologist to minimize the havoc he or she can wreak.

- Ask the person who is leaving to **ensure** that his or her **paperwork is updated**; such a paper trail is a key input to ISO 9000 and similar efforts, as well as providing data for metrics (see Chapter 9). If you know about the departure in advance, such as maternity leave or a transfer within the company, ask the person who is leaving to train the replacement and to provide detailed notes on what he or she is working on, where he is with the project, whether or not issues exist, and so on. Depending on where the person is going and why, you might be able to ask him to be "on call" in case the replacement has questions. Whatever you do, do not allow your personal disappointment or other feelings about the person's departure to cause you to make the person's life miserable for the remaining time. It will only cause you to lose face with the rest of the team, and you never know when you might need that person again.

Welcoming New Team Members

The advantage of a cohesive, tightly knit team is that the team tends to function very effectively. The disadvantage is that the team often becomes a bit cliquish and can make it difficult for new members to feel part of the group, particularly if the team has a long shared history and the stories that go with it. As a manager, you need to facilitate the integration of new team members into your team. Your attitude about the team member and how you treat that person will set the tone for the rest of the team. Some large teams have people who are designated as the "welcome wagon," peer mentors who facilitate the introductions, as well as the information-gathering, inevitable question-asking, and so on. The following sections provide specific recommendations for indoctrinating a new team member.

Preparing for the New Arrival

A little preparation can make a huge difference in how welcome new team members feel when they join the team. The power of small courtesies and kindnesses cannot be underestimated; this is particularly true if the new person is replacing someone who was well-liked or is coming in during a controversy. Making the following arrangements will ease a new person's transition onto the team, whether he or she is a long-time company employee or brand new to both the company and the team:

- **Identify the office space, equipment, and other infrastructure that the new person needs**. Make sure that it is ordered in time to be set up when the new person arrives. If the person will be working remotely, work with his or her office's facilities and IT team to ensure that the new person's access and setup meet the team requirements (software and security access, for example).

- **Create a welcome packet or binder** that you can give the new person. (Having this information as hard copy gives the team member a reference document in case there is a problem with accessing the system.) This binder should include the following items:
  - ❏ Contact information, short bios, and roles for all team members. Identify the "go-to" people.
  - ❏ Conference bridge phone numbers and codes
  - ❏ List of URLs, file locations, and other locations for all project-related information
  - ❏ Project history, including major decisions and redirects, major issues and how they were resolved, current status, team stories/inside jokes, and so on. For example, one software company taped its annual holiday skit program, which poked fun at the major company happenings (and sometimes upper management). The training staff showed these tapes to the new employees to help them get a feel for the company culture.
  - ❏ Schedule, times, and locations of standing meetings

❑ Team rules/guidelines
❑ Glossary and list of acronyms
❑ Gantt chart of most recent project schedule
❑ List of any outstanding action items that the new person will be responsible for
❑ Copy of position description and roles/responsibilities
❑ Copy of any training dates and times that the person will need; URLs for online training
❑ Agenda for the first week, including any appointments with human resources

- **Identify a team mentor** for the new person who will facilitate introductions, answer questions, and so on.

- **Provide the team with a bio and description** of the new person's skills so that the team has an idea of what to expect.

- **Schedule a team meeting** to introduce the new member (this can be brief, but helps ease the way).

Integrating the New Person with the Team

If your new team member is working remotely, and especially if he or she is also new to the company, it is helpful if you can be on-site to greet her upon arrival, to show her around, and to facilitate any paperwork or logistical things that tend to come up. If you are not able to be there, enlist the assistance of one of the local team members or one of the other managers. Make sure the person has received the team binder and system access, and verify that all the paperwork is being handled correctly and in a timely fashion. These efforts are particularly important if the new team member is coming from another country or is operating in a second or third language. By helping the new team member get acclimated and oriented quickly, you are facilitating the ramp-up period and ensuring a positive experience.

- Make a point of introducing the new team member to colleagues, support staff, and other team members.

- Make sure that the new person has a thorough understanding of her role and where the team fits in the overall organization.

- Provide the framework, context, and limitations of the project and the person's function on the project.

- Set aside time to meet regularly for the first couple of weeks so that the new person can ask questions and so you can get a feel for how things are going.

- Consider assigning a team buddy or mentor to help with the integration and acclimation.

- Encourage the new person to ask questions.

- Facilitate resolving issues with access, paperwork, or scheduled training.

If the new team member has been a company employee for a while, some of the above might not be applicable, so ask what he or she needs from you to expedite ramp-up time. (And do not forget to update your project schedule and budget to include the new person's ramp-up time.)

Handling Personnel Conflicts

A certain amount of conflict is inevitable in any team. However, during times of stress and big changes, seemingly minor issues often get blown out of proportion. As a manager, you can alleviate some of this by setting expectations appropriately, communicating proactively with team members about changes that affect them, and modeling the behavior you want. Chapter 6 provides more specific ideas on how to handle conflicts.

Product Design or Documentation Changes

(Adapted from "Integrating localization into change management," by M. Katherine (Kit) Brown in the June 2006 issue of *MultiLingual*. Reprinted with permission.)

(See Part II for information on relevant tracking tools.)

It is three weeks until the launch date for your new product, which will be distributed in 15 languages, and the quality assurance team finds a huge problem in the product. What do you do?

The answer, of course, is "it depends." For a company lacking effective change management, this scenario could result in delaying a product launch and could end up costing the company hundreds of thousands of dollars in lost revenue, added production costs, added localization costs, and so on. For a company with an effective change management process, however, such an issue might cause only a hiccup in the process.

Best Practices in Change Management

While different industries define the process slightly differently, change management is essentially the process of planning for, implementing, and evaluating alterations or updates in a product. Effective change management encompasses the following principles:

- **It is proactive**. To build an effective change management process, you must first acknowledge that product development is, by its very nature, iterative and that changes will occur during the product development cycle. Identifying the points in the process where changes are likely to occur enables you to plan for the impact of the change.

Chapter 8

- **It is systematic**. Not all changes are created equally, so you need a method for categorizing and prioritizing each change. By doing so, you can determine proactively when to introduce them into the system. For example, you may rate a change on a scale of 1 to 4, with 1 being critical and 4 being cosmetic. Critical changes are those that must be incorporated into the product before distribution (e.g., adding a safety guard to a movable part to prevent injury), whereas a cosmetic change does not affect the salability or effectiveness of the product (e.g., resizing the logo on the product's cover).

- **It is a team effort**. Not all changes affect all members of the team equally, so it is important that the change management team include representatives from each functional area on the project. For example, changing the product's name late in the product cycle might not seem like a big deal for the project manager, but it causes major headaches for documentation, localization, marketing, and packaging design.

- **It is synchronized with the product development cycle**. Early in a project, even cosmetic changes might be considered. However, three weeks before product release, only critical changes might be considered. By integrating change management with the product development lifecycle, you can decide when to bring changes into the process, rather than simply reacting as changes arise. When evaluating changes, you can determine if the cost/benefit of the change makes sense at a particular point in the product cycle.

- **It encourages effective quality assurance**. Tracking and managing changes enable you to identify points during the product development cycle where you may need to improve your quality assurance processes. For example, if you are always finding significant defects or changes after beta testing, you may want to perform more thorough system testing during the alpha release.

- **It facilitates tracking of enhancements between releases**. Some changes will not get implemented immediately, so you need a way of tracking them for consideration in the next product release cycle. Reviewing the change requests at the beginning of each project enables you to identify systemic issues, as well as get feature ideas, that you can incorporate into the new product design.

- **It results in cost savings**. The later in the product release cycle that changes are introduced, the more expensive it is to incorporate them. By having an effective change management process, you can manage the costs of incorporating changes. A related allegory involves a story about an engineer who was faced with recalling a product because of a serious flaw. The engineer calculated the cost of fixing the problem at each stage of the development process. He discovered the following: During requirements development, the change would have cost $10; during design review — $100; during alpha testing and initial prototyping — $1,000; during beta testing — $10,000. The cost of finding the problem after its release? Over $1,000,000, not including the bad publicity that the company received.

The tools you use to assist you in managing product changes can range from the simple, such as Microsoft Excel spreadsheets, Microsoft Word with Track Changes enabled, or Adobe Acrobat's notation features, to the complex, such as a relational database with a web interface or content management systems with version control, automated workflow, and mapping of content to system specifications. The specific tools depend on your needs and your budget.

Integrating Localization into the Process

(See also "Localization/Translation" in Chapter 6.)

I have good news and bad news. The bad news is that integrating localization into your change management process adds a layer of complexity and requires you to include the localization vendor earlier in the product development cycle. The good news is threefold:

- Like the documentation, which details how the product is supposed to work, the localization also describes the way the product is supposed to work.

- Identifying changes that affect localization early in the development process enables you to make the fix in the source, saving localization costs later on.

- Integrating localization into your change management processes can result in significant cost savings by reducing rework.

The keys to successfully integrating the localization team into the change management process include the following:

- Understanding where the localization process and product development process overlap

- Identifying information that was previously translated and designating that as off-limits for preferential changes

- Performing risk analysis on the product development process and flagging the least stable areas so that localization occurs last on those areas

- Prioritizing changes to the content and introducing them at appropriate times in the localization process
- Identifying changes that affect some languages and not others (e.g., a regulatory change in Japan only affects the Japanese translation)
- Keeping the localization team apprised of changes that might affect localization

A good localization vendor will work with you to create a system that works for both parties.

Chapter 8

Tools

Change control and tracking tools can be as simple as a shared spreadsheet or as complex as a relational database with automated workflow and version control. Your toolset depends on your specific needs and budget. However, with a virtual team, version control is vital, regardless of whether you use an application that requires check-in and check-out, use a wiki to develop project information collaboratively, or have a manual process to track changes. See Part II for more details on types of tools that can be used to assist you with change tracking.

Summary

Heraclitus, a Greek philosopher, once said that "nothing endures but change." Without an effective change management process for both personnel and product development, companies doom themselves to higher costs and lower quality, and to management by crisis. Effective change management, on the other hand, enables companies to integrate new people into the company, to control costs, to improve quality, and to determine the most effective time for introducing changes. When change is effected well, new team members have an easy integration period, products work better, and there are fewer support calls. Effective change management is even more critical when adding localization to the mix — a change that costs $100 (USD) to fix in the English source will require at least that amount to fix in each language. For example, if you are translating into 20 languages, that $100 change will cost you $2,000. Multiply that by all the changes required, and it does not take long for such changes to significantly increase your costs.

Related Resources

Bridges, William. *Transitions: Making Sense of Life's Changes*. Rev. 25th anniversary ed. Cambridge, Mass.: Da Capo Press, 2004.

Briggs, John, and F. David Peat. *Seven Life Lessons of Chaos: Timeless Wisdom from the Science of Change*. New York: HarperCollins, 1999.

Brown, M. Katherine (Kit). "Integrating localization into change management." *MultiLingual* (June 2006).

Carnegie Mellon Software Engineering Institute (http://www.sei.cmu.edu/).

Content Management Professionals (http://www.cmpros.org/).

Hackos, JoAnn. Center for Information-Development Management (http://www.infomanagement-center.com/) (verified September 2006).

McConnell, Steven C. *Software Project Survival Guide.* Redmond, Wash.: Microsoft Press, 1998. (See also http://www.construx.com/survivalguide/ detailedchangeproc.htm.)

Wikipedia. "Change Control." (http://en.wikipedia.org/ wiki/Change_Control) (viewed September 2006).

Chapter 9

Evaluating Project Success

> " *As a general rule the most successful man in life is the man who has the best information.*
>
> — Benjamin Disraeli, First Earl of Beaconsfield

When you travel somewhere, you have an idea of where you are going and how you are going to get there. As you drive, there are signs along the road that tell you where you are and how much farther it is to various destinations. If you take a train, there will be signs at each train station to tell you where you are at any given point along the journey.

If you think of your project as a journey, the plan is the map (see Chapter 5). There are signs along the route that show your progress; you just have to take the time to read them. In project management, metrics function as a type of road sign, telling you whether or not your project is moving in the right direction and if you will arrive on time. Watch the signs carefully so you can make course corrections before you get too far off track.

What Are Metrics?

"Metrics are a system of parameters or ways of quantitative and periodic assessment of a process that is to be measured, along with the procedures to carry out such measurement and the procedures for the interpretation of the assessment in the light of previous or comparable assessments." ("Metrics," Wikipedia, The Free Encyclopedia, http://en.wikipedia.org/w/index.php?title =Metrics&oldid=63367172 (accessed September 8, 2006)).

In Chapter 5, "Project Planning and Tracking," we talked about measuring data during the course of a project to better estimate future projects. When you store and analyze these measurements, you create metrics. Stand-alone numbers (two pages or six dollars or three printers) become metrics when expressed as a correlation between multiple numbers or items (two pages per hour or 0.5 percent of the budget or one printer for every four on-site writers). The fact that a project required 1,250 hours to complete is only important if you understand how the number 1,250 relates to lines of code, pages of text, number of new features, or whatever data points you choose to measure.

Just as the numbers are not enough without some analysis or comparison to other numbers, the metrics are not really worthwhile if you do not use them. Metrics can be used for a variety of purposes:

- To help team members and managers understand what is going on within a project

- To determine whether or not the overall project is on track when compared to original project estimates and to other similar projects
- To serve as input for creating more accurate estimates for future projects
- To identify problem areas so they can be corrected quickly

Where Do You Start?

In a mature or established company, you will be given a list of things you are required to measure and a set of metrics based on previous projects in your department. You may even be able to access the metrics created by other departments for comparison. In a young or growing company, you might have to come up with your own list of things to measure and metrics to calculate. To get to the list of things to measure, start with the end result (what do you want to know?), then work backward to figure out what you need to measure.

Metrics should relate to the original goals and purpose of the project. For example, a company trying to become more efficient (purpose) by creating a quicker method for processing customer calls (goal) might look at the percentage of different call types, the length of time per customer call, and the percentage of calls from different categories of customers (metrics). To do this, the company would have to count the number of calls, time each call, and record the call type and customer category for each call (the numbers or measurements).

When choosing which metrics to use, keep your ultimate goal in mind. Each number that you decide to track will add to the effort required, both while doing the work and in the later analysis. You want enough information to get a complete, accurate picture of the project, but not so much information that the gathering and processing of the tracking information requires more effort than the project itself.

Make sure that you start with numbers that you can act upon later. For example, if you are using a series of wiki pages to create a document, you might want to count the number of times each page is changed or the number of people who change each page. You could then compare these counts to determine if one particular page is taking a disproportionate amount of effort, or if only a few people are bothering with certain pages or topics when you really want the whole team fully engaged. These are problems that you can address and hopefully fix. Other counts, like the number of words or bandwidth per page, might be less useful for this particular type of project.

There are several types of information that can be measured:

- Time (how long does it take?)
- Resources (how much does it cost?)
- Process (what needs to be done and who does it?)
- Quality (how close does the output meet the initial requirements?)

What Do You Measure?

Each project will require different types of measurements. If you are writing a report, you might want to count pages or words, or record the time required for research. However, if your final output will be a piece of hardware, these types of measurements would be meaningless. Table 9-1 gives some sample items that might be useful for a variety of projects. Note that this is not a definitive list, but rather a starting point from which you can create additional measurements appropriate for your project.

Table 9-1: Raw measures

Time	Resources	Process	Quality
Number of hours Days or weeks elapsed Deadlines met or missed	Number of team members Bandwidth used Amount of storage space Cost of communications Cost of supplies Cost of employee labor (both salary and overhead) Cost of contract or consulting labor (include any agency fees)	Number of tasks Number of phone calls Number of virtual meetings Number of wiki or blog entries Number of comments entered Speed of communications	Number of bugs Number of errors Size of generated files Number of customer calls Percentage of improvement in customer satisfaction scores

Next, combine the numbers in a way that is appropriate for your project. Make these decisions early in the project so that your record keeping reflects all of the information you want to track. For example, it is likely that the team members are already reporting the hours spent on the project. For more detailed analysis, you might decide that you want to know how long it takes to perform a specific task, such as run a test, or what percentage of time the team spends on administrative tasks. Rather than estimate the number of hours or percentage of time, ask each team member to break down and report the number of hours by task. Similarly, if you are counting the number of bugs or errors reported, it is often useful to track the bugs by module or department as well as by severity. An accurate representation of this level of detail is only possible if you collect the numbers from the beginning of your project. Table 9-2 describes some examples of other information you might need to track. Note that most of these cross the boundaries of the categories above (time, resources, process, and quality).

Table 9-2: Calculated metrics

Time	Resources	Process	Quality
Number of hours per task Number of hours per meeting Number of hours to correct each error	Storage space per team member Personnel and other resources required for each task Bandwidth required to resolve each error	Number of meetings per week Number of team members per phone call Number of comments left by each team member Number and type of process changes required	Number of bugs corrected per team member Number of tasks completed on time Number of project change orders and priority level of the changes (for example, the implications of a high number of critical changes are different from the implications of a high number of minor changes) Stage of project Percentage of improvement in customer satisfaction scores

When selecting the information to measure, remember to account for the extra time required for measurement and analysis. If you try to measure too many data points, you might get bogged down trying to analyze them rather than focusing on the completion of your project. Aim for around 10 metrics to start, and include the number of metrics as something you evaluate periodically. You can always decrease the numbers you track if you find that you are spending too much time on the tracking tasks, or increase them if you find that you are not getting a full and accurate picture of the project status.

How Do You Measure?

Once you decide what you need to measure, you will need to figure out how to measure it. Your approach may vary depending on the type of information you are capturing.

Automatic Tracking Tools

Many of the numbers that serve as input to your metrics calculations are automatically tracked as you progress through the tasks outlined in your plan. Others need to be obtained from other sources and entered into your tracking system manually. For example, you can get cost of labor, overhead, and overtime cost information from your company's finance department, and have the team members submit information about the hours they spend on each task.

Project management software packages like Microsoft Project or 37signals' Basecamp generally allow you to enter the actual hours or actual completion dates into the same file where you store the estimated hours or dates. The software then calculates the variance between the estimated and actual numbers.

Many of the collaborative tools will track information for you. For example, our wiki for this project stores statistics on our usage of each of the separate components. Figure 9-1 shows that as of September 8, 2006, the pages in our wiki had been displayed 3,766 times.

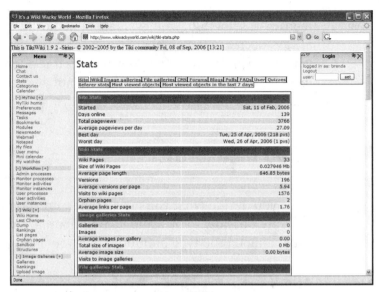

Figure 9-1: Tracking statistics with a wiki

This page displays statistics like the number of page views for each page and more. We can analyze these numbers to create metrics that might be able to help improve how we work together on our next book project or how we use the wiki functionality.

If you rely on your software to record data for you, run frequent reports so you can ensure that your project remains on track toward the goals you established up front.

Manual Entries

Though the collaborative tools will offer a lot of different statistics that you can use in your measurements, there are some things that still need to be tracked manually. For example, if your team consists of people from different companies, it is unlikely you can automatically obtain the hours expended. Instead, you need to set up a tracking system for the project and have each person manually enter the hours he or she has spent. Manual time tracking might be required even if your team members work for a single company, because sometimes the financial or payroll systems do not allow for the level of detail you need.

For the most accurate measurements, ensure that all team members enter information frequently into whatever system you set up, and check to make sure that you have data from everyone from whom you need it before beginning your analysis phase. Even if your team agrees to a regular schedule, such as entering their hours at the end of each day or by noon on Fridays, you will still need to ensure compliance with your schedule. Send regular reminders to the whole team if you need to, or personal notes, phone calls, or memos to those who turn in their information late. It only takes one procrastinator to skew your results!

Using Survey Tools

Sometimes you want to measure things that do not easily translate to numbers, like how easy something is to use or how satisfied your team members are with a particular process. For really quick surveys of one or two questions, you could just call team members on the telephone, send email, or use instant messaging systems. (See Chapter 13, "Meeting and Communication Tools.") For more detailed surveys, consider using one of the survey tools that are available as part of many wiki packages or as stand-alone applications. Survey tools help ensure that all team members are asked the same questions, and they can also help to compile the results.

Note: A well-designed, effective survey takes significant planning, design, and execution. If you are basing
product design decisions on survey results, take the time
to learn how to do surveys well or consider hiring an
expert in questionnaire design. (See "Related Resources"
at the end of the chapter.)

Before creating a survey, explicitly state the goal you are
trying to accomplish with the survey. What is it you are
trying to measure, and how will you use the information
you gain from the respondents? As you formulate the
questions for your survey, keep the following guidelines in
mind:

- **Be clear about what you want to know.** This
  might sound obvious, but people frequently create surveys that do not answer the questions that they think
  they are asking. Before you can write effective questions for the survey, think through and document what
  it is that you really need to know. It also helps to prioritize the list, so that you can more easily eliminate
  things if you need to.

- **Determine how scientific the survey needs to
  be** and what kinds of analysis you need to do on it. A
  survey that is intended to provide a "gut check" on a
  particular idea or course of action has a different level
  of validity than one that is being used to establish correlation. The less scientific the survey, the larger the
  margin of error and the more skeptical you should be
  of the results. News polls are a perfect example of this
  large error/low validity phenomenon. Such polls often
  show answer A as 52 percent and answer B as 48 percent, and in really tiny print next to the poll note a
  margin of error of 9 percent. Essentially, the news is
  reporting a non-event — if the margin of error is

greater than the difference between the responses, then there is *no* difference between the responses, and reporting the results is a bit misleading and dishonest.

- **Determine how you are going to sample the target population**. Are you going to send the survey to everyone on the team or in the company? Are you going to take a random sample (throw all the names in a list, scramble the list, and use a random number generator to determine which person is selected)? Are you going to do a systematic sample (determine the percentage of the population you need to sample, then count off that number on the list — a 10 percent sample of 100 people would mean selecting every tenth one, for example)? Are you just posting it on the web and letting anyone who wants to respond do so? (This is not recommended for volatile topics as the respondents tend to fall at the extremes in terms of interest in the topic.) How are you going to prevent people from responding more than once? The answers to these questions depend on how scientific your survey needs to be.

- **Write neutral questions**. If your question is biased, the answers will also be biased. For example, if you are trying to gather information about which instant messaging system the team uses most often, do not limit your question to just the two systems with which you personally are most familiar or that you think are the two most popular systems. Phrase the question so that it includes all the possible systems that your team may have, or allow team members to enter the name of an instant messaging system.

- **Verify that all your questions directly address the goal** of the particular survey. Unrelated questions will only distract respondents and clutter later analysis.

- **Make your questions specific, not general**, and for the purposes of gathering metrics, avoid open-ended types of responses (often used to gather comments). While it might be interesting to read text descriptions of the problems people are facing, and this information might be useful in resolving some types of problems, it will not give you the numbers you need to create metrics that can be easily analyzed later.

- **Choose the appropriate question type**. Most survey software packages allow you to create a variety of question types, such as true/false, fill-in-the-blank, multiple-choice, or "matrix" or "scale" questions.

- **Ensure that the answer options are appropriate** for each question. For example, if you want to find out why the team is not using a particular tool, you could set up a multiple-choice question that includes potential answers of "too hard to use," "too slow," and "no logging feature." But it is possible that the real reason team members are not using that software is that it is incompatible with their operating systems. By limiting the possible answers, you are not getting a complete answer to the question. Similarly, be aware that the scale you specify for matrix-type questions can have implications in the results. For example, if you set up a matrix with an even number of possible responses as shown in Figure 9-2, you force the respondents to be either positive or negative. If you use an odd-numbered scale as shown in Figure 9-3, you allow for neutral or "no opinion" responses. One way of checking internal validity in a survey is to ask for the same information in slightly different ways. For example, in one question ask how strongly a person agrees or disagrees with a particular statement, and then ask the respondent to rank items by importance.

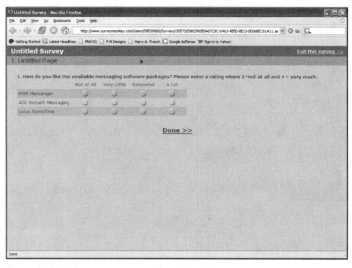

Figure 9-2: Using an even-numbered scale

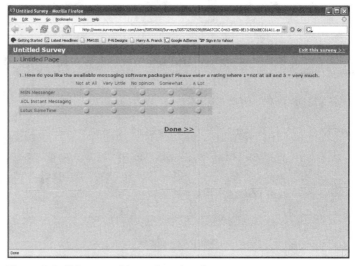

Figure 9-3: Using an odd-numbered scale

Chapter 9

- **Keep it short and simple**. You will get better responses from shorter surveys than longer ones. People can sometimes get tired if the survey is too long or complex, and they might not bother to complete it. Worse, they might begin to answer randomly just to get the survey over with, which will skew your results.

- **Assign numerical values to each possible answer.** (These numbers will be invisible to the respondent but are vital for you to be able to analyze the results.) Typically, higher numbers are used for more positive choices, e.g., strongly agree = 6, while strongly disagree = 1. The exception is ranking, where 1 = highest priority.

Before sending the survey to your whole team, run it past a small sample of respondents. Depending on the size of your team, the sample could consist of just one or two people. A test run will help to identify problem areas in the questions, validate the possible answers, and check the general clarity and usability of the survey.

Determine the timing of your survey. This includes how long the survey will remain "open" or available for team members to submit responses, as well as how often you want to conduct the survey. By repeating the same survey regularly, such as once a month or so, you can get a picture of the changes in your project and the team over the course of time.

After You Measure

What do you do once you have a stack of numbers from all your measurements? Convert them to metrics that you can then analyze and use to track your project's progress, using the following process:

1. Compare the numbers within categories and across categories.
2. Look for trends and trouble spots.
3. Store the information so your team and other teams can access it in the future.
4. Repeat steps 1 through 3!

1. Compare the Numbers within Categories and Across Categories

Some of the measurements you use will have obvious comparisons, particularly when looking at similar types of data within each of the categories of information you have measured (time, resources, process, and quality). For example, within the resources category, you can express the dollars spent on each category of expense (such as hardware, labor, or communications) as a percentage of the whole budget or a percentage of the estimated budget to date. Similarly, it is fairly simple to add the number of hours spent on each task or hours spent by each team member. The numbers become more interesting when you start to compare them across categories. As when choosing which data points to measure, choose the comparisons carefully. Perform enough analysis to get a clear picture of the project status, but do not try to overanalyze. You do not want to spend a higher percentage of your time calculating the metrics than you spend doing the work! There

Chapter 9

are several tools you can use in your analysis. Survey tools like Survey Monkey and Zoomerang include some simple analysis functions. Other tools allow you to export data in a CSV (comma separated values) format that can then be imported into and graphed by spreadsheet software like Microsoft Excel.

Start with the types of questions your management wants answered, because these will often generate more questions as you go along. The following list of questions is not comprehensive, but may help you start thinking about the types of information you want to gather.

- How does the actual output at a given time (lines of code, pages of text, web screens, functions, or whatever is appropriate for your project) compare to the estimated output?

- How much of your resources were used by each component of the process (such as planning, design, communication, or revisions)?

- How much time was spent on resolving quality issues such as bug reports or defects?

- How much of the project is complete at any given point when compared to the percentage of resources you have already expended?

- How does the percentage of resources expended compare to the elapsed time?

- Is the project going to be completed on time and within budgeted costs?

Many collaborative tools include mechanisms for tracking various statistics. Many web hosts provide statistics about sites, and can automatically track and graph information about site usage, visitors, paths through the site, and more. Survey software also compiles results and lets you export the numbers to spreadsheet applications for graphic and further analysis. Wiki software usually comes with a variety of measurements. Some even create graphics for you, like the following graph of usage on the wikiwackyworld.com wiki site.

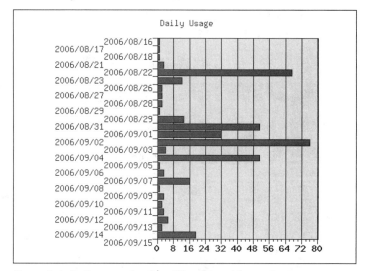

Figure 9-4: Daily usage for the wikiwackyworld.com site

2. Look for Trends and Trouble Spots

When initially analyzing a set of measurements, you are looking at a snapshot of the project. As you gather more information, you will also be able to evaluate trends. A trend can be defined as the direction of change between multiple measurements, usually expressed over time. For example, you might expect the number of outstanding errors to go down and the number of hours spent to go up as you progress toward the end of a project. If you find that you are getting more errors each time you measure or that the hours spent on a particular task (that is not yet complete) are not going up, there might be a problem in your process or with your team members.

Trends are often easier to see if you graph them. If you are measuring the usage of the pages on a site, you might start with the numbers of page views, visits, hits, and bandwidth for each day, as shown in Figure 9-5. This is a lot of numbers!

Day	Page Views	Visits	Hits	Bandwidth (KB)
8/1/2006	8,995	3,085	132,307	1,022,460
8/2/2006	6,809	2,953	132,363	895,814
8/3/2006	6,023	3,060	126,426	928,793
8/4/2006	5,426	2,824	105,586	782,083
8/5/2006	3,211	1,712	50,183	374,744
8/6/2006	2,514	1,537	44,273	347,338
8/7/2006	5,558	2,955	113,010	819,342
8/8/2006	6,015	2,834	119,621	884,085
8/9/2006	6,536	6,682	130,952	1,023,691
8/10/2006	6,152	3,793	129,299	1,009,009
8/11/2006	4,996	2,608	97,891	755,723
8/12/2006	2,264	1,663	47,040	356,363
8/13/2006	2,480	1,876	47,518	348,498
8/14/2006	6,342	2,855	133,919	959,274
8/15/2006	6,639	3,041	121,425	1,009,060
8/16/2006	6,425	3,391	123,499	868,397
8/17/2006	6,117	3,127	119,468	896,626
8/18/2006	5,116	3,140	103,572	753,990
8/19/2006	2,492	1,645	44,356	344,123
8/20/2006	2,443	1,915	46,004	360,258
8/21/2006	14,948	3,180	135,174	1,164,977
8/22/2006	15,980	3,272	142,418	1,257,106
8/23/2006	7,279	2,994	117,288	940,815
8/24/2006	6,632	3,201	130,552	972,441
8/25/2006	6,351	3,026	123,835	932,553
8/26/2006	2,908	2,073	54,119	385,797
8/27/2006	2,460	1,739	38,457	260,549
8/28/2006	6,120	3,350	133,968	912,716
8/29/2006	6,734	3,840	147,616	1,111,449
8/30/2006	8,189	3,594	143,858	1,269,330
8/31/2006	7,516	3,591	134,414	1,011,491
Total(s)	187,670	90,356	3,270,411	24,958,892
Average(s)	6,053	2,914	105,497	805,126

Top of Page

Figure 9-5: Site statistics for Microwaves101.com, August 2006

The graph in Figure 9-6 shows a comparison of visits to page views for one month. This clearly shows that the two numbers tended to remain roughly parallel, except for a spike in page views around August 21 and August 22.

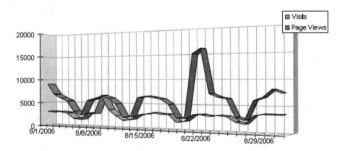

Figure 9-6: Graphic representation of visits and page views for Microwaves101.com, August 2006

To look for trends within your data, you have to take measurements several times over the course of your project. Each time you take any measurement, compare the resulting number to the prior numbers for that same measurement. For example, if team members are spending 15 percent of their time on communication during one month, and that number leaps to 25 percent or drops to 5 percent of their time the next month, you may want to investigate the cause of the change.

3. Store the Information so that Your Team and Other Teams Can Access It in the Future

As you measure and analyze your data, document your findings by creating a summary of your findings and sharing it with others in your team and in your company. The information you create at each step during the project will help you to adjust your process, schedule, or budget as necessary to ensure a successful completion. At the end of the project, use the interim reports as input to a final project report (see Chapter 7, "Conducting Reviews").

The final project reports, including the metrics that you create, become invaluable historical data that you and other project managers can use to increase the accuracy of estimation at the beginning of future projects (see "Planning" in Chapter 5).

4. Repeat Steps 1 through 3

Establish a regular schedule for taking measurements and performing your analyses. You need multiple measurements to establish trends and to find anomalies or problems as early in the process as possible. By continually measuring accomplished or completed tasks against the estimates in your plan, you should be able to identify overruns or schedule delays while there is time to make adjustments. As you make the adjustments, be sure to document them (see step 3, above) so that future project managers can learn from the things you did, both the efforts that worked well and those that did not.

Summary

To track a project's success, you must first understand the purpose of your project. Then track progress by taking measurements at various points throughout the project, and analyze your data frequently. Finally, ensure that you store the data and your analyses, and reference them at the beginning of future projects.

Related Resources

Alreck, Pamela L., and Robert B. Settle. *The Survey Research Handbook*. Boston: McGraw-Hill/Irwin, 2003.

Dillman, Don A. *Mail and Internet Surveys: The Tailored Design Method*. 2nd ed. New York: Wiley, 1999.

Grady, Robert B. *Practical Software Metrics for Project Management and Process Improvement*. Englewood Cliffs, N.J.: Prentice Hall, 1992.

Kan, Stephen H. *Metrics and Models in Software Quality Engineering*. 2nd ed. Boston: Addison-Wesley, 2002.

Kirakowski, Jurek, comp. *Questionnaires in Usability Engineering: A List of Frequently Asked Questions*. 3rd ed. Human Factors Research Group, University of Cork,

Cork, Ireland (http://www.ucc.ie/hfrg/resources/qfaq1.html).

Rico, David F. *ROI of Software Process Improvement: Metrics for Project Managers and Software Engineers*. Boca Raton, Fla.: J. Ross Publishing, Inc., 2004.

Society for Technical Communication Usability Special Interest Group resource page on surveys (http://www.stcsig.org/usability/topics/surveys.html).

Chapter 9

Evaluating the Tools

Hundreds of tools exist for different types of collaboration — from open source to really expensive, and from one tool/one task to integrated suites. With all these options, adding a tools section to a book on concepts is an interesting challenge, one that is almost guaranteed not to succeed.

Unlike books that describe how to use a product (such as *How to Use This Most Amazing Software, Version 2*), this book has a fairly broad audience. We determined that we could expect managers, educators, trainers, senior technical staff, localization vendors, and team members themselves to read this book. (We know that some of our family members will also skim through it, but we do not consider them our target audience.)

In our estimation, those who read this section will fall into one of three areas:

- Novice folks, who may be a bit overwhelmed by the number of tools we have included

- Those somewhere in the middle, who will recognize some of the tools we have listed but possibly not all

- Experienced tools folks, who will tell us which tools we should have included (and they will probably be right)

However, novices are only novices for a short time. As they learn, they move to the middle, and the list of tools will not be quite as overwhelming. And experienced folks can use our wiki to add other tools that should be considered.

Before you start, you need to be aware of a few things:

- Vendors update their tools regularly, although only they know the exact schedule. Unfortunately, this can seriously affect a section on tools. (During the months that we were working on this book, several instant messaging applications distributed upgrades, new web-based collaborative software was released, and several companies released new applications and devices.)

- Accessibility options vary by tool. Most web-based tools state how accessible they are somewhere on their website. If you search the web for "accessibility issues [tool name]" or "accessibility problems [tool name]," you should be able to find out about any existing problems.

- We are not recommending any specific tools because we do not know exactly what you need. In fact, we only recommend tools after we see the results of a needs analysis (in which we may or may not participate). What we have done is suggest possible features that you might be interested in, and list some tools that you might want to investigate. You need to create your own needs analysis, based on the types of tasks that you need to perform and the constraints of your team members. Be aware that you might need to create a different needs analysis for every project.

For example, we needed to perform a needs analysis ourselves before starting this book. The following chart shows the types of tasks we thought this project might require and the tools we chose. When choosing our tools, we had to work with three time zones, one native language, and a limited budget. Your mileage *will* vary!

Note: Some tasks are associated with more than one tool because other factors had to be considered, such as immediacy.

Table II-1: Needs analysis

	Task	Tools	Comments
1.	Create outline of topics (table of contents)	Wiki	http://www.wikiwackyworld.com. The wiki let us modify the TOC as necessary.
2.	Assign chapters to each author, and discuss status and schedule	Skype	This tool has both VoIP and text chat capabilities, and it is free.
3.	Report status to publisher	Wiki Email (as necessary)	All three authors have full wiki permissions to read, write, and edit. We granted our publisher read-only rights so that he could view our progress whenever he wanted to. We also set the wiki up to send notifications to all of us when any pages were changed.
4.	Create chapter files	Microsoft Word	Publisher's request. (We used the wiki for all other information.) (Note: If we were prioritizing, this would be a priority 1.)
5.	Keep informed of each other's schedules	Wiki (calendar) Email	We never remembered to use the calendar.

	Task	Tools	Comments
6.	Resolve inter-chapter (inter-author) content conflicts	Phone Skype	Particularly useful when we were not all online.
7.	Participate in one-on-one discussions	AOL Instant Messenger (AIM) or Skype	We all had AIM accounts before beginning this project.
8.	Share revised chapter files	Wiki	We uploaded files to a file gallery, and then updated a page that sent notices out.
9.	Deliver finished chapters to publisher	Wiki	We created file galleries for documents.

If you want to create your own needs analysis:

1. Create a list of tasks, using any application that lets you create a four- or five-column table. Brainstorm with your team and include everything you can think of, no matter how silly it seems. The chances are slim that any tool will match every item on your list.

The four columns in the above table are:

- **Number.** Start at 1 and stop when you are finished. The number is used for reference during the brainstorming and the prioritizing sessions.

- **Task.** List the specific functionality that you want. You need to get really granular when describing the items. For example, "chat" can mean "having a conversation with another person by typing," "having a conversation with multiple people by typing," "having a conversation with another person by voice," "having a conversation with another person by voice and video," and so on.

- **Tools**. As you research your tasks, use this column to indicate which tools include the specific feature.

- **Comments**. Use this space to explain why you think the item is important.

2. Consider prioritizing the tasks. First, add a fifth column to your table. Then, after you have finished your list (which can be extremely long), you and your team need to prioritize it. Choose a ranking scheme, such as 1 to 3, 1 to 4, 1 to 5, or 1 to 6.

   Ranking priorities is similar to setting up surveys (see Chapter 9, "Evaluating Project Success"). Odd-numbered schemes include a midpoint, which is the "do not care" rank. Even-numbered schemes force people to choose their preference. More than seven choices are too many.

   When ranking the items, think about the items that you must have, that you would like to have, and that would be nice to have. All stakeholders should be involved when prioritizing the list, and the items from some stakeholders might automatically be assigned a priority 1. For example, our publisher required that we deliver our chapters in Microsoft Word files.

3. Use your priorities to help determine which tools are required. If you have a situation like we did, where an absolute requirement determines a tool, mark it as a priority 1 and specify the tool that you must use.

4. If your needs analysis shows more than one possible tool for a task, download trial versions or install web-based applications locally for testing. Make sure you know what the restrictions are, if any, when using a trial version. Some trial applications set a timer (typically 30 days). Some cripple the output.

Some do both. If you are looking at open source software, no trial versions are available.

5. Test the software. Set up some scenarios that match how you want to work, and test those scenarios.

6. Run a pilot after you have determined which software is best for your team. The type of software that you are testing will determine what happens during the pilot. For example, for any content-based tool, start moving some material into the new tool.

When you are testing the software, be sure to check out all available support options. For example, visit user forums to see how quickly questions are answered and what kinds of complaints current users have. One of the best forums to visit is the one called something like "suggested enhancements," as this will let you know what features most users think are missing.

Note that support options for free tools tend to be limited to user forums and knowledge bases.

In our case, we had already used most of the tools on our list. We all had AIM installed before we started writing the book. None of us had Skype installed, but we had all used Microsoft Word, phones, and email. Only Char had really used wiki software before, and she chose the package we ultimately used (TikiWiki).

To help you determine which tools you should use, Part II includes the following information:

- Chapter 10, "Comparing Features, Tools, and More," includes a matrix comparing tasks and the categories we used for organization.

- Chapter 11, "Installation, Customization, and Security," includes some basic information that should be of use to novices and those somewhere in the middle.

- Chapters 12 through 18 describe the tools in the different categories in more detail and provide a partial list of tools laid out in a matrix with some of the more common features.

We hope you enjoy learning about the tools in this section. Should you have any questions, comments, or suggestions, please visit our wiki at http://www.wikiwackyworld.com for the latest updates, corrections to the book, and more. And please feel free to modify wiki pages, as described on the site.

Chapter 10

Comparing Features, Tools, and More

Your true value depends entirely on what you are compared with.

— Bob Wells, contributing editor for *Windows IT Pro*

Use the following matrix to determine which types of tools you need to investigate based on the functionality you want to use.

Comparing Tasks and Categories

We use categories to describe the different types of tools. However, many of the tools include more than one function. For example, some meeting and communication tools let you chat with one or more people (by typing), hold voice and video conversations, share files, share applications, and save meeting notes on a whiteboard. Some collaborative software suites let you assign role-based permissions, share files, and chat. The tools in just about all of the categories provide different types of alerts to immediately notify everyone when changes have been made.

Our categories and the tools they include are:

- Collaborative software suites include many tools as part of the default installation or include modules for tools that can be added. Typically, the core function of the suite is documentation. (See Chapter 12.)

- Meeting and communication tools include instant messaging applications, Voice over Internet Protocol (VoIP) applications, and meeting-based websites. (See Chapter 13.)

- Information broadcasting tools include blogs, podcasts, and webinars. (See Chapter 14.)

- Information sharing tools include calendars, file sharing, forums and bulletin boards, and application sharing. (See Chapter 15.)

- Information gathering tools include surveys, project management and scheduling software, and time-tracking software. (See Chapter 16.)

- Wikis can include just the software itself, although many wiki packages that are available are collaborative software suites. (In the following matrix, the indicated features are for wiki-only software.) (See Chapter 17.)

- RSS feeds and other "push" technologies include emails, faxes, voice mails, newsletters, and RSS feeds, although only RSS feeds themselves are described in the chapter. (See Chapter 18.)

The matrix in Table 10-1 indicates the functionality available.

Table 10-1: Tools matrix

	Collaborative Software	Meeting and Communication	Information Broadcasting	Information Sharing	Information Gathering	Wikis	RSS Feeds and "Push" Technologies
Chat (type) with one or more people in real time	X	X	X				
Talk (chat application or VoIP) with one or more people in real time		X	X				
Run an application on someone else's system		X	X	X			
Share thoughts, opinions, decisions, and more	X		X			X	
Share voice and/or video recordings			X				X
Present a slide show to one or more people		X	X	X			
Hold a scheduled online meeting or training session	X	X	X	X			
Share dates for deadlines, meetings, and more	X			X			
Share files with team members (documents, graphics, and spreadsheets)	X	X		X			
Maintain long-term discussions about concepts, comments, and more with team members	X		X	X	X	X	X
Collect information from team members	X				X	X	
Track tasks, assignments, and due dates	X			X	X		

Chapter 10

	Collaborative Software	Meeting and Communication	Information Broadcasting	Information Sharing	Information Gathering	Wikis	RSS Feeds and "Push" Technologies
Collect feedback online from team members	X			X	X	X	
Set up an editable website that team members can use	X					X	X
Distribute information to team members	X		X	X		X	X
Notify team members when information has been updated	X		X		X	X	X

Chapter 11

Installation, Customization, and Security

" *The great successful men of the world have used their imaginations, they think ahead and create their mental picture, and then go to work materializing that picture in all its details, filling in here, adding a little there, altering this a bit and that a bit, but steadily building, steadily building.*

— Robert Collier, motivational author

Once you have decided which software you want to use, it has to be installed and, if desired, it has to be customized. You also need to set all applicable security options.

It is impossible for us to include detailed installation and customization instructions for all the tools that we have referenced (or even a fraction of them). Instead, we have included some general information about the different types of tools.

Installing Applications

Collaborative tools, like most types of software, come in three flavors:

- Web-based and installed on your server. However, you can install these tools locally for testing purposes.

- Web-based and installed on the vendor's server. You license this software and are required to set up an account.

- Local, which is installed on your hard drive. If you are not allowed to install software on your system, contact your IT department and see what kind of arrangements can be made.

Before installing any software, verify the following items:

- Your system and server meet the minimum hardware and software requirements (and, if possible, more than the minimum). Install any necessary software, such as PHP or Perl, before installing the application. If necessary, make sure a Java Virtual Machine is installed.

- You can access any web-based software through your company firewalls.

- Your connection speed is fast enough.

- You have the required permissions to install additional software that might be needed (such as ActiveX).

- You have tested your microphone and headset.

Using Fantastico

Fantastico, which is included with some cPanel servers, includes more than 50 open source applications that can be installed on your server. (cPanel, a proprietary graphical website management tool, helps administrators update and maintain their servers.)

These applications include:

- Blog software (b2evolution and WordPress)
- Wikis (TikiWiki and PhpWiki)
- Calendar (WebCalendar)
- Image galleries (4images Gallery, Coppermine Photo Gallery, and Gallery)
- Discussion boards (phpBB2)

Open the Fantastico panel, select the software you want to install, and follow the directions (which usually requires accepting the defaults and clicking OK).

Note: A blog entry at Drupal strongly suggests Fantastico not be used for the installation. More information is available at the Drupal site at http://drupal.org.

General Installation Notes

Some general notes on installation:

- Collaborative software suites tend to be a bit more complicated to install on your own server, but only because there are more pieces involved (such as PHP, Perl, SQL, and so on, which must be installed first).
- Software that is installed on your server could require root access or extra permissions.
- Most instant messaging (IM) applications are installed locally on your system after downloading the

Chapter 11

executables from the websites. Windows Live Messenger (formerly MSN Messenger) will be included with Microsoft Vista, and iChat is included with Macintosh systems. (Previous versions of Microsoft Windows included MSN Messenger and Windows Messenger.)

If you are not allowed to install applications because of company policy, check into browser-based clients or see if a security application resolves the issues. For example, AIM Express (http://www.aim.com/get_aim/express/aim_expr.adp), a chat application available to anyone with an AIM or AOL account, does not require ActiveX or Java.

Customizing Applications

After the software has been installed, you might want to customize it. How you customize an application varies, depending on the tool and its functionality. For example, templates let you change the "look and feel" for wikis and blogs, but you cannot customize how RSS feeds display. Some applications, like collaboration software suites, wikis, and hosted blogs, let you apply standard themes, changing the "look and feel" without having to modify any files.

You might need to use the services of an expert for some customizations. For example, the changes you want to implement might require someone who knows HTML, cascading style sheets, PHP, or Perl.

For more information on customizing a specific application, see the Help file, the user documentation, and the user forums for the specific application.

Implementing Security

These days, everyone is concerned about security (and rightly so). Most web-based applications typically include some type of security that you can implement, such as:

■ Challenge emails

■ CAPTCHA

■ Verification

■ Whitelists

■ Role-based permissions

Some applications, such as Yahoo! Groups (http://groups.yahoo.com), use both challenge emails and CAPTCHA to prevent computer programs called "bots" from registering accounts. Yahoo! Groups then goes a step further by letting group owners set different permissions (which are similar to role-based permissions): public (searchable) or private archives, approving new members or automatic acceptance to the group, moderated posted privileges, and more.

Challenge Emails

Challenge emails are emails sent to new registrants automatically so that they can prove who they are. Many sites now use challenge emails to reduce the number of fake users and to prevent bots from registering numerous fake users automatically.

When a user receives a challenge email, typically he or she just needs to reply, although some systems require that the email's body content be cleared. Once the system has received this acknowledgment, the user can access the system.

Challenge emails do not completely stop spammers from attacking a site, but it requires more time than spammers want to spend, as they want to "hit and run." For example, someone registered an email with a dubious email address on a wiki. Shortly thereafter, one page on the site was spammed by that user. However, the account was quickly deleted and the page was restored within minutes.

Most spammers do not want to go through that much effort. They want to take advantage of any loopholes in security so that they can modify the largest number of pages in the shortest amount of time (and, preferably, automatically). Our wiki (at http://www.wiki-wackyworld.com) uses a challenge email system to register users.

CAPTCHA

CAPTCHA stands for "Completely Automated Public Turing test to tell Computers and Humans Apart." CAPTCHAs display distorted text as a graphic or display an icon to play a sound file (which tend to be more accessible to non-sighted users) that must be interpreted before proceeding, typically with a registration process. Like challenge emails, CAPTCHAs help prevent automated registration from computer programs. However, many visitors have found CAPTCHA codes difficult to read, and some systems require that the CAPTCHA code is typed exactly as it is shown (using the same capitalization), while others do not. CAPTCHA sound files can be hard to understand.

Verification

Some applications require verification before one user can accept information from another user. For example, many chat programs let buddies transfer files to one another. However, you can customize your chat program to prompt you when someone is sending you a file so that you can approve it. Some also allow you to specify an anti-virus application that scans all incoming files.

Microsoft Outlook has added a type of verification by preventing graphics from displaying until you explicitly allow them. You can approve graphics on a case-by-case basis or by approving all graphics in emails from a specific domain.

Whitelists

Whitelists indicate the email addresses of the people who are allowed to contact you. A whitelist includes email addresses or user names that will not be blocked by various spam traps. Most whitelists let you specify either a domain name (*.example.com) or an email address (person@example.com). Many spammers take advantage of free email accounts, and as a result, many spam trap applications automatically block those domain names. You can add a friend's email address at a free account domain to your whitelist, which allows email from that account to get to you.

Another type of whitelist is the contact, or buddy, list in chat applications. Chat applications include options that let you set global controls based on your contact list. For example, you can specify that only folks on your buddy list are allowed to contact you, and others must be approved. You can specify that anyone can contact you, but that tends to lead to trouble.

Role-based Permissions

Role-based permissions control what users are allowed to do by assigning permissions according to their role. Many web-based tools (and some desktop tools, too) use role-based permissions to easily define security settings. For example, our wiki uses the following roles:

- The authors belong to the group "authors," and we can do anything: post, upload files, delete members, hide pages, and so on.

- Visitors belong to one of two groups: "registered" users are allowed to read and post, while "anonymous" users are allowed to only read the content.

Role-based permissions are assigned by an administrator, who creates whatever groups are necessary. For example, we have seen systems with groups for administrators, writers, editors, legal, QA, and more, and we have seen systems with administrators, registered, and anonymous. Each group (and therefore every member of the group) was assigned high-level permissions. In some cases, specific users in a group were assigned more permissions than others in the same group.

Users who are assigned to multiple groups function under the least restrictive set of permissions. For example, if a system were set up with groups for writing (can create new information pages) and editing (can only edit existing pages), then a user assigned to both the writing and editing groups can both create new pages and edit existing pages.

Chapter 12

Collaborative Software Suites

> " *It is not a question of how well each process works; the question is how well they all work together.*
>
> — Lloyd Dobyns and Clare Crawford-Mason,
> *Thinking About Quality*

What we categorize as "collaborative software suites" is sometimes known as "groupware" or "computer-supported cooperative work." According to Wikipedia (http://en.wikipedia.org/wiki/computer_supported_cooperative_work), some authors see a difference between cooperation and collaboration because of the way tasks are divided. *Cooperation* is when the results of independent subtasks are merged to create a final deliverable. *Collaboration* requires teamwork for each subtask as members work toward a common goal.

This book is an example of both collaboration and cooperation, and the tools we chose reflect that. We used TikiWiki for most of our non-voice communication, taking advantage of the wiki, blogs, directory, and file galleries. We even played with TikiWiki's online chat (although we were on the phone at the time). We also used AIM and Skype. See the Part II introduction for the complete list of tools we used.

Collaborative software suites include many of the features described in the glossary, and thus include many tools. As a result, collaborative software suites can save you time and effort when compared to installing many individual tools, but lead to more decisions, because now you have to analyze all the tools, as well as the suite itself.

When choosing a suite, first find out the primary purpose of the suite. For example, TikiWiki is built around a wiki; Basecamp's primary purpose is project collaboration; Drupal is a content management system. Then, look at the secondary tools and see if they are of interest to your group.

The following describes the primary purposes of the categories that we have chosen:

- **Communication applications** primarily include instant messaging, online chat, or VoIP. Suites might also include application sharing, chat rooms, and video chat.

- **Broadcast applications** primarily include blogs, podcasts, and presentations. Suites might also include wikis, surveys, "push" mechanisms, and comments.

- **Sharing applications** primarily include calendars, file galleries, forums, bulletin boards, and application sharing. However, many of these features can be found in suites from other categories. For example, Windows Live Messenger includes applications from the communication and information sharing categories. Some wiki software includes "push" mechanisms, security, calendars, RSS feeds, and email. Some meeting software includes application sharing and chat.

- **Gathering applications** primarily include surveys, project management, feedback, and time tracking. While these applications might be included in some other suites (like wikis and blogs), it is more likely that you have to install stand-alone versions.

- **Wikis** are either stand-alone (such as MediaWiki) or part of a suite (such as TikiWiki). Wiki suites might include workflow management, blogs, image and file galleries, chat, a calendar, surveys, and more.

- **RSS feeds** are never the primary purpose of a suite. However, most web-based applications, such as blogs and wikis, include RSS feeds.

You must also determine what type of software you want to use:

- **Web-based** (also called *managed* or *hosted*) software, where you select a plan and create an account. With web-based software, such as Kavi or Basecamp, your information is stored securely on the vendor's server. You and your team log in when you want to make changes, report progress, or upload files. The vendor is responsible for maintenance, support, upgrades, and backups. However, if you cannot connect to the Internet for any reason, you cannot access your account. Typically, you can use the latest version of

Chapter 12

any browser to access web-based software. (For example, you can typically use Internet Explorer 6 or later, Netscape Navigator 8 or later, Mozilla, Safari, and Opera.)

■ **Server-based software**, which requires that the software is installed on your server. With server-based software, such as TikiWiki or Drupal, you are responsible for making sure that your server meets the installation requirements and updates are applied in a timely manner. These installations tend to be a bit more complicated because of other requirements (like PHP or SQL). If you have an IT department, talk to them first, because they will be installing the software and all updates.

Instead of using a suite, you might want to use individual communication tools like those found at Google (http://www.google.com/intl/en/options, which is the English site):

■ **Blogger** lets you create a blog for yourself or for your team, letting all team members post on individual blogs. You can post photos, customize the layout, and set the options for syndication (RSS feeds). You can also specify whether your blog is public or is only available to those readers you have chosen.

■ **Google Calendar** lets you create multiple calendars, which you can view individually or as a group. You specify the name of the event, when it is (and if it is an all-day or limited-time event, and if it repeats), where it is, which of your calendars it belongs to (if you have multiple calendars), and a description. You can also give permission to others to view your calendar along with theirs, and they can do the same for you. (However, you cannot make changes to their calendar unless they give you permission, and they cannot make changes to your calendar unless you give them permission.) Like Blogger, you can specify whether your calendar is public or only available to specific guests.

■ **Google Groups** lets you create mailing lists and discussion groups. Groups can be one of three types: Public (open to all), Announcement-only (only moderators can post messages, but all members can read them), and Restricted (only those who have been invited can join the group, post, and read). Restricted groups are not listed in Google's public directory.

■ **writely** (http://writely.com) lets teams collaborate on documents, which can be saved as HTML, RTF, Microsoft Word, Open Office, and PDF. It also includes an option to create an RSS feed, although the feed is added to a public site, so you might not want to use it for private documents. writely documents include revision history and blog posting (to a hosted provider like Blogger or to your own server).

You can also use Google Talk as your primary communication tool if all team members have a Google or gmail account.

Chapter 12

The suites listed in Table 12-1 include different collaborative features.

Table 12-1: Partial list of collaborative software suites

Software Suite	Requirements	Features
Basecamp http://basecamphq.com Prices range from free (one project) to $149 a month (unlimited number of projects).	Hosted	Administrative privileges Export messages and comments to XML File sharing (not included with free account) Message boards Message and file categories Milestones Time tracking (not included with free account) To-do lists
Drupal http://drupal.org Open source; donations welcome	Multi-platform (Apache is recommended) MySQL or PostgreSQL PHP version 4.3.3+ Client systems require that JavaScript is enabled.	Administrator and user permissions Collaborative book Content management Forums Online help Optional modules Polls Threaded comments Version control
eGroupWare http://egroupware.org Open source; donations welcome	Multi-platform MySQL, PostgreSQL, or MaxDB PHP version 4.3+ (version 5 recommended)	Address book Calendar Email File Manager Projects Manager Trouble Ticket System Wiki (WikkiTikkiTavi)

Chapter 13

Meeting and Communication Tools

> *True interactivity is not about clicking on icons or down-loading files, it's about encouraging communication.*
>
> — Edwin Schlossberg, founder of ESI

Meeting and communication tools provide ways to communicate in real time with other team members by typing, by voice, or by video (or by all three). Some tools include chat rooms, file transfers and application sharing, among other features. Typically, all participants must have compatible software installed, and may need a headset, a microphone, and a video camera.

The following types of tools are included in this category:

- Instant messaging (IM) applications
- Voice over Internet Protocol (VoIP) (covered in the "Instant Messaging (IM) Applications" section)
- Web-based meeting programs

The connection speed that is required depends on what tool you are using and what capabilities you want to use. If you are typing in an IM window, you can use a dial-up connection. However, if you are using VoIP, video, or audio, a high-speed connection prevents lags and improves buffering. Therefore, if you are stuck in a hotel room with a dial-up connection (something that is becoming rare, as most hotels now provide high-speed access), you can still keep in touch with team members, at least through text messaging.

Instant Messaging (IM) Applications

Instant messaging (IM) applications let two or more people "talk" in real time by:

- Typing messages in a chat window
- Using a headset to carry on a conversation
- Using a video camera and microphone to both talk and see other people

Some common IM applications include Windows Live Messenger, AIM, Yahoo! Messenger, Skype, Trillian, Adium, ICQ, Jabber, and Gaim. If you cannot install software, check out AIM Express, which is web-based. See "Comparison of instant messaging clients" (http://en.wikipedia.org/wiki/Comparison_of_instant_messaging_clients) at Wikipedia for multiple comparison charts of more than 60 IM applications, many of which are free.

Most IM applications include the ability to set up a conference room for multiple people. Trillian and Adium X, which are multiprotocol applications that let you connect to AIM, ICQ, Windows Live Messenger, Yahoo! Messenger, and others, only allow conference rooms for the same protocol (that is, you cannot have a chat room with contacts using two different IM applications).

However, interoperability (that is, the ability to talk to contacts using different chat applications) is increasing. Google Talk provides interoperability with other Jabber clients. Yahoo! Messenger with Voice and Windows Live Messenger let users chat with members of either service (but they must be using the latest versions). Trillian has started development on an update that includes interoperability. eWeek's Messaging & Collaboration Center (http://messaging.eweek.com) provides news, reviews, white papers, resources, and more on the latest collaboration efforts.

Voice over Internet Protocol (VoIP) is becoming much more popular, and many IM applications now include the option to use VoIP to contact others with your computer and high-speed connection. Some, like Skype, include the VoIP network, while others, like Windows Live Messenger, require an external service to connect to a VoIP network. Prices vary by provider and are based on location, with one price for national calls and another for international. (Audio and video chat through an IM application are free.) AIM Triton includes the new, free AIM Digits, which gives you a telephone number and allows you to receive inbound phone calls. It also works with AIM Phoneline, which lets you make outbound phone calls.

Most IM applications will let you know if updates are available and provide links directly to the upgrade, as well as a "Check for Updates" menu option.

Customizing IM Applications

Most IM applications let you customize the interface in the following ways:

- Choose a picture to display in chat windows and next to your name
- Modify the font (size, family, style, and color) and background color
- Specify alert sounds (played when contacts log on or log off, etc.)
- Specify folders for file transfers
- Enable virus protection
- Indicate your status

Many applications let you use status messages (and, in some cases, status icons), which lets your contacts know if you are logged in but away, in a meeting, eating lunch, and so on. You can use the default status messages or create your own.

Look for the Options dialog box in the IM application to see what options you can customize.

Adding Security to Instant Messaging

Many companies require security for any IM applications. If you want to add third-party security to your IMs, some products you might want to check out are:

- Akonix's L7 product line (http://www.akonix.com)
- WiredRed's e/pop product line (http://www.wiredred.com)
- FaceTime product line (http://www.facetime.com)
- IMlogic's product line (http://www.symantec.com/enterprise/imlogic/index.jsp)

Or you could use AIM Pro (http://aimpro.premium-services.aol.com), which includes encrypted messages, integration with Microsoft Outlook, and access to WebEx voice and video conferencing to help teams collaborate securely.

IM Applications

For more information about instant messaging applications, see the individual websites or visit BigBlueBall ("Everything about instant messaging," http://www.bigblueball.com).

Table 13-1: Partial list of IM applications

IM Application	Operating Systems	Compatible with...	Features
AIM Triton http://aim.com Free	Microsoft Windows Mac OS/OS X Linux Windows CE Palm OS	AIM AOL CompuServe ICQ Netscape	Address book AIM Digits (telephone number) (free inbound calls) AIM Phoneline (inbound and outbound calls, including international) Audio chat Bots Chat rooms Email File transfer Instant messaging IM forwarding (to mobile phone) Internet search Mobile IMs (text message) Photo sharing Radio

IM Application	Operating Systems	Compatible with...	Features
AIM Triton (cont.)			Video chat Voice conferencing (up to 20 people at one time)
Adium X http://adiumx.com Free	Mac OS X	AIM Google Talk ICQ Jabber Windows Live Messenger Yahoo! Messenger	File transfer (limited) Instant messaging Message logging Off-the-record messaging
Gaim http://gaim.sourceforge.net Free	Microsoft Windows Mac OS X Linux	AIM Google Talk ICQ Jabber Windows Live Messenger Yahoo! Messenger	File transfer Instant messaging Message logging Multiple accounts
Google Talk http://google.com/talk Free	Microsoft Windows	Adium X Gaim iChat Trillian Pro	Audio chat Email (gmail) File transfer Folder transfer Instant messaging Message logging Music status Off-the-record messaging Voice mail VoIP

IM Application	Operating Systems	Compatible with...	Features
ICQ http://icq.com Free	Microsoft Windows Mac OS X		Audio chat Email File transfer ICQ Universe Instant messaging Mobile IMs (text message) (including people not on ICQ) Off-the-record messaging Video chat Voice message VoIP
Skype http://skype. com Free	Microsoft Windows Mac OS X Linux Unix		Audio chat Chat rooms Conference calls (up to four people) File transfer Instant messaging Message logging Mobile IMs (text message) SkypeIn (inbound calls) SkypeOut (outbound calls) Video conferencing (one-to-one) Voice mail VoIP

IM Application	Operating Systems	Compatible with...	Features
Trillian/Trillian Pro http://cerulean-studios.com Free/$25 a year	Microsoft Windows	AIM ICQ Jabber (Pro only) Rendezvous (Pro only) Windows Live Messenger Yahoo! Messenger	Audio chat Instant messaging Mass messaging (ping several users regardless of service used) Message logging Other features through individual IM clients Video chat (Pro only)
Windows Live Messenger (formerly MSN Messenger) http://messenger.msn.com Free	Microsoft Windows	Xbox Yahoo! Messenger with Voice	Alerts Application sharing Audio chat (PC-to-PC) File transfer Folder sharing Instant messaging Message logging Mobile IMs (text message) Video chat VoIP (requires Verizon Web Calling) Whiteboard

IM Application	Operating Systems	Compatible with...	Features
Yahoo! Messenger with Voice http://messenger.yahoo.com Free	Microsoft Windows Mac OS X Linux Unix	Windows Live Messenger	Address book Audio chat (PC-to-PC) Calendar Conferences (text only; including people not on Yahoo! Messenger) Contact search bar Email File transfer Games Instant messaging Internet search Mobile IMs (text message) Music (LAUNCHcast plug-in) Photo sharing Radio (personal selections) Video chat VoIP (with voice mail, call history, and custom ringtones; requires subscription with Yahoo! Communications USA Inc.) Yahoo! Search
Zoho Chat http://zohochat.com Free	Web-based		Conferences ("Scheduled Chat"; including people not on Zoho) History Instant messaging Public room Schedule chat

Web-based Meeting Programs

Web-based programs like WebEx, GoToMeeting, Elluminate, Microsoft Office Live Meeting, Adobe Breeze, and Hewlett Packard Virtual Rooms let you:

- Hold online meetings, which might include a presentation
- Conduct conferences, training sessions, and presentations

These applications require either a Java Virtual Machine or installation of an ActiveX control. WebEx includes a pre-meeting test that verifies that you have all the necessary components before attending an online event.

These types of meetings typically have a moderator who controls not only the agenda but the mute button, which prevents interruptions. However, even when the moderator does not mute attendees, most will mute themselves so as to prevent background noise at their location from interfering with the meeting. The difference is whether or not they have permission to break into the ongoing conversation.

Prices vary by provider, and while they might include a telephone bridge for calls into the meeting, many do not provide a bridge for international calls. One possible solution is to use an IM application because some let you create conferences for 4 to 20 people. However, all attendees would need accounts with the specific IM application.

You can customize the display of the meeting room, such as branding and customized color schemes, and you can customize the presentation itself. Those attending the meeting cannot customize their display (other than the usual control over the browser window). Adobe Breeze lets the presenter add a photo, name, logo, biography, contact information, and title to the speaker's area on the screen.

You can control various settings when holding meetings:

- Let attendees view the attendee list.

- Let attendees chat with each other and with the organizer and presenter during the meeting.

- Send a customized "welcome" message when attendees join the meeting.

- Control system messages.

- Change the viewer color.

Some meeting software includes the ability to add quizzes, with or without SCORM and AICC compliance.

Windows systems include NetMeeting, which includes various communication applications such as conferencing, chat, file transfer, program sharing, remote desktop sharing, and a whiteboard. However, be aware of the following limitations:

- NetMeeting must be installed on everyone's computer first.

- Macintosh users must use Virtual PC.

- *nix users must install other software first.

Web-based Meeting Tools

For more information on the features that the tools in Table 13-2 include, visit their websites.

Table 13-2: Partial list of web-based meeting tools

Meeting Application	Requirements	Purchase Options	Includes
Adobe Breeze http://adobe.com/products/breeze Monthly plans range from $375 per month for five users to $750 a month for 10 users. (Contact the sales department for information about an annual subscription.) Pay-per-use plan costs $.32 per minute per user.	Macromedia Flash Player 6 Other requirements determined by purchase type (hosted or licensed)	License (licensed server) Annual subscription (hosted server) Monthly use (hosted server) Pay-per-use (hosted server)	Communication Server Breeze Training Breeze Meeting Breeze Presenter Breeze Events
Elluminate http://elluminate.com 10-seat Lite Office costs $49.95 a month. Contact the sales department for other editions.	Java Static IP address Firewall access	Elluminate Live! Academic Edition (up to 100 concurrent users) Elluminate Live! Enterprise Edition (up to 100 concurrent users) Elluminate Live! Lite Edition (up to 10 users)	Live web conferencing Content development Management and usability Accessibility and security Breakout rooms (Academic and Enterprise editions) Instant messaging Full duplex VoIP (no phones required) Room available 24x7, for up to the maximum number of users

Meeting Application	Requirements	Purchase Options	Includes
GoToMeeting http://gotomeeting.com GoToMeeting costs $49 a month; annual plan available. GoToWebinar costs $99 a month; annual plan available. GoToMeeting Corporate is licensed based on a set fee per organizer; there are no other meeting or attendee fees.	High-speed Internet connection Java Virtual Machine enabled	GoToMeeting (up to 10 attendees) GoToWebinar (single organizer; up to 1,000 attendees) GoToMeeting Corporate (multiple organizers; up to 1,000 attendees)	Application sharing Changing presenters Desktop sharing Drawing tools Multiple monitor support
Hewlett Packard Virtual Rooms http://education.hp.com/hpvr Pricing starts at $1,800 for a 10-seat bundle for three months and ranges up to $8,400 for a 50-seat bundle for three months, or $75 per month per seat.	High-speed Internet connection	HP Virtual Meeting Room HP Virtual Training Room	Application sharing File transfer Presenter profile Reporting and logging

Meeting Application	Requirements	Purchase Options	Includes
NetMeeting http://microsoft.com/ windows/NetMeeting/ Features/default.asp Free	Internet Explorer version 4.01 or later High-speed Internet connection	Free (included with the Windows operating system)	Video and audio conferencing Chat Internet directory File transfer Program sharing Remote desktop sharing Security Whiteboard
WebEx http://webex.com WebEx Meeting Center pricing starts at $75 per month per host, with a minimum of five hosts required. Pay-per-use accounts start at $.33 per minute. WebEx MeetMeNow costs $49 a month; annual plan available.	ActiveX (Internet Explorer only) JavaScript Cookies	WebEx Meeting Center (per month or pay-per-use) WebEx MeetMeNow (up to 10 attendees)	AIM integration Application sharing Document sharing Outlook scheduling Recording VoIP

Chapter 14

Information Broadcasting Tools

" *Knowledge is of two kinds. We know a subject ourselves, or we know where we can find information on it.*

— Samuel Johnson

Information broadcasting applications are used to distribute information to team members and others.

The types of applications that we include in this category are as follows:

- Blogs (short for *weblogs*) are online journals that let you combine text, images, and hyperlinks.

- Podcasts (audio) and vodcasts (audio-video) let team members retrieve information on demand, unlike presentations and webinars that are typically scheduled. With very little equipment, you can create a podcast for distribution.

- Webinars are covered in the "Web-based Meeting Programs" section of Chapter 13.

If you are not sure whether to blog or create podcasts, check out BlogTalkRadio (http://blogtalkradio.com). The service lets you extend your blog by adding real-time interaction with your readers (or your team). (However, it does not look like it is possible to control who listens to those blogs.)

Blogs

Blogs let people share information personally and casually, typically in a journal format. *Bloggers* (those who write a blog) might write about a specific subject, personal information, or a combination of these.

If you are looking for blogs about a specific topic, visit Technorati (http://technorati.com). This site tracks over 52 million blogs, organizes them by popularity and subject, and lets you track your favorite blogs (after registration).

Most blogs allow the author to categorize the entries, which lets visitors see only those posts related to a specific topic. Some blogging software lets multiple bloggers post, either to the same blog or to multiple blogs that are linked together (called a *blog farm*). Blogs can be hosted on the blogging software's server or installed onto a company server.

If the URL refers to the blogging software's site, the blogger is using that server (for example, see Brenda's blog at http://vagabond.blogsome.com), which is called "hosted services." If the URL refers to the blogger's home page or domain, the blogger has installed the software on his or her personal server (for example, see Char's blog at http://helpstuff.com/blog), and is called "self-hosted." The difference between hosted services and self-hosted blogs is maintenance: Hosted services manage all maintenance (including installation and updates).

You can customize your blog by modifying templates and style sheets, or by selecting a different theme.

Team members can stay up to date with the latest blog entries by using an *aggregator*, which lets you specify the sites that you want to track. (The sites must have RSS or Atom feeds enabled.) See Chapter 18 for more information.

Blog Software

To create a hosted blog, you need to create an account.

Table 14-1: Partial list of blog software

Blog Application	Hosted/Self-hosted	Features
Blogger http://blogger.com Free	Hosted and self-hosted (Hosted requires Google accounts)	Access control (public or specific readers) Audioblog (.mp3) Categories Customize layout Dynamic pages from a database FTP to specific website Google Data API Localization (UTF-8) Post from your phone Syndication (of posts and comments, in Atom or RSS) Team blogs Templates

Blog Application	Hosted/Self-hosted	Features
Blogware http://blogware.com Sold and installed through resellers; pricing varies.	Hosted (through resellers)	Access control Categories Localization (two languages) Photo album Post from your phone Spam blocking Statistics Syndication (posts, RSS) Templates WYSIWYG editor
b2evolution http://b2evolution.net Free	Self-hosted (included in Fantastico)	Access control Blogger API Bookmarklet blogging Categories (multiple) Localization Multi-page posts Statistics Sub-categories Syndication (posts, in Atom or RSS) Team blogs (can be displayed on same page) Templates Themes
Movable Type http://movabletype.org Ranges from five users and one year of support for $199.95 to 50 or more users (call for price)	Self-hosted	Categories Customize layout Localization (UTF-8) Syndication Team blogs Templates

Blog Application	Hosted/Self-hosted	Features
WordPress http://wordpress.org Free	Hosted and self-hosted (included in Fantastico)	Access control Blogger API Localization Team blogs Templates Themes Workflow control

Chapter 14

Podcasts

Podcasts have been around for several years now, providing a way to distribute audio-video files across the Internet. The term might refer to audio only or both audio and video (which are sometimes called "vodcasts"). Podcasts are recordings that can be played through any MP3 player, such as Windows Media Player or QuickTime. If the podcast includes video, you have to use a video player like Windows Media Player, QuickTime, or RealPlayer. For either, you can also use a portable MP3 player, such as an Apple iPod, the Sony PSP, and the new Microsoft Zune. (See http://en.wikipedia.org/wiki/History_of_podcasting for the history of podcasting.)

While you can watch a podcast over the Internet (by visiting the site with your browser), many people use podcatchers to retrieve the latest updates. Podcatchers are applications installed locally that check podcast websites periodically for updates. Some common podcatchers that you can use are iTunes (http://www.apple.com/itunes) and Juice (http://juicereceiver.sourceforge.net/index.php). Both are free.

Creating a Podcast

If you have not created a podcast before, see the introductory "Four Minutes about Podcasting" (http://www.cadence90.com/wp/index.php?p=3548). Follow that with CNET's "Podcasting 101" video (http://reviews.cnet.com/4660-12443_7-6533367.html?tag=nl.e501). For a more detailed overview, read *The Art & Science of Podcasting* by Peter Prestipino (http://magazine.websiteservices.com/blogs/posts/articles/podcasting_overview.aspx).

Before creating a podcast or vodcast, it is a good idea to create a storyboard. And practice. (A lot.) When you first start recording, you might be amazed at how much background noise the microphone picks up or how much you say "ummm."

To create a podcast, you need a microphone and headphones (or a headset), and recording software like Audacity (http://audacity.sourceforge.net). If you want to create a vodcast, you also need a digital video camera and video editing software (to fix any mistakes) like Ulead VideoStudio or Adobe Premiere. Podcasting requires lots of hard drive space (to store the sound and video files).

After you have created and edited your podcast or vodcast, you want to a) publish it on the Internet and b) tell the world (or at least your team). You can send everyone an email with the link to the recording, or you can syndicate your podcast with an RSS file that you upload to the Internet. Podcatchers download the updated podcasts when the site has been updated.

If you use Blogger to create your blog and want to add MP3 files to your blog, you can use Blogger's audio-blogging feature.

Finding Existing Podcasts

If you are looking for podcasts about a specific topic, visit Podcasting News (http://podcastingnews.com/forum/links.php). You can view lists of podcasts by categories or use the search feature. The main site (http://podcastingnews.com) contains frequently updated news articles on various technological issues, along with instructional articles on podcasting. You can also visit YouTube (http://youtube.com) or the Podcast Directory (http://podcastdirectory.com). Many sites, such as NPR, BBC, and ZDNet, create specific podcast directories for their content.

The Future of Podcasting

If you have already started creating podcasts, attend a PodCamp (http://podcamp.pbwiki.com), which is also known as an unconference. The biggest differences between an unconference and a conference are unconferences are free, registered attendees receive gifts, and everyone who attends is encouraged to contribute.

Podcast Software

If you are going to create a podcast, you need video editing software.

Table 14-2: Partial list of podcast software

Podcast Application	Features
Ulead VideoStudio 10 http://ulead.com $69 (Plus version $99); volume discounts available	Chroma key (background substitution) Dolby Digital 5.1 Surround Sound DVD authoring MPEG-4 support Multiple overlay tracks Multi-Trim Editor with AccuCut Editing
Adobe Premiere Pro http://www.adobe.com/products/premiere/ $849	Dolby Digital 5.1 Surround Sound Complex edits possible Multiple nested timelines Project manager Real-time playback Scalable format support

Information Sharing Tools

> " *I want to share something with you: The three little sentences that will get you through life. Number 1: Cover for me. Number 2: Oh, good idea, boss! Number 3: It was like that when I got here.*

> — Matt Groening, creator of *The Simpsons*

Virtual teams need to share information, or the concept of "teamwork" disappears. Use collaborative software such as calendars, file sharing, forums, bulletin boards, and application sharing to do so.

Calendars

Calendars let individual team members indicate important dates. Management can specify deadlines, meeting times and dates, and more. Typically, users toggle between their individual personal calendars and the team calendar, although some calendar software lets users view multiple calendars at one time.

Calendar Software

Many collaboration tools come with a calendar feature that could preclude the need for a separate type of software. If you are already using a wiki with a calendar function, or software such as Lotus Notes, the benefits of compatibility might outweigh other considerations. Ensure that whatever tool you choose can handle the number of users you expect to have, and that it includes the desired security functions. Do you want desktop-based software, or do you need to access calendar entries through an Internet connection? (Note that if either the server or your connection is down, you cannot access the calendar.) You also need to consider whether or not the calendar information can be easily imported (such as from email) or exported (such as to a PDA).

Table 15-1: Partial list of calendar software

Software	Platform	Tools	Features
CyberMatrix http://cyber-matrix.com/prosched.html Price ranges from $100 for a single license to $3,500 for a site license.	Desktop	Pro Schedule Standard Pro Schedule Client/Server Pro Schedule Enterprise Pro Schedule Web	Access control Appointment scheduling Database Drag-and-drop appointments Scalable number of users Share data over a network or Internet Synchronize with PDA Team calendars View appointments for multiple team members
Enlista http://enlista.com Enlista costs $49 a year; Enlista Live costs $99 a year; quantity discounts available.	Internet	Enlista Enlista Live	Access control Automated reminders Automatic time zone adjustment File sharing Instant messaging (secure) Team calendars View appointments for multiple team members
Google http://google.com/calendar Free	Internet	Google Calendar	Event reminders Guest comments Mobile access Multiple calendars Requires Google account Send invitations Team calendar View appointments for multiple team members

Chapter 15

Software	Platform	Tools	Features
Tucows http://kiko.com Free	Internet	Kiko Calendar	Contact management Drag-and-drop appointments Import from ICAL and VCARD Localization Reminders through email, AIM, and SMS RSS feeds Synchronization

File Sharing Software

File sharing software (also called "file galleries") allows team members to upload any kind of file for use or review by other team members, including graphics, documents, spreadsheets, and more. Anyone can download and edit the files, and then re-upload them. However, the team needs to institute a system so that two people do not make independent edits to the same file at the same time, · because then two different files result.

A key element of collaboration is the ability to share files. Sometimes you might want to simply allow team members to view files belonging to other team members. In other instances, you might want to allow team members to edit each other's files directly. Most wikis include file sharing, as do most collaboration software suites. This category also includes the "version control" systems that "lock" the files as team members check them out. This prevents people from undoing each other's work, and also allows you to track changes to show exactly who did what (and when).

When choosing file sharing software, you need to determine exactly how many levels of security are needed and whether each file needs different levels. File security usually involves setting up unique permissions for each file, based on either user passwords or group identities. This can generally allow team members to create, view, edit, and/or delete files (or can be used to prevent any of these activities). You should also look at file size limits (both in terms of storage and file transfers) and, as with any collaboration software, the number of users allowed per license.

Table 15-2: Partial list of file sharing software

Software	Security	Features
Intranet or website Free, once you have a website	Optional, by user login	Customizable to your needs, but requires some programming for customization File size limits determined by your system setup No version control capability
FTP (team members upload or download from your server) Typically free, once someone uploads the files to the specific folder	Optional, by user login	Customizable to your needs, but requires some programming for customization File size limits determined by your system setup No version control capability
bigVAULT http://bigvault.com Costs vary based on storage plan	Two levels (owner and guest), which can be applied to files and/or folders	Access files online or from a desktop Fees determined by file size required No version control capability
CryptoHeaven http://cryptoheaven.com Costs range from $2.42 a month (prepaid for the year) to $49.92 a month for a personal account, and $7.98 to $624.98 a month for a business account.	One login per account	Desktop software Secure storage No version control capability

Software	Security	Features
FilesAnywhere http://filesanywhere.com/Features.htm Costs range from free to $8.95 a month for single users, from $13.95 a month to $25 a month for multi-user accounts, and from $99 a month to $2,000 a month for corporate accounts.	Multi-user plans are available	Check-in/check-out capability and file locking
iBackup http://ibackup.com Costs range from $9.95 a month to $299.95 a month.	Sub-accounts for multiple users	Online access No version control capability

Forums and Bulletin Boards

Forums and bulletin boards let team members discuss specific topics. This centralized area lets team members decide which information they want to investigate and which they do not.

This category involves creating a space where team members can post and respond to messages. There are lots of names for this type of technology, depending on the vendor, such as message boards, bulletin boards, forums, and discussions, but they all have several properties in common. There is usually a way to categorize the messages, there is a mechanism for tying responses to the original messages (often called "threading"), and all team members can view all of the messages and responses. The messages remain on the board or forum, and team members can refer back to them later. There is usually a mechanism for searching through older messages.

A message board system can be useful, but remember that it requires the team members to check regularly for new messages or responses. Also, you should assign a single person to be the board moderator to ensure that topics are categorized the way you want them to be, that the messages stay on topic, and that information that needs to be escalated or handled in some other way gets noticed and addressed properly. For example, if the team is discussing a problem and determines that it can be resolved by additional funding, the request for funding would most likely need to be submitted through some other communication path (such as email, online forms, or even on paper).

If you want the message boards to reside on your system server, ensure compatibility with your existing system and allow for the appropriate system resources (disk space, memory, and so on).

Table 15-3: Partial list of forum and bulletin board software

Software	Features
Anyboard http://netbula.com/anyboard/ Costs range from free to $2,995.	Access control Changelogs Chat room Comments Customization Event scheduling Polls Post messages by email Site management Templates WYSIWYG editing

Software	Features
phpBB http://phpbb.com Free	Database choices: MySQL, MS-SQL, PostgreSQL, or Access/ODBC Localization Multiple language interface Public and private forums Requires PHP Templates
PunBB http://punbb.org/ Free; donations welcome	Database choices: MySQL, PostgreSQL, SQLite Modules Open source Requires PHP

Application Sharing

Application sharing means that one person links to another member's system, and then takes control while running a specific application (which includes the Windows desktop). This lets one person show the other how to accomplish a specific task, apply settings, or make backups of the other system (typically when the first person is not around). Two popular application-sharing applications are Windows Live Messenger (see Table 13-1) and WebEx, including WebEx MeetMeNow (see Table 13-2).

Chapter 16

Information Gathering Tools

" *I find that a great part of the information I have was acquired by looking up something and finding something else on the way.*

— Franklin P. Adams, American journalist

Surveys, project management and scheduling, feedback, and time tracking let team members collaborate on the current deliverable(s).

Feedback further identifies areas of strength and weakness. Use feedback to adjust your project plan and identify topics for future surveys. Most information gathering applications include feedback mechanisms.

The tools discussed in this chapter can be installed as part of a collaborative software suite or as a stand-alone version.

Surveys

Surveys allow you to collect information, usually without verification, about a specific activity or concept. They help you better understand the activity or concept (or, at least, people's concepts of it), identify areas of concern, and see if more information needs to be gathered.

The surveys we refer to are simply used to gather information. While you can take advantage of the features required in more complex surveys (such as specifying the sampling frame, sampling method, data collection, and weighted analysis), it typically is not necessary when gathering information from your team or your end users.

Make sure that you word the survey questions so that you get valid answers. For example, a recent survey included the question, "How effective is our marketing?", with possible answers ranging from "very effective" to "not very effective." However, the question cannot be quantified because "effective" and "marketing" are subjective. A better question would be, "Did you see our TV ad?" Ranges (also known as "Likert scales"), rankings, and multiple-choice questions work better than true/false or yes/no questions. For more information, see Chapter 9, "Evaluating Project Success."

Table 16-1: Partial list of survey software

Software	Features
SurveyMonkey www.surveymonkey.com Basic Subscription (free), includes 10 questions and 100 responses per survey Professional Subscription ($19.95 per month or $200 per year), includes up to 1,000 responses per month	Basic: limited to 10 questions and 100 responses per survey Professional: unlimited number of surveys with unlimited number of pages and questions; additional charge for more than 1,000 responses per month Answers required option Conditional logic Custom redirect Customization Download responses to Microsoft Excel Email list management Filter and share results Localization Randomized answer choices Response tracking
Zoomerang http://info.zoomerang.com Basic (free), includes up to 100 participants, 30 questions, 10-day window zPro ($599 per year) (nonprofit and education versions available)	Basic: unlimited number of surveys with up to 30 questions limited to 100 responses per survey; results available for 10 days zPro (any version): unlimited number of surveys, questions, and responses; can download responses to Microsoft Excel Conditional logic Customization (branding and design) Filter and share results Localization (40 languages) Templates (survey questions)

Project Management

Project management and scheduling software let you monitor progress on specific tasks and those assigned to the task. Project management identifies both strengths and weaknesses on the team by letting you see who is (and who is not) meeting deadlines, how complete (or incomplete) the project is, and how deliverables compare to milestones.

Table 16-2: Partial list of project management software

Software	Features
@task http://www.attask.com Prices range from $50 per user ($2,500 unlimited per year) for help desk end user to $395 per user	Audit trails Critical path analysis Document management Dynamic list grouping Issue management Milestone tracking Multiple timeline options Organizational charts Project collaboration Reporting and analysis Security Task approval Time tracking Timesheets
Basecamp basecamphq.com Prices range from free (one project, no file sharing) to Max ($149 per month; unlimited number of projects)	Chat (via Campfire) Encryption Feedback File sharing Milestones Number of projects limited by chosen plan

Software	Features
Basecamp (cont.)	Task assignment
	Time tracking
	To-do lists
	Unlimited people and clients
	Writeboards
EMC eRoom http://emcinsignia.com/products/smb/eroom/ Prices range from $495 for five users (electronic) to $2,395 for 25 users (physical media)	Alerts and notifications
	Archives
	Calendar
	Discussions (threaded)
	File sharing
	Instant messaging integration
	Milestones
	Polls
	Tasks
	Templates
	Version tracking
	View relationships
eProject http://www.eproject.com/products/index.htm $45 per user per month or $495 per user (quantity discounts available)	Automated approvals
	Document management
	Project estimates
	Project request forms
	Project scoring
	Reports
	Resource planning
	What-If modeling

Chapter 16

Software	Features
Kidasa Milestones	Earned value calculations
http://www.kidasa.com	Earned value reports
Simplicity costs $60; Professional costs $239 (electronic versions); quantity discounts available	Import from Microsoft Project
	Integrates with Microsoft Word and Microsoft PowerPoint
	Microsoft Outlook import/export
	SmartColumns
	Templates
Microsoft Project	Assign resources
http://www.microsoft.com/project	Calendar wizard
Stand-alone (Project Standard or Professional), $599/$999; EPM, contact reseller	Compare versions
	Convert task lists from Excel or Outlook
	Cross-project critical path
	Customizable
	Grouping
	Guided planning and management
	Material resources
	Presentation wizard
	Reports
	Reschedule uncompleted work
	Smart Tags
	Task deadlines
	Templates
	Track performance

Time Tracking

Time tracking, which is sometimes part of project or workflow management, lets you see how much time is being spent on specific tasks and projects, and helps you identify problem areas before the situation interferes with the schedule.

Some packages include time tracking functionality. However, stand-alone packages typically include more features (including integration with billing). See "2006 Time Tracking & Management" (http://time-tracking-management-software-review.toptenreviews.com/) and "Comparison of time tracking software" (http://en.wikipedia.org/wiki/Comparison_of_time_tracking_software) for comparison charts of some popular time tracking packages.

Table 16-3: Partial list of time tracking software

Software	Features
BillQuick http://www.bqe.com Lite (free); Basic ($395) includes two users. Additional users extra.	Alerts
	Billing arrangements (e.g., hourly, flat, etc.)
	Budgets and estimation
	Customization
	Database wizard
	Extensible modules
	Industry-specific templates
	Microsoft Outlook integration
	Multi-currency
	Peachtree Accounting integration
	QuickBooks integration
	Report Designer (limited unless you have Crystal Reports)

Chapter 16

Software	Features
BillQuick (cont.)	Retainer history
	Scheduled backup
	Stopwatch timer
	Team time tracking
	Time and expense slips
	Timesheet entry
Timeslips http://www.timeslips.com Prices start at $449.99 for Single Station (additional users extra; value packs available). Network stations extra.	Alerts
	Billing arrangements (e.g., hourly, flat, etc.)
	Customization
	Database wizard
	Email timeslips
	Extensible modules
	Industry-specific templates
	Microsoft Outlook integration
	QuickBooks integration
	Peachtree Accounting integration
	Report Designer
	Scheduled backup
	Split bills
	Stopwatch timer
	Team time tracking
	Time and expense slips
	Timesheet entry

Chapter 17

Wikis

Wikis are collaborative websites that allow users to add and edit content. The word "wiki" (Hawaiian for "fast") can refer to the site or to the software installed on the site. Wikis, which are similar to word processors, were created by Ward Cunningham in 1994. He called it "WikiWikiWeb" after being told to catch a Wiki Wiki shuttle bus that ran between the terminals of the Honolulu International Airport. (He preferred WikiWikiWeb over his second choice, "QuickWeb.")

All work in a wiki is done through a browser in real time. Most wikis disable JavaScript and HTML tags to help keep the results more secure. One of the largest wikis is Wikipedia, an online encyclopedia with over

1 million articles in English alone, and a continuously expanding library in other languages.

Wiki software can be described as coming in one of two flavors:

- **Wiki only**, with a minimal feature set (minimal registration process, history, page locking, and IP blocking). MediaWiki, the wiki software used for Wikipedia (http://wikipedia.org), is wiki-only.

- **Full-featured management set**. This includes challenged registration (visitors have to confirm their email address before modifying pages), workflow management, user permissions, image and file galleries, surveys, and a full administrative panel, plus more. TikiWiki, the wiki software used for WikiWackyWorld (http://www.wikiwackyworld.com), is a full-featured management set.

Installation requires that you upload or copy files to your server, create a MySQL database and user account, and run the installation scripts. Installation packages are available for some wikis. Be sure to read the installation requirements and any posts about problems at the wiki's site. You do not usually need to know anything about (X)HTML, SQL, or CSS to set up a wiki, but some knowledge of PHP is required for customization.

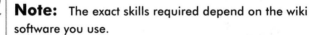

Note: The exact skills required depend on the wiki software you use.

Most wikis allow for customization, but how this is implemented varies. In some cases, you must modify the underlying files. In others, you modify a select group of templates. Several wikis let you select from existing themes (and you can set the permissions so that users may choose a different theme if they like). When first starting, it is easier to accept as many default settings as possible, and worry about the look and feel after you are more comfortable using the software. (Of course, if this will be a public-facing wiki, then the look and feel must be finished by the time it goes live.)

One strength of a wiki is its revision history. Every time someone makes a change to a page, no matter how small, the previous version is stored. This helps prevent problems because unwanted changes (like spam) can be removed quickly by restoring the best previous version.

Spam has always been an issue with wikis. However, most wiki software has been upgraded to require registration before visitors can post to prevent spamming problems. You can also set global email alerts to notify administrators when a page has been changed, and registered users can select to "watch" a page for any changes. ("Watch" means that the user is notified by email when the page is changed.)

Also, some wikis have been enhanced to include content management capabilities, such as user permissions, categories, workflow management, image and file galleries, surveys, forums, newsletters, articles, and more. See Chapter 12, "Collaborative Software Suites."

While wikis can be installed locally, they are almost always run from a server (either Internet or intranet). Wiki farms provide hosting specifically for individual wikis.

Most wikis include the following features:

- **Registration**. Some wikis require registration before content can be added or edited. Others are open (and require constant monitoring because of hackers).

- **History**. Tracks changes over the life of the page and lets you revert to a previous version. You can usually choose the versions that you want to compare.

Chapter 17

- **Locking pages**. The wiki administrator can lock specific pages against changes. Lock pages that only an administrator should modify, such as a home page.

- **Search**. Some wikis let you search titles only, but many include full-text search.

- **Recent changes**. This lists the pages that were most recently changed. A quick glance at any recently changed pages indicates which topics are the most popular.

- **IP blocking**. This feature prevents visitors from specific IPs from accessing the site. An administrator must add IPs to the list, although this is usually a moot exercise (hackers change their IPs too frequently for a lock to work).

Some wikis include a WYSIOP (What You See Is One Possibility) editor, while others use text editors that require a custom markup language, sometimes called "Wikitext" or "wiki syntax." However, every wiki uses slightly different syntax, which can make it difficult to switch between wikis.

For example, early wikis used CamelCase (sometimes called "WordsSmashedTogether") to create links and page names. But as wikis matured, CamelCase has been dropped for freelinks, created by using either parentheses or square brackets:

- (General Questions) is a freelink to the General Questions page on It's a Wiki Wacky World.

- [http://www.wikiwackyworld.com | It's a Wiki Wacky World] is a freelink to the Wiki Wacky World website that displays the website title and not the URL.

Today's wikis may accept both CamelCase and freelinks, or may only accept freelinks. If you have a preference, read the documentation at the wiki site.

The following table shows some of the different wiki syntax possibilities for formatting text.

Table 17-1: Wiki syntax

	TikiWiki	MediaWiki
heading	!Heading 1 !!Heading 2	=Heading 1 ==Heading 2
unordered (bullet) list	*bullet item *another bullet item	*bullet item *another bullet item
ordered (number) list	#item 1 #item 2	#item 1 #item 2
bold text	two underscores	three single quotes
italic text	two single quotes	two single quotes
underlined text	three equal signs	<u></u> (HTML tags)

Some sites include a style guide page that provides quick access to the specific rules. For example, the MSHelpWiki (http://www.mshelpwiki.com/wiki) includes a page called Formatting Rules, which shows examples for different types of formatting (headings, images, text formatting, horizontal rules, and so on). Each example demonstrates both the raw code (from the editor) and the final results.

Many wikis do not allow the use of HTML tags. Some, like TikiWiki, leave the decision to the administrator. And others, like MediaWiki, allow for a very limited number of tags. This prevents visitors from wreaking havoc with malicious HTML.

Many wiki sites include a Sandbox, which is a page where visitors can "play" with the wiki syntax. The easiest way to use the Sandbox is to open two browser windows: one for the Sandbox and one for the page that describes the wiki syntax.

Chapter 17

More detailed matrices can be found at the following sites:

■ WikiMatrix (http://wikimatrix.org) lets you select from more than 60 wikis to produce a custom side-by-side comparison chart, and includes a wizard. You answer questions about the features you want in a wiki, and the wizard then lists the wikis that match the selected features so you can investigate further.

■ Wikipedia (en.wikipedia.org/wiki/Comparison_of_ wiki_software) includes features for more than 25 wikis.

Table 17-2: Partial list of wiki software

Wiki	Hardware/Software	Features
MediaWiki mediawiki.org	Apache PHP 5 MySQL or Oracle	Administrator permissions Categories Extensible (with plug-ins) Freelinks Namespaces Right-to-left support RSS feeds Security/anti-spam Subpages Unicode support

Wiki	Hardware/Software	Features
TikiWiki http://tikiwiki.org/	Apache PHP MySQL, PostgreSQL, Oracle	Administrator modules Articles Blogs Calendar CamelCase links (also known as WordsSmashedTogether) Categories Chat File galleries Forums Freelinks Image galleries Newsletters Role-based permissions RSS feeds Save as PDF Security/anti-spam Subpages Surveys Themes (customizable) Unicode support Workflow management
Twiki http://twiki.org/	Apache Perl Text files	CamelCase links (also known as WordsSmashedTogether) Extensible (with plug-ins) Freelinks Themes (customizable) Unicode support Variables Workflow management

Chapter 17

RSS Feeds and Other "Push" Technologies

❝ You create your opportunities by asking for them.

— Patty Hansen, coauthor of
Chicken Soup for the Kid's Soul

❝ Cats seem to go on the principle that it never does any harm to ask for what you want.

— Joseph Wood Krutch,
U.S. author and critic

"Push" technologies deliver information from a server to users. Users may initially request the information, but then it is delivered when ready, and users have no control over when the information arrives. With "pull" technologies, such as websites, users search for and request the information.

Push technologies include emails, faxes, voice mails, newsletters, and RSS (originally defined as "Remote Site Syndication," then as "Really Simple Syndication," "Rich Site Summary," and "RDF Site Summary").

Emails, Faxes, and Voice Mails

Emails, faxes, and voice mails are technologies familiar to many people. However, there are some things that you should be aware of when using these technologies to send information to your team:

- Never send more than one fax per day (or per couple of days). In many cases, it is a waste of resources (like paper), and of the three technologies, faxes tend to be the most irritating when received too frequently.

- Using the information in Chapter 4, "Communicating with the Team," design a communication system. Make sure everyone knows if a system has been defined for emails (for example, starting the subject line with "ANN" for announcement or "MTG" for a scheduled meeting), when they should respond to an email or voice mail (upon delivery to indicate that they read it? as soon as they can answer any questions? before the next meeting?), and anything else that has been designed to increase team communication.

- When leaving a voice mail, keep it short. Provide your name, phone number, reason for your call, and your phone number again. Be sure to say your name and phone number slowly so that the other person can understand it.

Newsletters

Electronic newsletters let you share information with your team, your company, your customers, and the public. You can use a simpler format and layout for team-only newsletters than those prepared for your company, your customers, or the public. Successful newsletters provide recaps of past work, introduce different team members, provide previews for upcoming products and events, and set expectations.

Newsletters can be sent through email or posted on a website. If you send them through email, they are stored on the recipient's hard drive until permanently deleted. If team members use the same server for email, then multiple copies will be stored, making a case for posting newsletters to a website. If you post them on a website, you can send an email to announce them (or people can use RSS, discussed next, to find out when the latest newsletter has been posted).

RSS

RSS is different from the other technologies mentioned earlier. Based on XML, RSS notifies those who want to know (subscribers) when information has changed. This information includes:

- Pages on a website (including blog entries and wiki pages)
- Headlines, article excerpts, schedules, and so on
- Weather alerts
- Announcements (for example, read the latest newsletter, welcome our newest members, and so on)

Chapter 18

The sidebar shows how RSS works, using blogs as an example. However, the general concepts apply to any updated information: Someone publishes new or changed information; the RSS is created, either manually or automatically; and once the RSS file is finished, it is distributed to syndication servers.

In addition, visitors might use an RSS aggregator (sometimes called a "feeder" or "reader") that searches for updated RSS files on a regular basis. Visitors choose which RSS feeds they are interested in. For example, Brenda uses Feedreader to keep an eye on the Society of Technical Communication website (http://www.stc.org), Scriptorium's blog Palimpsest (http://www.scriptorium.com/palimpsest), Darren Barefoot's blog (http://www.darrenbarefoot.com/), and Rahul Prabhakar's blog (http://2brahulprabhakar.blogspot.com/), among others. Char uses CITA's RSS Aggregator to watch many of the same sites Brenda does, plus the STC Forums (http://www.stcforums.org), the MSHelpWiki (http://www.mshelpwiki.com/wiki), and Microsoft Watch (http://www.microsoft-watch.com). We also watch each other's sites, as well as our own. (If you watch your own site with an aggregator, you know that the RSS file was updated correctly and that your aggregator is working!)

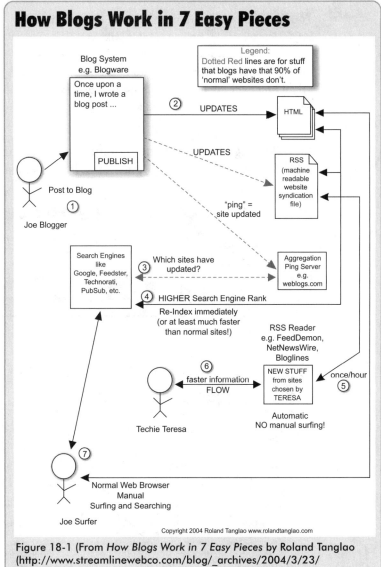

Figure 18-1 (From *How Blogs Work in 7 Easy Pieces* by Roland Tanglao (http://www.streamlinewebco.com/blog/_archives/2004/3/23/28903.html))

Note: RSS feeds are not the same as "watching" a page. For example, on our book's wiki at http://www.wikiwackyworld.com, you can click the "watch this page" icon at the top of a page to receive email notifications when that page is changed. The watching process does not use RSS.

The following screenshots help demonstrate the differences between the pieces. Figure 18-2 is a screenshot of the RSS file for the helpstuff blog:

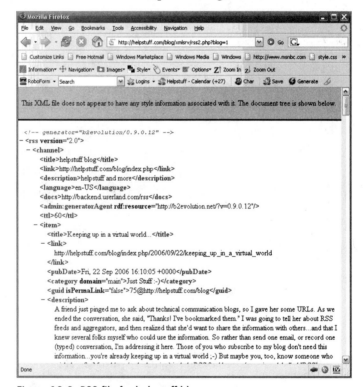

Figure 18-2: RSS file for helpstuff blog

After the blog has been updated, aggregators find the updates:

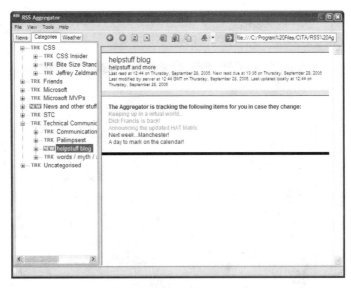

Figure 18-3: CITA's RSS Aggregator showing updates

Finally, you can view the updates through your aggregator. Figure 18-4 shows the blog entry as seen with CITA RSS Aggregator (a desktop application):

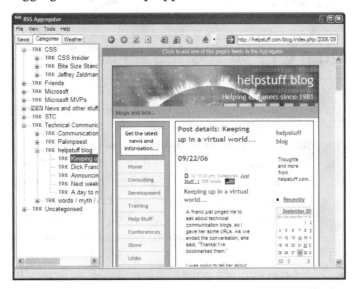

Figure 18-4: Viewing the web page through the CITA RSS Aggregator

Chapter 18

Figure 18-5 shows the blog entry as seen with Feedreader (another desktop application):

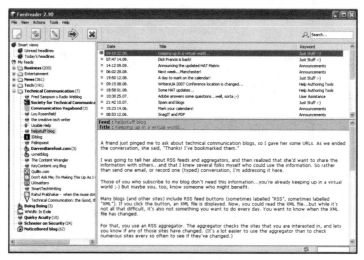

Figure 18-5: Viewing the same content through Feedreader

The rest of this chapter discusses creating and validating RSS files.

Creating and Validating an RSS File

Reading this section is only necessary if you want to add an RSS file to your own site, and you are not using an application that automates the process.

To manually create an RSS feed, you can use a web-based tool like RSS Creator (http://www.web-reference.com/cgi-bin/perl/makerss.pl), or you can use any editor that saves the results as plain text. The file includes information about the site that has been updated and what the update is, using the <item> tag. RSS feed files can contain notices for up to 15 updates.

RSS comes in several flavors:

- **RSS 0.9x**. Originally created by Netscape (when it was known as "Remote Site Syndication"). The various 0.9x versions have been adapted and enhanced by different companies.

- **RSS 1.0**. Based on RDF (Resource Description Framework), a universal format for the Web. RDF is a W3C specification and is part of the Semantic Web.

- **RSS 2.0**. The update to version 0.9x. Now known as "Really Simple Syndication," this version was released under a Creative Commons license.

  For more information, see "Web RSS (Syndication) History" at http://goatee.net/2003/rss-history.html.

RSS files must contain the following elements:

- The XML declaration. This tag starts with `<?xml version`, and identifies the document as XML. It might also include the encoding standard and language.

- `<rss>` element. Identifies the document as RSS *x.x*. The version attribute is required.

- `<channel>` element. This identifies your feed content.

- The tags that make up the feed information, including `<title>`, `<link>`, `<description>`, and `<language>`. The `<lastBuildDate>` tag is optional, and identifies the date and time when the RSS feed was changed. The `<ttl>` tag is also optional, and represents the number of minutes that a feed reader should wait before checking the feed again.

Chapter 18

- The tags that identify the feed content, including
  `<item>`, `<title>`, `<link>`, `<guid>`, `<pubDate>`,
  and `<description>`. Other optional tags, such as
  `<category>`, can also be included.
- Finally, add the closing tags for the feed, including
  `</channel>` and `</rss>`. (Note that all other tags
  must also be closed when used.)

If you create your RSS file, you must validate it or it will
not display correctly. The RSS Specifications list several
validators at http://www.rss-specifications.com/
feed-validators.htm.

For more information on creating RSS feeds, see
"RSS Workshop: Publish and Syndicate Your News to the
Web" (http://rssgov.com/rssworkshop.html) and
"Making an RSS Feed" (http://searchenginewatch.com/
showPage.html?page=2175271). This page also includes
links to other resources, including the RSS Headline
Creator (a wizard that takes your information and
produces a valid RSS feed).

Because there are several versions of RSS (and a lot of
forking through the development cycles), a new protocol,
called Atom, was developed. Even though it is still in
draft form, Atom was published as a proposed standard in
RFC 4287 (http://tools.ietf.org/html/rfc4287).

Many of the tags in Atom are similar to those in RSS.
To learn how to create an Atom feed, see "The Atom
Syndication Format" (http://www.atomenabled.org/
developers/syndication/atom-format-spec.php).

Using HTML in RSS and Atom Feeds

Both RSS and Atom feeds let you include HTML tags in
your RSS file to provide formatting and layout. A special
tag called "[CDATA]" indicates information that is not

parsed (that is, the content is not validated). [CDATA] lets feed creators pass HTML tags through to the readers.

Applying Formatting to RSS and Atom Feeds

If you have used HTML tags in your feeds, you can use a cascading style sheet (CSS) to format them. First, you must create the CSS file and save it to your server. Then you must add a second XML tag to the RSS feed to specify the CSS:

```
<?xml-stylesheet type-"text/css"
href=http://helpstuff.com/rss.css ?>
```

Alternatively, you can use an XSL stylesheet. (XSL tends to be a bit more complex than CSS.) If you are not familiar with XSL, you can find samples on the web (for example, "Making RSS Pretty" offers sample CSS and XSL files at http://interglacial.com/~sburke/stuff/pretty_rss.html). The XML tag for the XSL is:

```
<?xml-stylesheet type-"text/xsl"
href=http://helpstuff.com/rss.xsl ?>
```

Vulnerabilities in RSS Feeds

Because RSS feeds can include both HTML and CSS, it is possible to create a malicious RSS feed. RSS aggregator developers have already started dealing with these issues, which is described more fully later in this chapter. (Aggregators let you accumulate RSS feeds for those sites that you want to track.)

Chapter 18

Syndicating an RSS Feed

If you are using an application that includes RSS feeds, such as blog or wiki software, the updated RSS information is distributed automatically once the content is published.

"Syndication" is how multiple sites share content. People subscribe to the channels that they want to read using an aggregator. Thousands of RSS channels already exist, and some sites publish content to multiple channels (for example, MSNBC offers channels for U.S. news, U.S. politics, world news, business, sports, entertainment, and more).

However, if you are manually creating your feeds, use a site like FeedBurner (http://www.feedburner.com) or Technorati (http://www.technorati.com/ping/) to let people know about your content.

To make sure that your feed went out correctly, subscribe to it. When you receive the notice, you know that everyone else did, too. To subscribe to feeds, you use a reader or aggregator.

Using an RSS Aggregator

Many blogs (and other sites) include RSS feed buttons (sometimes labeled "RSS," sometimes labeled "XML," and almost always orange or blue). If you click the button, an XML file is displayed in your browser. This XML file contains the latest highlights from the site: headlines, hyperlinks, graphics, metadata, articles, and more. (If you right-click the button, you can add the file to your browser's bookmark list.)

To receive these updates automatically, use an RSS aggregator. The aggregator checks the sites that you are interested in, and lets you know if any of those sites have changed. (It is a lot easier to use the aggregator than to check numerous sites every so often to see if they have changed.) Follow the instructions in your aggregator to add the feeds you want to follow.

Dozens of RSS aggregators exist, and most are free. You can use an RSS aggregator that integrates with a browser, or you can visit websites specifically designed to store your information, or you can install a local application. The choice is yours.

For example:

- **Firefox** includes "live bookmarks." If you visit a site that has RSS enabled, a small web feed icon is displayed to the far right of the address field. Click the icon to add the site to your live bookmarks. Other options are Internet Explorer 7, Opera 8, and Safari. To see if the sites have been updated, click the appropriate bookmark icon.

- **Bloglines** is a website where you subscribe to blogs, email groups, and websites (after creating an account). You can blog, collect clippings from other blogs, and share your clippings. Everything is organized on a personal web page. Other options are Technorati, FeedBurner, NewsGator (http://www.newsgator.com), and My Yahoo! (http://my.yahoo.com/index.html; requires a Yahoo! account). Websites usually indicate new entries by making them bold.

- The **CITA RSS Aggregator** is a Windows application that runs in the background. When any watched feeds are updated, a small window is displayed on the screen (you can choose to read the feed then, read it later, snooze, or ignore the feed). Other options

Chapter 18

include SharpReader (http://www.sharpreader.net), Feedreader (http://www.feedreader.com), and NetNewsWire (http://www.apple.com/downloads/macosx/internet_utilities/netnewswire.html). Desktop applications indicate new entries by making them bold or by using icons.

Each aggregator type has its pros and cons. Website aggregators like FeedBurner and Technorati mean that you can see the latest news from any computer, but you have to visit the website to see the updates. Browser-based aggregators let you gather RSS information without installing any applications, but you have to launch a browser and click the bookmarks. Desktop aggregators are installed locally and run in the background, but you cannot use any other computer to access your information.

See NewsOnFeeds (newsonfeeds.com/faq/aggregators) for lists of web-based, desktop, built-in, email, command line, and mobile aggregators.

Vulnerabilities with Aggregators

While no cases of malicious HTML in RSS feeds have been reported yet, the general consensus is that it is probably just a matter of time. Robert Auger of SPI Dynamics published "Feed Injection in Web 2.0" (available at http://www.spidynamics.com/assets/documents/HackingFeeds.pdf), which discusses the different types of possible attacks.

After the report was published in August 2006, many vendors took notice. James Snell developed a series of tests to check aggregator security (see his blog at http://www.snellspace.com/wp/?p=448). Microsoft's Internet Explorer 7 developers ran the tests and blogged about it at the Microsoft Team RSS Blog (http://blogs.msdn.com/rssteam/archive/2006/09/09/

747111.aspx). Other developers picked up on this and have tested (and are fixing, as necessary) their aggregators, including FeedDemon's Nick Bradbury. Steven Garrity of silverorange posted test results on the company blog at http://labs.silverorange.com/archives/2003/July/privaterss.

Some vendors have already implemented security. For example, the CITA RSS Aggregator strips scripts, ads, and tracking mechanisms, and includes a sample control file that prevents applications from being downloaded. It also encrypts passwords required for restricted RSS feeds.

To keep your computer as safe as possible:

- Request feeds only from sites you trust.
- Disable scripts, applets, and plug-ins. These options can affect functionality.
- If an "Active Content" warning is displayed, click No so that no applications are installed.
- Change your security settings to add more restrictions to both the Remote and Local zones.

However, it is possible to use so much security that legitimate functionality is impacted. If you request feeds from sites you trust, use a virus checker, and regularly remove spyware, your vulnerability should be limited.

Chapter 18

Appendix A

It's a Wiki Wacky World

As we mentioned in the earlier sections, we used a wiki as a collaboration tool while writing this book. Now that we have finished writing the book, we are opening the site so that you can see a real-life example of a wiki at work. Our wiki is implemented using TikiWiki (www.tikiwiki.org), but other wiki software packages have similar features.

From the home page, you can look at our wiki and use the Sandbox to practice editing pages. You can view the blog and forums, participate in our surveys, or send an email to us.

If you want to actually make and save edits to the pages, or participate in any of the other wiki features (such as leaving comments on pages or messages in the forums), then you need to register on our site.

Looking Around

To see our wiki, go to http://www.wikiwackyworld.com.

> **Note:** Like all wikis, Wikiwackyworld is constantly changing. Features are added or upgraded, content gets edited, and registered users participate in modifications throughout the wiki pages. The graphics here and throughout this section display what the site looked like as of this printing, and may vary slightly from the screens you see on the site.

Figure A-1: The Wikiwackyworld home page

On the left side of the screen are the features that are enabled. For the most part, these functions are available to anyone who views the site (you, our readers). This might be useful for a project where you have a large number of reviewers who need to know what is going on but do not necessarily need to make edits or comments.

Announcements

The announcement page looks and acts much like a standard web page that only displays information. Not all wiki pages have to be interactive! Check here for the latest information about the book, the site, and the authors.

Wiki Rules

This page describes the things you are (and are not) allowed to do on our site.

Figure A-2: Wiki Rules page

Formatting Rules

This page is a handy reference page for the TikiWiki formatting. Remember, every wiki software package has slightly different syntax and formatting rules.

Sandbox

The Sandbox allows you to practice editing pages and to see exactly what the wiki editing interface looks like. Anyone can edit the Sandbox, but none of the changes are saved. This is a good way to learn about the wiki syntax and to experiment with links and other types of pages. See the section titled "Using the Sandbox" later in this chapter for details on how to play in the Sandbox.

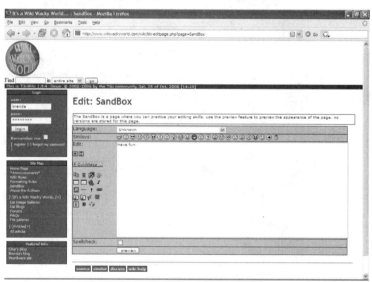

Figure A-3: The Sandbox page

About the Authors

This web page has information about the authors, including a biography, photos, and links to our home pages.

List Image Galleries

This option displays a list of the galleries that contain images that are uploaded to the site. To view an image, first choose a gallery by clicking the gallery name. For example, we have a gallery of press kit photos.

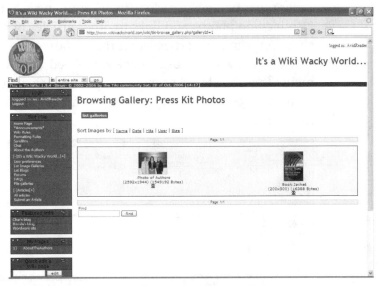

Figure A-4: List of image galleries

This particular gallery had two photos in it on the day we captured the screen. If a gallery has a lot of files in it, you may find the Find feature valuable. Enter a word in the Find text box, and then click Find to display all images that have that word in their descriptions. You can also sort the images in the galleries by Name, Date, Hits, User, and

Size, by clicking the appropriate link across the top of the thumbnails.

You can get an idea of what the photos look like from this screen, or you can click the image to see a larger version. Once you open the larger image, the actual image name appears. This is the text string to use if you want to link to the image from another page in the wiki.

Articles

Articles are similar to standard web pages available on other types of sites. Articles are primarily text, but can also include photos and links to other articles or other sites. You can view articles that the authors have posted or that other registered users have submitted, read comments that registered users have left for each article, add your own comments, and click links that are embedded in the articles.

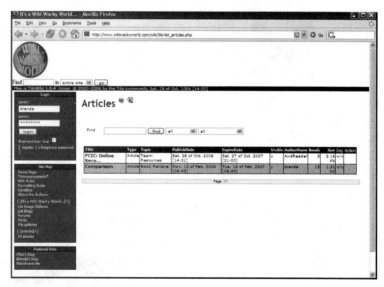

Figure A-5: List of articles

List Blogs

This option displays the Wikiwackyworld blog, where the authors post news, events, and commentary about our book and our other projects. You can search the blog, read old posts, read comments that registered users have left for each post, and post a comment.

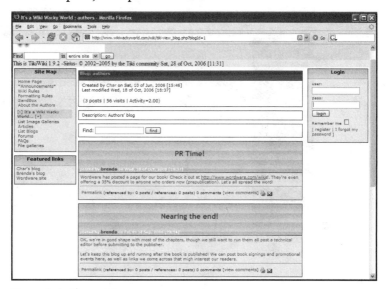

Figure A-6: Blog entries

Forums

The Forums section of the wiki is a message board where registered users can post and answer questions from each other. The forum is sorted by topic; for example, there is a board just for tool discussions and another specifically for comments on the book.

If you are not logged in as a registered user, you can view the forum, but you cannot post messages.

To read messages in the forums, click the topic name to display just the subject line for each message. To read the full message, click the subject line. Replies are listed below the message.

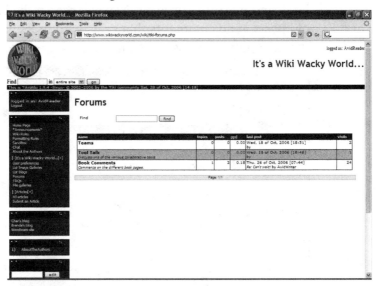

Figure A-7: List of forums

FAQs

FAQs (Frequently Asked Questions) are lists of common questions and answers. We currently have several categories of FAQs, and may add more as time goes on. To see the questions and answers, click FAQs from the Site Map.

Click the FAQ title to see the actual questions and answers. You can click the question itself to go straight to the answer, or you can scroll down the page to browse through all of the questions and answers.

If you have a question that is not answered here, send it to us in an email to authors@wikiwackyworld.com, and we will do our best to answer you.

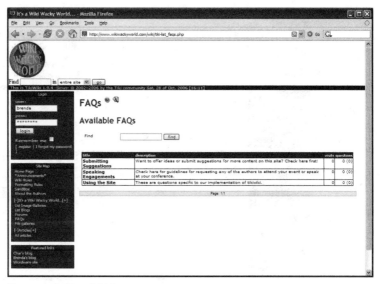

Figure A-8: List of FAQs

File Galleries

This page lists the files available for download. This may grow to include presentations we have given, references, handouts, or other types of files. Like the image galleries, this option displays a list of the galleries that contain files that are uploaded to the site.

To view a file, first choose a gallery by clicking the gallery name to open it. The gallery page lists the names of the available files, sizes, and number of times the file has been downloaded.

Figure A-9: List of file galleries

To open a file, click the file name. Note that you must have software on your system for the specific file type (such as a graphics program to view images or Adobe Acrobat Reader to view PDF files).

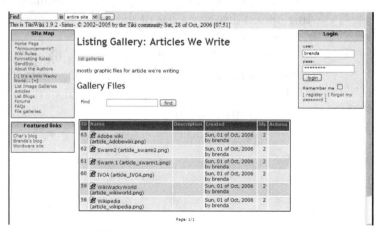

Figure A-10: List of files in a gallery

RSS Feeds

Wikiwackyworld automatically generates RSS feeds whenever any of our content changes. If you have software that reads RSS feeds, you can set it up to automatically display the new or changed components of our site. (See Chapter 18, "RSS Feeds and Other 'Push' Technologies," for more information.) The primary available feeds are displayed across the bottom of the screen (you may have to scroll to see them), as shown below.

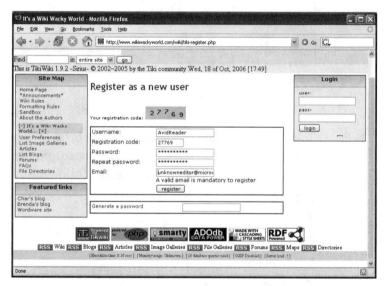

Figure A-11: RSS feed buttons at the bottom of each page

Click any of the orange RSS buttons to display the feed code and display the exact URL of the feed in your browser. For example, the feed for wiki pages might look like the figure on the following page.

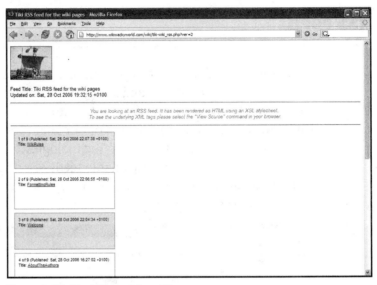

Figure A-12: The RSS feed for wiki pages

You can then place the URL from the browser's address
bar into your feed reader software for automatic update
notification. This is available for the following types of
pages:

- Wiki
- Blogs
- Articles
- Image galleries
- File galleries
- Forums
- Maps
- Directions

If you are a registered user, you can also "watch" pages
and get an email whenever a watched page changes.

Using the Sandbox

The Site Map includes an option for the Sandbox. This is a special area of the wiki that anyone can view or edit. You do not need to log in and you do not need special permissions. However, nothing you create in the Sandbox will be saved. Other than that, the Sandbox works exactly like other wiki pages.

Use this as a practice page to get used to the TikiWiki editing syntax, or as a training page where you can teach or learn without fear of deleting existing content or causing links to break on other pages.

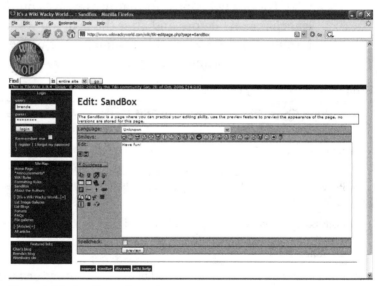

Figure A-13: Sandbox edit mode

TikiWiki Syntax

When you first open the Sandbox, a normal editing page appears. As you can see, there is a large blank area where you can type your text and wiki codes, and a series of icons that represent "smileys" or emoticons that you can use when creating pages or leaving comments on other pages.

The simplest way to start is simply to type some text in the center of the edit area (like "Have fun!" above).

Formatting Text

The method for formatting text varies a little from wiki to wiki. For our wiki, most formatting involves putting special characters before and after the text you want to format. The following table contains some of the more common formatting characters.

Table A-1: Formatting characters

Formatting Characters	Syntax in Edit Mode	Appearance in the Wiki
For bold text, use double underscores	__this text will be bold__	**this text will be bold**
For italic text, use double quotation marks	"this text will be italic"	*this text will be italic*
For both bold and italic, use underscores and double quotation marks	__"both bold and italic"__	***both bold and italic***
For underlined text, use triple equal signs	===underlined text===	underlined text
For centered text, use double colons	::centered heading::	centered heading
For monospaced text, prefix each line of text with a space	monospaced text	`monospaced text`

Colors

By default, all text appears black on the wiki, but you can change the color of the font. If you know the hexadecimal code (a pound sign and eight characters) for the color you want, you can precede the code with two tildes, and then follow it up with a colon, the text you want in the specified color, and finally another pair of tildes:

```
~~#FF0000:This text is red~~
```

```
~~#800080:This text is a lovely shade of
purple~~
```

You can look up the hexadecimal codes for different colors at http://www.gate.net/~barbara/color3.htm.

TikiWiki also has the ability to use some color names instead of the hexadecimal codes:

```
~~red:This text will display in red~~
```

```
~~purple:This text will display in a
lovely shade of purple~~
```

Note: Using names instead of hex codes may make it easier for you when creating the wiki page, and easier when viewing the page code, but it is not good practice. Some browsers may not recognize the names correctly.

Lists

TikiWiki can create two kinds of lists. Use an asterisk to create bulleted lists if the order of things does not matter. Use a pound sign to create numbered lists if the order is important. To create sublists, use multiple asterisks or pound signs.

For example, type the following to display a nested bulleted list:

```
* Flavors
** Chocolate
** Vanilla
** Strawberry
** Rocky Road
* Sizes
** Small
** Medium
** Large
** Family Size
```

The bulleted list would have two levels as follows:

- Flavors
  - Chocolate
  - Vanilla
  - Strawberry
  - Rocky Road
- Sizes
  - Small
  - Medium
  - Large
  - Family Size

The following example shows a combination of numbered and bulleted items:

1. Choose the size.
2. Choose the flavor you want.
   - Chocolate
   - Vanilla
   - Strawberry
   - Rocky Road
3. Pay the appropriate amount of money.
4. Enjoy!

Images

To insert an image on a wiki page, you must know the exact URL of the image. Images are identified by the letters "img," followed by the image location and any optional parameters you want to include. The optional parameters, shown in Table A-2, define specific information about the image, such as display dimensions, alignment, or a text description of the image. Surround the whole string with curly brackets to indicate that these are instructions, not text to be displayed.

Table A-2: Available image parameters

Parameter	Description
src=	URL for the image
height=	Display height in pixels
width=	Display width in pixels
align=	Alignment of the image on the page (left, center, or right)
desc=	Text that will be displayed below the image on the page
link=	Makes the image itself into a link that, when clicked, displays the entered web page (on this wiki or elsewhere)

For example, to display our logo and to link it back to the home page, enter the following:

```
{img src="http://www.wikiwackyworld.com/
wiki/img/tiki/www-small.jpg"
"link=http://www.wikiwackyworld.com"
alt="it's a wiki wacky world..."}
```

Links to Other Pages

The easiest way to create a link to another page within the wiki is to type the name of the page using "WordsSmashedTogether" (sometimes called CamelCase). If the page exists, the wiki automatically puts in a link. If the page does not exist, then simply using this syntax will create the page as well as the link.

The other way to create a page is to type the page name in between double parentheses like this:

```
((Page Name))
```

Like smashing words together, these parentheses will create a link to the named page, and create the page if necessary.

> **Note:** Sometimes you may need to use CamelCase, but do not really want to create a page (this often happens with product or company names). To prevent the wiki from creating a page for a word with internal capital letters, enclose the word in backward brackets, like this:
>
> ```
> ))WikiWackyWorld((
> ```

Links to External Pages

To insert a link to a page not on our wiki, surround the URL with square brackets:

```
[http://www.hat-matrix.com]
```

The URL appears as a link on the page, and if the viewer clicks the URL, the specified site appears. If you want to create a text link — that is, to display a word or phrase that can be clicked — use a vertical bar after the URL and then follow it with the text:

```
[http://www.hat-matrix.com|View the HAT
Matrix]
```

Quicktags

On several pages throughout the wiki, there is a Quicktags link that provides shortcuts for some of the wiki syntax that you need to create or edit pages. When the Quicktags link is available, click it to display the available shortcut tags.

Figure A-14: Quicktags

As you move your cursor over each icon, a small text description of the icon displays. You can use many of these tags in two ways:

- Select your text first, and then click the Quicktag to surround the text with the appropriate symbols (such as underscores for bold).

- Click the Quicktag first to insert the appropriate tag surrounding the word "text" and then replace the word "text" with your information.

Whichever method you choose, it is a good idea to play around with these tags in the Sandbox before editing pages.

Table A-3: Quicktag descriptions

Quicktag	Description
Copy	Select text and then click this tag to copy the selected text to your clipboard.
Underline	Inserts underline tags.
Title Bar	Inserts a title bar in your text. This will display the text in a light color on a dark background across the entire page.

Quicktag	Description
Tagline	Displays the current cookie.
Table New	Inserts a table.
Table	Inserts a row in a table.
RSS	Inserts a link to an RSS feed. You must specify the exact feed ID.
Italic	Inserts the code for italic text.
Image	Inserts the code for importing an image. You must enter the image URL and any optional parameters.
Horizontal Rule	Inserts a horizontal line across the page.
Heading 1	Inserts the wiki code for a heading 1 style, which is transformed to heading 1 HTML tags.
External link	Inserts the tag for a link to a URL not on the wiki.
Dynamic Content	Inserts the code indicating that you are using dynamic content. See the TikiWiki documentation for more details.
Dynamic Variable	Inserts the code for variables. You must enter the variable name.
Colored Text	Inserts the code for red text. If you want a different color, you must enter the correct hex code.
Center	Inserts the tags that center the text on the page.
Boxed	Inserts the code that places a box around the text.
Bold	Inserts the code for bold text.
Special Characters	Displays a box from which you can choose special characters like vowels with accents or ampersands.

Print

To print a wiki page, click the Print icon ( ) at the top of the page. The page, formatted for printing, appears in your browser window.

You can save or print the results.

Create PDF File

Tikiwiki includes the software required to create PDF files that can be viewed by Adobe Acrobat Reader. The results are a snapshot of the wiki pages, and can be used as a record of what each page looked like at a given time. This feature also allows you to pull several wiki pages into a single file, which is handy for printing or emailing.

To convert any page or set of pages to a PDF file, follow these steps:

1. Click the PDF icon () at the top of the page to display the PDF options.

Figure A-15: Print to PDF options

2. Enter the appropriate settings. The PDF Settings section lets you specify how you want the content to appear in the PDF file. The Filter section changes the displayed wiki pages to only those pages that contain the filter word. For example, if you are looking for

pages about tools, enter the word "tools" in the Filter box, then click the Filter button. Only those pages will be displayed in the Select Wiki Pages area.

3. To specify the pages you want included in the PDF, click the page name and then click Add Page. The page name will be displayed on the right side of the screen. The page from which you originally clicked the PDF icon is automatically included on the right side of the screen.

4. To remove a page from the PDF, click the name of the page on the right side of the screen and then click Remove Page.

5. Click Create to generate a PDF file containing the pages you specified.

Register and Sign In Please

While there is plenty of content to view on Wikiwacky-world, you can do even more as a registered user. Instead of just reading the forums, you can post your own questions or answer other people's questions. Instead of just reading our blog, you can post comments to each entry.

As a registered user, you can create a profile for yourself and choose the image that displays by your name when you post to the wiki. More importantly, registered users get access to the "watch" functionality. When you set a page to "watch" — any page, on a blog or forum or throughout the site — the system automatically sends you an email whenever that page changes.

Registration

Registration is quick and easy, but it requires three things:

- A user name. This must be unique within our wiki, so if your name is Kit, Brenda, or Char, you need to use something else.

- A password. Passwords must contain both letters and numbers, and must be at least eight characters long.

- A valid email address. This is the address where you want to receive email notifications, administrative information, and notifications that your watched pages have changed. It is also required to verify your registration.

To register, follow these steps:

1. From the wikiwackyworld.com home page, click Register to display the registration screen.

Figure A-16: Registration page

2. Enter your user name. Remember, this must be unique, so if your chosen name is already in the system, an error message appears.

3. Type the registration code from the gray square graphic in the Registration Code box. This is a security feature to ensure that a human is registering, rather than an automated computer system.

4. Enter your password twice. You must enter the password exactly the same way in both boxes!

Note: The wiki software generates a password for you if you click Generate a Password. The generated password is a random string of letters, numbers, and special characters, and is entered automatically in the two password fields for you.

5. Enter a valid email address. If the address is not valid, you cannot register.

6. Click the Register button. A request is sent to the system administrators, who will validate your information and activate your account. Once your account is activated, you receive an email.

Logging In

After registering, you can log in from the home page at wikiwackyworld.com by entering your user name and password in the Login box on the upper-right corner of the screen. Then simply click the Login button.

As soon as you log in, a couple of features appear on the left of the screen that are only available to registered users. The My Pages area displays pages that you have created on the wiki. The Quick Edit a Wiki Page area allows you to edit pages in the wiki when you know the page name.

User Profile

Your user name and password are all you need to access most of the Wikiwackyworld site. However, the TikiWiki software also has a variety of personalization features that can identify you and your contributions throughout the site. Having user profiles builds community and lets registered users get to know each other. This section is entirely optional.

To set up your user profile (or to make changes at any time), follow these steps:

1. Click the User Preferences link in the Site Map on the left side of the screen.

    Three tabs appear where you can enter your information and set your preferences, starting with Personal Information. Use this area if you want to include your home page as part of your profile or upload an avatar. An avatar is a graphic that will be displayed

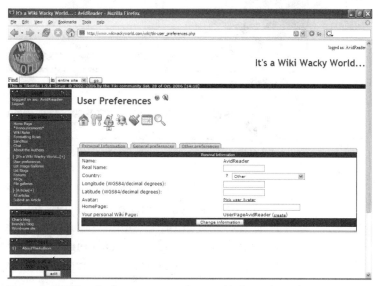

Figure A-17: User Preferences page, Personal Information tab

with your comments on various pages throughout the wiki to identify you. A graphic uploaded for your avatar must be in JPG format, and will always display as a square no matter what shape your original graphic is.

2. Click the General Preferences tab to see more information in your profile. This page lets you specify how much information is displayed to you as you use the site and how much information is displayed about you to other users. This is also where you can change your email address or password.

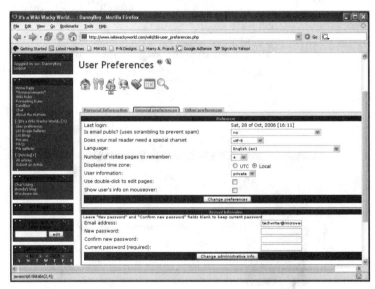

Figure A-18: User Preferences page, General Information tab

3. To make changes to any of the displayed information, type the new information in the appropriate boxes. All passwords must be at least eight characters long, must contain both letters and numbers (or special characters), and must be typed exactly the same way in both the New Password and Confirm New

Password boxes. Passwords are case-sensitive. Finally, you must enter your current password before you can make any changes to this screen! Click the Change Administrative Info button to store your changes.

4. The third tab in the User Preferences area defines which of your contributions to the site you want tracked on your personal welcome page.

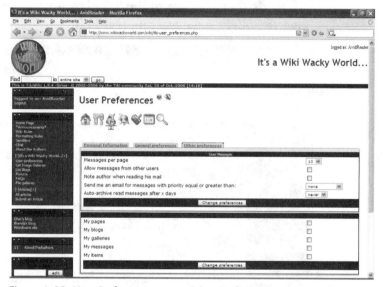

Figure A-19: User Preferences page, Other Preferences tab

5. Click the check box next to the type of content you want displayed, and then click the Change Preferences button to change your settings.

Creating and Editing Wiki Pages

Once you are signed in as a registered user, you can create and edit any pages for which you have permission. In addition to the syntax and features available in the Sandbox (see "Using the Sandbox" earlier in the chapter), you can save pages, edit saved pages, or leave comments on other people's pages.

Editing an Existing Page

As you display different pages in the wiki, pages that you are allowed to edit contain an Edit icon (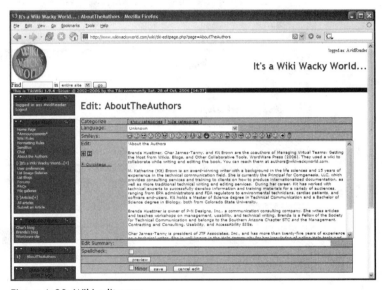). When you click the Edit icon, the page displays in the same type of edit mode that you saw in the Sandbox area. This page, however, might have existing text in it.

Figure A-20: Wiki edit page

You can use the same editing features that you practiced in the Sandbox. When finished editing, you can click the Preview button at the bottom of the screen to see what your page will look like, or you can save or cancel your changes.

Creating a New Page

To create a new page:

1. Start by creating a link to the new page on an existing page. Type the name of the page with a text string where there is at least one uppercase letter in the middle of the string. You can use either the "WordsSmashedTogether" syntax (sometimes called CamelCase) or double parentheses such as ((link name)) to create a link to another page.

2. Click Save. A question mark appears after the new page name to indicate that the new page has been created but has no content yet.

3. Click the question mark to display the new blank page in edit mode.

Watching Pages

If you see a page in which you are particularly interested, you can specify that you want to "watch" the page. The wiki sends you an email whenever that particular page changes. As a registered user, the wiki already knows your email address. To watch a page, click the Watch icon (⬤) to begin monitoring the page. The icon will change to the Stop Watch icon (⬤). Click the Stop Watch icon to stop monitoring the page.

Personal User Pages

Registered users each get a personal page on Wikiwackyworld. The page is automatically named with the format "UserPage*name*" where *name* is the user login, such as "UserPageKit" or "UserPageAvidReader." Only the user and the administrator of the wiki can edit personal pages.

Articles

Articles are similar to wiki pages, except that other users cannot change them. Even users who have write permissions in other areas can only enter comments on an article; they cannot change the article page itself.

To view the available articles, click the Articles link. You can sort the list by any column, or you can filter the articles to display only those containing a specific word. To view an article, click the article title.

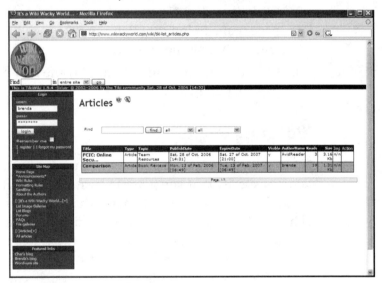

Figure A-21: List of articles

This page displays the title of each topic, along with other information about the articles in a table. You can sort the listed articles by any of the table columns, or you can use the Find feature to search through the list of articles to display only those articles that fit your entered criteria.

Once you have identified the article you want to view, click the article title to open it and read it.

As a registered user, you can also upload articles for consideration to the site. Uploaded articles will be stored until one of the administrators can review the article and either accept it or decline to publish it.

Figure A-22: Article view

To submit an article for possible publication, click Submit an Article to display the submission page.

Enter the information about your article in the top portion of this page.

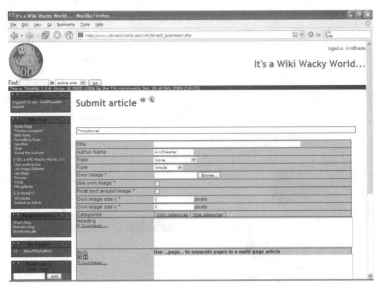

Figure A-23: Article submission page

Table A-4: Article information

Element	Description
Title	This displays at the top of the completed article.
Author Name	This defaults to the user name under which you are currently logged in.
Topic	Choose from the drop-down list of available topics, such as Tools or Team Resources. This allows readers to sort the articles later, but is not necessary.
Type	Choose from the drop-down list of available article types, such as Review, Event, or Classified. If you do not enter anything, this will default to Article.
Own Image	If you want to include a graphic with the article, upload it by entering the location or using the Browse button. If you want to use your own image, you must also check the Use Own Image check box just below.

Element	Description
Use Own Image	Check this box to use your own image with the article. You must specify the image location (as described above).
Float Text around Image	Check this box to allow text from the article to display next to and around your image. If this box is not checked, the image will be on a line by itself.
Own Image Size x	Specify the display width of the image. If you do not specify a size, the wiki displays the original image size.
Own Image Size y	Specify the display height of the image. If you do not specify a size, the wiki displays the original image size.

The lower two sections of the Articles page work the same way that the wiki page editing and Sandbox features work. Type your text and use the special formatting, or whatever else you want to use. Articles have two additional features:

- You can separate text in an article into multiple pages by entering a manual page break. To do this, enter the string **...page...** where you want the page break to be.

- You can specify a date when you want the article to be published. This allows you to create several articles, and then have them released once a week (or on whatever dates you specify). To do this, enter the month, day, year, hour, and minute that you want the article released at the bottom of the screen.

Like other wiki pages, you can preview your article by clicking Preview. When you are ready to submit the article, click Save.

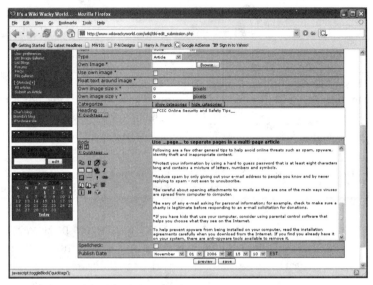

Figure A-24: Article submission preview page

Comments

When you edit a page, you are changing the page itself
and only the edited version displays. If you want to comment on something but leave the original page as is, you
use the comment feature. As a registered user, you can
leave comments in several areas of the wiki. Other users
can read your comments and respond, if they choose to do
so. Comments can be left on pages that contain articles,
blogs, and image or file galleries. Wherever comments are
allowed, you will see the Add Comment button. Click this
to display the comment screen.

You must enter a title for your comment. You may
click any of the smiley face icons to include that in your
comment. The rules for typing comments are basically the
same as for editing pages (see "Using the Sandbox" for
details).

add comment

Post new comment

Post new comment	preview post
Title: Required	
Smileys	😀😃😄😁😆😅😂🤣😊😇🙂🙃😉😌😍🥰😘😗😙😚😋😛
Comment	

Posting comments:
Use [http://www.foo.com] or [http://www.foo.com|description] for links.
HTML tags are not allowed inside posts.

Figure A-25: Comments area (available on many pages)

You can also reply to comments left by other users. All replies will be displayed as links underneath the original comment.

Searching the Wiki

If you are looking for something specific in our wiki, use the search feature. This allows you to enter a word or phrase, and then scan either the entire site or just a specific type of page for that word or phrase. To begin a search, type the word you are looking for in the Find box, which appears at the top of every wiki page.

Figure A-26: Search box

Use the drop-down box to specify whether you want to search the whole site, or limit the search to just pages, articles, blogs, or other types of pages. Click Go to display a list of the pages that meet your criteria.

Figure A-27: Search results

Forums

A Wikiwackyworld forum is a form of message board where registered users can post questions, comments, or announcements for everyone to see, and respond to messages that other people have posted to the forum. Each forum has a specific subject or theme, such as tools or discussion about the book. Within each forum, there are topics, and within each topic there are messages.

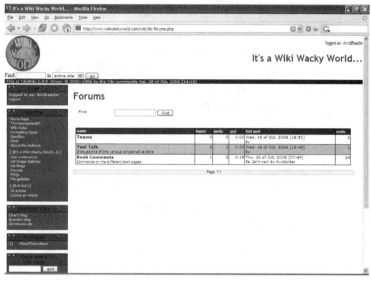

Figure A-28: List of forums

Click the name of the forum you want to read to display
the list of topics within that forum.

Figure A-29: List of forum messages

The title for each comment displays as a link, and this page also displays the number of times each comment has been read and the time and date of the most recent response to each post. The responses are listed beneath the topic, prefaced by "Re:". To display the actual text of the comment, click the title of the comment.

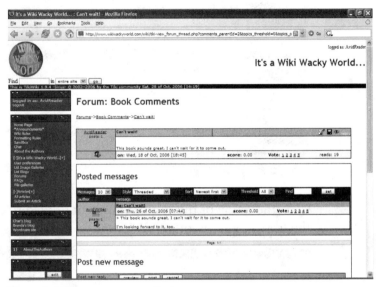

Figure A-30: Forum message display page

If you are a registered user, the message will be followed by an editing screen that lets you post a response. You will probably have to scroll down to see the Post New Message section.

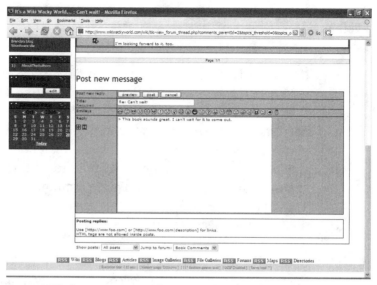

Figure A-31: Forum message edit page

You must enter a title for your post in the Title box. This is the field that displays when someone generates a list of messages. For the body of the message, enter your text the same way you would edit a page, then click Preview, Post, or Cancel.

TikiWiki Help and Documentation

If you need help remembering TikiWiki format, there is a wiki help button at the bottom of many editing screens that displays a summary of the formatting for you. If you need more help than this summary, you can view the Formatting Rules page available from the menu on the left side of every page. This page has links to additional resources throughout the TikiWiki community. For general TikiWiki information, you can get answers at the TikiWiki documentation site at http://doc.tikiwiki.org. The documentation is structured as a wiki, so it is constantly being updated and improved. This site also has tutorials, demonstration videos, and a user community including message boards.

Figure A-32: TikiWiki help

Appendix B

Glossary

The following terms are used throughout the book. If you do not find a term that you think should be in the glossary, log in to our companion wiki (www.wikiwackyworld.com) and add it.

accessibility

Measurement of how well websites can be accessed by those with disabilities. Many countries have passed laws that require that all websites are accessible. (At the time of publication, the United States only required that websites being accessed by government employees be accessible. However, a recent court decision against Target's online store on behalf of a blind user indicates that this may change.)

adaptable organization

A company where all the units understand how they fit into the larger whole so that the organization can coordinate its goals and efforts as a unified whole. The organization remains flexible and effective in the face of challenges.

address book

An application or feature used for tracking contact information (user name, "real" name, address, email address, and so on).

adjourning

The final stage of the team lifecycle, according to Tuckman's model. In the adjourning phase, the team members begin to disengage and move on to other projects and capture lessons learned. An orderly adjourning phase helps the team disband on a positive note. (See Chapter 1.)

administrator and user security

Permissions assigned by group within several tool types (like content management systems, wikis, and blogs). For example, basic users may have permission to read content, while authors can add content and editors can modify content. *See* role-based permissions.

agile programming

A methodology for software development where the project team releases iterations in a two- to four-week cycle. Regular, ongoing communication with all members of the project team is emphasized over written requirements, and face-to-face communication is the typical model for these communications (which makes this methodology a particular challenge for virtual teams). At the end of each iteration, the team re-evaluates progress and goals.

AICC

Aviation (All Encompassing) Industry CBT (Computer-Based Training) Committee, an international organization that develops evaluation guidelines for the aviation industry for computer and web-based training technologies.

alerts

Notices that are either displayed or emailed. Alerts are typically sent when something has changed, such as when content is added, edited, or deleted. Other applications also include alerts, such as instant messaging applications that tell you when someone has logged on or off.

anti-spam

Features that include ways to reduce the amount of spam (unwanted and unsolicited email), typically for blogs, wikis, or content management systems. The following list describes some of the more common methods:

- Blacklists, which track domain names that have been reported as sending spam

- IP blocking

- Challenge emails, which require registrants to reply to an email before letting them post any comments or content

- User permissions

- Privacy settings, typically in instant messaging (IM) applications, to prevent folks who are not on your buddy list from contacting you

application sharing

Tool that allows a person to log onto another person's system to run a specific application or to take over the other person's desktop. This is useful during training sessions or for customer support.

approval review

The final sign-off for a project. This review is a final check that the item under review is ready for the customer. In most cases, it should be a formality because previous reviews should have caught any errors or omissions.

assessments

Formal evaluations of personnel, products, or services. Assessments are usually scheduled at regular intervals, and often use formal surveys, forms, and other materials to ensure consistency and to document the results.

asynchronous

Communication activities that do not occur in real time. For example, email, bulletin boards, blogs, articles, and so on are forms of asynchronous communication. *See also* synchronous.

audio chat

An application that lets two or more people talk in real time while using a computer. All parties are required to have headsets, or speakers and a microphone. Many instant messaging (IM) applications include audio chat as a feature.

bands of involvement

The level of participation each team member type has with the project team. For example, the core team members might have 100 percent involvement in the project team, while the subject matter experts might be in the 10 percent band.

bandwidth

The capacity of a data line. Often used colloquially to mean the amount of time a team member can spend on a particular activity.

benchmark

Depending on context, it is either the measurements taken to establish a point of reference for the future, or the results expected when following best practices; in the latter case, the team measures how close it comes to meeting the results expected.

blog

An electronic journal (short for *weblog*). Blogs can cover any subject, from personal to professional, and are typically available to the public, although they can be password protected for private access only. Free blog sites (like Blogger) let you sign up for a public blog, but for virtual collaboration, you will probably want to check out blogging software (like b2evolution or WordPress) that can be installed on your server. See Blog Software Breakdown (http://www.asymptomatic.net/blogbreakdown.htm).

blog farm

A site that links multiple blogs together. Some software, like b2evolution, includes the functionality to create multiple blogs on one site. Other software requires that the blogs are linked together.

blogger

A person who blogs. ("Blogger" with a capital B is blogging software that is now owned by Google.)

bot

An automated web-based application (short for *robot*). Many search engines use bots to search different websites and follow the links. A newer type of bot is an instant messaging (IM) application that can be programmed to display the weather, monitor security settings, and more.

boundary-crossing interaction

Any communication between organizations or that requires access to another's firewall. Examples include communication between consultants and clients, bots that access a client's data and add it to the localization team's workflow, and so on.

brainstorming

An activity intended to generate ideas. Brainstorming is typically a group activity. When facilitating a brainstorming session, it is important to track all ideas that come up and to avoid evaluating their viability until the brainstorming is complete. Brainstorming sessions are creative and tend to build their own energy as one person takes a tidbit of someone else's idea and builds on it. Humor and fun are key aspects of successful brainstorming.

branding

The effort made by any organization to distinguish itself from the competition and from other organizations. This effort involves the logo, labeling, and marketing materials, as well as the "personality" of the organization — the intangible feeling that people have when they think about or interact with the organization. Most companies that want to play in the global market work to develop a global brand for the organization, one that has positive connotations, regardless of locale. Given cultural diversity, this is a huge challenge. *See also* corporate identity.

bulletin board

Software that lets people post messages to others who have permission to read the entries. Sometimes referred to as "newsgroups" or "discussion groups," bulletin boards store messages on a server.

bureaucracy

A system of administration, policies, procedures, and rules that a person is required to navigate in order to accomplish a goal. While some process is necessary to ensure consistency and efficiency, excess bureaucracy can derail the project and can cause unnecessary frustration and delay.

calendar

E-calendars let team members create online schedules that can be viewed by all. This makes it easier to schedule meetings and conference calls, track deadlines, and more. Some calendars can send notifications to mobile phones and email inboxes.

CD-ROM

Compact Disc-Read Only Memory. Medium for storing data and other electronic information.

change management

The process of determining the priority and timing of alterations to the product, process, service, documentation, or other element. Effective change management is critical to the success of projects with many components, particularly if the product and documentation are being localized.

channels

Method for tracking types of content for RSS feeds. Channels can refer to a specific category from a site (such as "local news" from any news station's website) or can refer to the site itself. Thousands of channels exist.

charter

An agreement between teams or entities that defines the working relationship at a strategic level. From the charter, statements of work and other documents can be derived. This is also known as a memo of understanding.

chat (and chat rooms)

Application that enables real-time, synchronous communication between two or more people. While "chat" typically refers to typing, many applications also let you use a microphone and headset to hold real-time conversations over the Internet. Skype, Windows Live Messenger, and Yahoo! Messenger with Voice also let you make phone calls (rate plans available on the individual sites). You can hold conversations with one or more people, depending on your needs. *See also* instant message.

coaching

The process of providing encouragement, direction, and feedback to an individual. Coaching does not necessarily involve a formal relationship between the individuals involved and can occur as peer-to-peer, as well as leader-to-team member, or even team member-to-leader. Coaching is similar to mentoring, but has been popularized as a term because of the connotation of play and team sports associated with it.

collaboration

The process or act of working with individuals to produce an outcome, product, or service. Collaboration occurs in the context of completing a particular task.

collaboration technology

Applications and websites that let individuals work together to complete a task.

comments

Feature that allows users and visitors to add notes to information that has been published (like blog entries).

communication tools

Applications, processes, or hardware that facilitate interaction between two or more individuals or teams.

competency network

Forum for sharing expertise, knowledge, and information, as well as exchanging ideas. These networks facilitate innovation and collaboration among cross-functional teams, professionals in a variety of disciplines, and so on. List serves and special interest groups can be competency networks.

competition

The effort of independent individuals, teams, or businesses to secure limited resources or the business of a third party.

conference call

Conversation with three or more people on the line. Conference calls might have a moderator who facilitates the call. Often, conference calls are used as virtual team meetings.

conflict management

The process of handling problems, grievances, and disagreements. With virtual teams, it is important to be explicit about the expectations for such interactions, as well as ensuring that an escalation path is clearly defined to ensure that the issue is resolved at the lowest level possible. (Ideally, two individuals negotiate their own resolution to the conflict, but sometimes, others need to be involved to achieve an equitable solution.)

consensus

Agreement derived as a result of collaborative problem-solving and discussion. Consensus implies active willingness to go along with a solution, even if it was not an individual's first choice.

constructive conflict

Creative disagreement that ultimately results in a better idea or result than any of the original ideas that precipitated the conflict.

content management

The process of creating, storing, and retrieving content for use, such as graphics, text, hyperlinks, tables, and other data. At a minimum, effective content management includes version control, naming conventions, and a specified storage structure (through either a manual or automated process). Most enterprise-level content management systems store information in a database and provide at least some automated workflow.

content review

Evaluation of documentation, requirements, or other information to determine technical accuracy, completeness, organization, or grammatical correctness.

continuous improvement

A philosophy that involves evaluating a product, service, activity, or document in an effort to iteratively make it better. No matter how good something is, it can always be improved.

cooperation

The act of working together toward a common goal. While collaboration implies that the people involved are contributing directly to complete a specific task, cooperation is broader and means that the individuals involved are supportive of each other, even if they are not working together on a specific task.

core team

The members of a group who are required for success of a project. Typically, core cross-functional teams include representatives from each functional area that is needed to do the project.

corporate identity

The brand and personality of a company or organization that is easily recognizable to outsiders. *See also* branding.

cPanel

Graphical web-hosting management software. cPanel lets site administrators add users, change passwords, and more.

cross-functional team

Group of people from a variety of disciplines and specialties who are brought together for a project or task force.

cross-references

Also known as hyperlinks or links. Cross-references provide access to other parts of a system, to URLs, and so on.

cultural iceberg

Model for explaining cultural differences. The iceberg analogy is used because much of our cultural biases, assumptions, beliefs, and worldview are deeply ingrained and unconscious, much like the underwater portion of the iceberg, which is not visible from the surface.

culture

According to Merriam-Webster, the customary beliefs, social forms, and material traits of a racial, religious, or social group. Culture also includes the set of shared attitudes, values, goals, and practices that characterizes an institution or organization. Culture can apply to all levels of society from nations down to families or couples.

customization

The process by which users modify output to match a corporate look and feel, or to assign a custom theme (predefined or one that a user has created).

distributed team

See virtual team.

domain name

Unique name that identifies a domain on a network (which can be a computer on an intranet or a website on the Internet). This name must correspond to the assigned numeric IP address.

editable content

Content that anyone with permission can modify, such as information found in a wiki.

elearning

Any training or educational process delivered using electronic media, such as the web, CDs, DVDs, or other methods.

empowerment

The process of encouraging and authorizing team members to take the initiative for accomplishing tasks, making improvements, and determining priorities.

face

One's public self-image or status. To "give face" means to increase status or respect for someone. To "lose face" means to reduce one's status or self-image in front of others.

facilitation

The act of making something easier for someone else. Also the act of managing the flow of ideas, information, and schedule of a meeting.

facilitator

A person who keeps meetings and discussions on task, and who guides the discussions to elicit relevant information.

Fantastico

An automated script installer, included with some installations of cPanel. Fantastico reduces installation of blogs, wikis, and more to a couple of clicks.

feedback loop (or feedback mechanism)

The process by which communication is responded to. For example, when a project manager requests that team members provide a report on their activities, the report is the feedback for the request. Another example is active listening techniques where the listener reflects back the statements heard from the speaker.

File Galleries

Feature that allows you to upload and download electronic files. Many web-based systems let you save files (documents, photos, graphics, etc.) for archival or review purposes. If the team has access to the same network, this might not be a priority.

file transfer

To send a file from one system to another. File Transfer Protocol (FTP) lets people upload files to a website (*see* File Transfer Protocol). A generic file transfer lets users share files across a network.

File Transfer Protocol (FTP)

Copies files from one location to another. Some websites allow for anonymous file transfers, which means that users can upload files without logging in. Most sites, however, require a user name and password for security reasons.

file upload support

Permissions that allow visitors to upload files to a site for others to access.

flat organization

Companies that lack a strict hierarchy and have few layers of bureaucracy between the lowest and highest levels. These organizations typically have more interaction across functional groups and more communication both up and down the levels of the organization than do more hierarchical organizations.

folder sharing

Ability for users to share one set of folders. Folder sharing means that more than one person can make modifications to the files in the folder.

forming

The initial phase of Tuckman's team lifecycle, where the ideas are discussed, alliances made, and the leader selected. (See Chapter 1.)

forums

Forums and bulletin boards are similar, even though they have different purposes: Forums are considered open discussion groups, while bulletin boards tend to be focused around a central theme. Typically, conversations are threaded, and most applications include a search function.

game theory

A method of analyzing strategic behavior, particularly in situations where the parties involved may have conflicting interests. John von Neumann developed the theory, which has applications not only to board games, card games, and video games, but also to economics, military strategy, business, and behavioral studies.

gatekeeping

The process of filtering information for other members of the team. Depending on context, this activity can be helpful (as in filtering extraneous information to identify the important data) or not (as when a manager neglects to pass on important information to the team).

globalization

The process of aligning the product design, marketing, packaging, and support materials with a global product strategy. Globalization is a company-wide endeavor and affects all aspects of the business.

goal

An objective that a team or individual works toward. Effective goals are SMART: specific, measurable, attainable, relevant, and time-delineated.

groupthink

The tendency of people who interact with each other frequently or who work closely with each other to begin thinking alike rather than finding innovative solutions to problems.

groupware

The combination of applications, infrastructure, and processes that facilitates collaborative work.

hierarchy

An arrangement of people or organizations by social or professional status, rank, grade, or other criteria. The higher the placement in the hierarchy that an individual attains typically means that that individual has more authority and responsibility than lower ranking individuals.

history

See version control.

hosted

System or application provided by a third party that owns the underlying infrastructure and makes it available to others on a subscription basis.

in-country review

The process of comparing translated materials to the source materials and ensuring the localization's technical accuracy and completeness. In-country reviewers are typically employees of the client company who are located in the target locale, speak both the source and target languages fluently, and have a deep knowledge of the product or service that is being localized.

indexing

The process of extracting meaningful keywords from a set of text so that users can more easily find the information.

installation

The process of placing an application on a computer system so that the user can access and work with the application. Installation can involve configuring both the application and the underlying computer system to optimize usage.

instant message

Application that facilitates interactive text exchange in real time. When more than two individuals are using the same window to interact, the activity is typically called chatting. *See also* chat.

internationalization

The process of creating a flexible system architecture and processes for the product and documentation so that they can be easily customized to meet the needs of a specific locale. Generally, internationalization focuses on the technical side of globalization. The key idea is that this process is accomplished in the source.

Internet search

The process of using a search engine to find information that is stored on the Internet.

interoperability

The ability of a system to interact with other systems without special effort on the part of the user.

knowledge management

The process of creating, collecting, storing, and retrieving organizational memory, data, documentation, and other information so that the members of the organization can access it easily and work more effectively.

line management

The person to whom the team member reports for purposes of personnel evaluations, raises, and so on. Line managers typically have responsibility for a profit area or line of revenue for a company.

link

A connection on a web page that leads to another web page, graphic, email, and so on.

list serve

A mailing program that enables subscribers to the list to communicate with all other list members using a single email address.

locale

The combination of culture, region, and language that make an area unique. Some countries have multiple locales (for example, Switzerland has German, Italian, and French areas).

localization

The process of taking a product or service, and then reviewing and modifying it so that it is acceptable to a specific locale. The key idea here is that this process creates the target.

logistics

The organization of a project to track and manage the flow of information and resources.

meeting applications

Applications that let you hold virtual meetings. WebEx is one such application.

message logging

The process of storing text exchanges so that they can be reviewed later.

metrics

Methods and specific indicators used by an organization to assess progress toward a goal, process improvement, quality, or other characteristics. Most metrics are tracked over time so that companies can identify trends.

milestone

A flag in the project schedule that indicates a time by which key activities should be completed. Milestones give team members a deadline to work toward, and break a large project into more easily completed phases.

mobile IMs

Functionality included with some mobile phones that allows instant messaging (short messages exchanged in real time using an IM application like AIM). Most mobile phones also allow text messages, which are short messages sent directly to your phone. However, IM applications also include the ability to see who is online and what their status is (available, busy, and so on).

moderator

See facilitator.

multi-language support

The capability of a product to accommodate the needs of two or more languages.

needs assessment (or needs analysis)
The process of identifying the current situation compared to the optimal situation so that you can determine what activities, technology, and processes need to be changed or added in order to achieve the goals.

newsletters
Periodic publications that provide information, news, and announcements specific to an audience. The tone and style tend to be casual and informal.

norming
Phase three of Tuckman's team lifecycle. During this phase, teambuilding begins in earnest and team members begin working together as a cohesive unit. (See Chapter 1.)

objectives
Statements of direction and expected results that are connected to the overall goals of a project or program.

off-the-record messaging
Functionality included in some IM applications that delivers messages sent to offline buddies. When the buddy logs on, the message is delivered.

organizational development
The study of how human groups work effectively, and how they improve and evolve over time.

performance appraisal
The formal evaluation performed by one's supervisor. Typically, performance appraisals are scheduled events, usually annually. The results of the appraisal should not be a surprise to the employee, as feedback should occur throughout the year. (See Chapter 7.)

performing

Stage four of Tuckman's team lifecycle model. During this phase, the teams are working at peak effectiveness. (See Chapter 1.)

personnel appraisal

Also known as "personnel assessment" or "review." *See* performance appraisal.

podcast

Podcast (sometimes referred to as *webcast*) are passive presentations typically available on demand. RSS or Atom feeds indicate when new podcasts are available, or they can be stored on a site and delivered through direct download or streaming video. Podcasts are a form of "push" technology.

poll

A one- or two-question survey that typically has a large margin of error and limited statistical validity. They are useful for identifying trends, but the results should not be the only datapoint that you use to make a decision. *See also* survey.

post-project evaluation

The process of capturing lessons learned and evaluating areas of success at the end of a project. This process involves all of the key players on the project team and helps to guide future projects. (See Chapter 7.)

procedure

An ordered list of steps required to complete a task. Procedures often include graphics and other supporting information to assist the user in completing the task.

process

"A naturally occurring or designed sequence of operations or events, possibly taking up time, space, expertise or other resource, which produces some outcome. A process may be identified by the changes it creates in the properties of one or more objects under its influence." (Wikipedia)

programming language

Code used to translate an algorithm or process into instructions for the computer. Programming languages form the basis of the code used by software applications. Examples include PHP and Python.

project management

The process of organizing the resources, logistics, schedule, and goals of an activity. Effective project management involves regular interaction with the team; proactive risk and change management; a well-defined purpose, scope, and schedule; and achievable goals.

project manager

The person responsible for ensuring that the project is completed on time and on budget. This person also allocates resources, tracks costs, creates schedules, and so on.

project review

The process of evaluating components of a project for technical accuracy, completeness, organization, or other criteria.

reciprocity

Balanced exchange of goods or services. Actions, both good and bad, are mirrored by the recipient. For example, if one team member goes out of her way to assist another team member with a problem, the second team member will then look for an opportunity to help the first team member.

remote team

See virtual team.

requirements analysis

The process by which organizations determine what functionality will enhance the user experience or solve a particular business problem.

risk

The potential for a negative event to occur during a project. Effective risk management involves identifying risks and proactively determining a course of action that will likely mitigate those risks.

role-based permissions

Access levels based on the user's function on the team.

RSS feed

XML file that includes information about an updated entry on a website (from a blog or web page, or about a podcast, and so on). An RSS feed can include an introductory blurb about the content or the entire piece. Aggregators search user-defined sites for updates and display notifications when a site has been updated.

scheduling

The act of planning the project using a timeline to identify deadlines and milestones.

SCORM

Sharable Content Object Reference Model. This model includes the standards and specifications for e-learning, and defines how components are combined and used.

S-curve

The standard curve ubiquitous in systems theory and in the natural world. When graphed, the growth of a population or the efficiency of a team generally follows an S-shaped pattern, with a relatively flat start, exponential acceleration, and eventual plateau.

search

The act of looking for information, usually through a search engine application.

security

Measures taken as a precaution against theft, viruses, spam, and so on.

self-assessment

The process of evaluating your own work, successes, failures, strengths, and weaknesses. Typically, team members are asked to conduct a formal self-assessment as part of their performance appraisals.

servant leadership

Also called "service leadership." The concept of the manager or team lead as steward of resources and facilitator of tasks. Robert Greenleaf coined the term and several others have since built on it, though the concept has been around for thousands of years. Servant leaders seek first to make the world (or their organization) a better place, and in doing so, facilitate teamwork, improve product quality, and meet the organization's goals.

social networks

Set of relationships, both formal and informal, between two or more people. These networks foster the acquisition and distribution of information and knowledge within the network.

source

The locale in which a document or product originates.

spam

Unsolicited email, usually advertising or solicitation for inappropriate activities. Spam is basically electronic junk mail.

storming

Second stage of Tuckman's team lifecycle. This stage is characterized by conflict as team members figure out how they fit in the overall team structure and defining how they will work together. (See Chapter 1.)

strategic planning

The process of determining direction for a company or department. This process involves figuring out where you are now and where you want to be, as well as high-level goals for getting to where you want to be. Good strategic plans include cost/benefit analysis, a timeline, high-level goals, metrics for measuring success, and priorities for which goals are most important to the success of the plan. Such plans are also "living documents," with the flexibility to make changes should the need arise.

subject matter expert (SME)

A person with a specific set of knowledge related to a project or discipline.

survey

A research methodology that uses a questionnaire to elicit data from a specific population. You can use surveys and polls to gather opinions from other team members, and possibly from other employees. When done well, surveys can provide a statistically valid benchmark for quality improvement and other activities. *See also* poll.

SWOT

Strengths, Weaknesses, Opportunities, Threats. Marketing-speak for a form of analysis that helps you examine your company's current status. This process is often used as part of a needs analysis.

synchronous

Activity that occurs in real time. Examples of synchronous activities include telephone calls, instant messaging, and chats. *See also* asynchronous.

syntax

Rules that govern how to order the formulae and commands in software code.

systems theory

The interdisciplinary study of how an organization or entity works within the larger whole, with the assumption that the whole is not only greater than the sum of its parts but different from the sum of its parts. This theory examines the relationships among components of the whole as well as within the hierarchy of systems.

target

The locale into which the document or product is transferred.

task

A job or piece of work that must be completed.

task force

An ad hoc team that is formed to solve a specific challenge, and that typically dissolves once the challenge has been identified and resolved.

teambuilding

Any activity that has as its primary purpose the goal of encouraging team members to work together effectively.

team lifecycle

The flow of events and relationships that occur during team formation, performance of tasks, and adjournment. See the discussion of Tuckman's team lifecycle in Chapter 1.

technical review

Evaluation of a product, service, document, or other project component by subject matter experts for the purpose of determining technical accuracy and completeness.

template

A format or pattern used to create other documents or products. Using templates helps to ensure consistency, particularly when multiple people are working on the same component.

template support

Functionality included in an application (like a wiki) that lets administrators and users assign templates to specific areas (like articles) or pages. Typically, administrators define the templates, which can be assigned site-wide (for example, all articles use the same template), or can be assigned by the user to specific pieces of content.

testing

Fifth stage of Tuckman's team lifecycle. The process of ensuring that a product or process works the way it is designed to work and that it meets the needs of the user. (See Chapter 1.)

time to market

The length of time it takes to get a product from design to availability to the customer.

time tracking

Application that records how much time a person spent on a particular task. Use the time tracking results to set benchmarks, analyze productivity, and more.

TQM

Total Quality Management. A quality improvement methodology popular in the 1980s and still used today that attempts to completely eliminate product defects.

The primary premise is continuous, incremental improvement.

track changes

The process of identifying and managing changes needed in the product or documentation. Also known as bug tracking and error tracking.

translation

The process of taking information in one language and transferring it to another language. A good translator considers not only the text itself, but also the conventions, idioms, and expectations of the audience for the target language.

translation memory

A database tool that allows the human translator to connect the translated segment with its corresponding source segment. This capability facilitates consistency by pre-matching segments that have been translated previously and flagging them for approval.

valid (X)HTML

(X)HTML coded according to standards defined by the World Wide Web Consortium (W3C). The latest HTML standard is 4.01, and the latest XHTML standard is 1.1. See the W3C website at http://w3.org for more information.

vendors

Companies that supply products or services to you. Usually, vendors operate according to a contract with your company for a specified set of goods and services.

version control

Method for tracking history and for ensuring that the master copy of a component represents the current iteration. Wikis include automatic version control, saving all older pages according to limits set by the administrator.

video chat

A method for holding meetings using a video camera and headset (or microphone and speakers). Video chats allow the participants to see each other in real time. They work best with high-speed Internet connections.

virtual private network (VPN)

Virtual private networks enable remote employees to access files that reside behind the company's firewall.

virtual team

A group of individuals who work together toward common goals primarily by using computer technology, and who are usually located remotely from each other.

vodcast

Technical name for a podcast that includes video. However, many people refer to vodcasts as "podcasts."

voice conferencing

Also known as "conference calls," a method for holding meetings, either over the web or a phone line. Various companies offer the capabilities, although prices vary.

voice mail

A way to capture phone messages. Some companies use answering machines, but many use a computer-based system that records the caller's phone number, the date and time of the call, and the message.

If leaving a voice mail, be sure to speak slowly when reciting your phone number, especially if the other person is not familiar with it.

Voice over Internet Protocol (VoIP)

Voice over Internet Protocol lets you connect a digital telephone line (using a standard telephone) to your computer for telephone calls. Prices vary by vendor, as do the applicable calling areas. In some cases, the service is portable, letting you use your VoIP telephone from anywhere.

webinars (presentations)

Web-based presentations. Such presentations are effective for one-to-one or one-to-many meetings that need audio and video, and possibly interaction between the presenter and the participants. Typically, audio is provided through a conference call, which is usually muted while the presenter is talking and then opened for a question-and-answer period.

web portal

Another name for a website. Typically, portals include an area for uploading and downloading files, as well as forms and other methods of working collaboratively.

whiteboard

Electronic application for taking notes. Whiteboards can be saved and distributed after meetings.

wi-fi

Wireless fidelity. Refers to the capability of a product for sending and receiving data over a wireless network, as well as to the wireless network itself.

wiki

Software for websites that anyone can edit, if they have the appropriate permissions. Some wikis are set up so that only a select group of users can edit the content, while anyone can read it. Other wikis are completely open, and any registered user can edit any page.

wiki farm

Wiki hosting service. Wiki farms let you host your wiki for less than the cost of a traditional website, and include installation, updates, upgrades, and backups.

WYSIOP (What You See Is One Possibility)

The best way to describe an editing environment. What you see in development will probably not match every possible output, but could match one, because the final layout is dependent on all the presentation factors. Chris Lilley of the World Wide Web Consortium (W3C) coined the term in 1998 when discussing XML transforms: "The idea was that visual editing was done with the firm understanding that structure was being generated underneath; and that the styling being used for the editing was just *one possible way* to present the information."

WYSIWYG (What You See Is What You Get)

Technically, an incorrect term used by many vendors to describe their editing environment. Because the final display is determined by cascading or extensible style sheets, the editing environment may or may not match the final deliverable.

Index

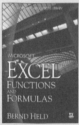

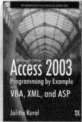